THE COMPLETE
RIPPING YARNS

THE COMPLETE RIPPING YARNS

MICHAEL PALIN AND TERRY JONES

ART DIRECTION & DESIGN: KATE HEPBURN

COVER PHOTO: MIKE PRIOR
PHOTOGRAPHS: AMY LUNE & BERTRAND POLO

Mandarin

The Complete Ripping Yarns
First published in Great Britain in 1990 by Methuen London
This edition published in 1991 by Mandarin Paperbacks
Michelin House, 81 Fulham Road, London SW3 6RB

Mandarin is an imprint of the Octopus Publishing Group,
a division of Reed International Books Limited.

Copyright © 1978, 1980, 1990 by Michael Palin and Terry Jones

A CIP catalogue record is available from the British Library

ISBN 0 7493 1222 X

Ripping Yarns (Tomkinson's Schooldays, Across the Andes by Frog,
The Testing of Eric Olthwaite, Murder and Moorstones Manor,
Escape from Stalag Luft 112B, The Curse of the Claw) first published in 1978
by Eyre Methuen Copyright © 1978 by Michael Palin and Terry Jones.

More Ripping Yarns (Whinfrey's Last Case, Golden Gordon, Roger of the Raj) first
published in 1980 by Eyre Methuen
Copyright © 1980 by Michael Palin and Terry Jones.

Printed and bound in Great Britain
by BPCC Hazell Books Ltd.
Members of BPCC Ltd. Aylesbury, Bucks.

To Terry Hughes, Jim Franklin, Alan JW Bell, Sidney Lotterby
and everyone at the BBC who made Ripping Yarns possible.
And to Nigel Parry Jones for an idea that grew.

Introduction by a very famous man

The collection of outrageous and offensive erotica which fills these pages does no credit to its "authors" — Sandy and Knud Urkstrom — and even less to a publisher of Oxford University Press's reputation.
I only wish it possessed a fraction of the brilliance and insight of the "Complete Ripping Yarns" collection, for which it was my privilege to write an introduction earlier today.

Regretfully yours,
An Extremely Famous and Charismatic Personality

P.S. Could you send me twelve more copies for some friends who I know will be equally offended.

A Viewer* Writes:

Hello. Unfortunately I missed the first of the Ripping Yarns, but I caught most of the last five minutes of the second one when the tuning knob on my old Murphy stuck on BBC-2. But the third I saw from beginning to end apart from a phone call in the middle from old Archie MacIntyre in New Zealand whom I hadn't seen for absolutely ages. Turned out that a huge bottle had fallen on his head in the night and he'd become a missionary. Amazing — didn't remember a thing. One moment a ventilation consultant in the Midlands, the next beloved by thousands in a small Fijian township. He, too, had missed most of the Ripping Yarns but some of his wives had seen them whilst at a 'Polygamy Now!' conference in London.

---

* 'A Viewer' is the pen name of Sir Humphrey de Vere Oldcastle Bart., author of the very popular 'By Camel' series: *By Camel Through Solihull, By Camel from Solihull to Wednesbury, By Camel to Castle Donnington via Beverly, Camels and the Law, Camels — Lunchtime Snack or Lifelong Friend?.* He also writes under the pseudonym 'Graham Greene'.

TOMKINSON'S
SCHOOLDAYS

Adapted from the novel *Atkinson's Schooldays*
Based on the story *My Schooldays* by Robinson as told to Blenkinsop
From an original idea by Jenkinson, Gorringe, Potter, Venables,
Simpson Minor, Tookey and Timms
Translated from the Swedish, cleaned up, put in a nice green folder and
sent to the BBC by:
Michael Palin and Terry Jones

TOMKINSON'S SCHOOLDAYS

England 1912

The scene is Graybridge School; it stands totally isolated amidst empty wastes, a fee-paying mausoleum beside which Dartmoor would look convivial. Pubescent voices are heard in the distance uncertainly singing the School Song, as if no one had ever properly learnt it.

> My school, my school, how bravely she stands,
> Long steeped in the memories of
> Time's ageing hands.
>
> My school, my school, how oft I recall
> The comrades, the wisdom,
> The bat and the ball.
>
> The bails and the wickets,
> The stumps and the pads,
> The athletic supporters . . .

The song fades, and the scene moves to a corridor at Graybridge School. It is a dark, heavily panelled corridor. A line of four boys sit nervously on a bench. From behind the heavy oak door opposite them comes the sound of measured whacks of a cane. The boy at the head of the queue is TOMKINSON. *We hear his thoughts as he listens to the frightful sound from within the Headmaster's study.*

I had been at Graybridge for two weeks . . . and the dour, forbidding place had produced such misery in my soul and fear in my heart as I had never known in my whole life . . . Everything about the place seemed designed to crush the soul and break down any reserve of pride I ever had . . .

The door of the Headmaster's study opens, and the HEAD *shows out a remarkably composed boy.*

3

HEADMASTER   (*dishevelled and a little breathless*): Thank you, Foster! Next!

TOMKINSON goes in. The door shuts . . . and after a moment the sound of caning begins again.

Beating the Headmaster was just one of those ghastly chores which produced such depression within me . . . There was also the compulsory fight with the grizzly bear which all new boys had to go through . . .

TOMKINSON sees the scene in his mind's eye as a huge grizzly bear charges in and attacks him, trying to tear him to pieces. He is in a corner of the quad, surrounded by a crowd of fellow schoolboys urging him on. Around him the ground is littered with the bones of other new boys, blood-stained mortar boards, torn books, gowns ripped apart and dismembered logarithm tables.

And there was St Tadger's day, when, by an old tradition, boys who had been at the school for less than two years were allowed to be nailed to walls by senior prefects.

A senior boy's face concentrating hard as he hammers. With one final blow he finishes and steps down the ladder to admire his handiwork. Five boys are nailed to the wall of the Main School building, rather haphazardly and at strange angles. At the bottom of a ladder a queue of boys waits to be nailed up, TOMKINSON is at the front of the queue. Beside the school buildings the SCHOOL CHAPLAIN is engaged in fairly heavy manual labour, digging an eight feet deep hole, prior to laying a length of pipe.

The days always began the same way. We were woken by alsatians at three-thirty and after two games of football, we assembled for morning prayers in Big Hall.

In the School Hall, the HEADMASTER is on stage, a slightly shambolic man with a lot of chalk on his gown and profusely creased trousers. He is one of those people who pray rather violently with their eyes all screwed up, in that sort of sing-song way masters develop when they've been at it for more than thirty years.

HEADMASTER: O Lord, we give thee humble and hearty thanks for this thy gift of discipline knowing that it is only through the constraints of others that we learn to know ourselves and only through true misery can we find true contentment. We ask Thee to remember especially today the owner, trainer and rider of Doncaster Boy in the 4.15 at Chepstow, and may the fire of thy just and awful wrath fall upon — (*Here he consults a clipboard.*) Biggs, Normanton, Potter Minor and Tookey. Amen . . . Amen . . .

His voice fades. It's a few minutes later. Boys come out of the main door of the school buildings, clutching books, mortar boards, etc. Some of the boys walk normally, some are hopping and TOMKINSON *and the youngest boys shuffle along as best they can, as their legs and arms are tied together.*

How I longed to be able to hop like the second-year boys and not have to ask permission to breathe out after 10.30 and how I dreaded, as we all did, the sight of Grayson, the school bully.

Suddenly TOMKINSON *is pushed in the rush. He falls in front of an elegant, disdainful, monocled figure, wearing a top hat and morning dress.*

. . . He was said to be the most successful bully in the school's history. He had twice won the Public Schools Bullying Cup and last year beat the extraordinarily vicious Ackroyd of Charterhouse at a kick-in of fags at the Hurlingham Club.

GRAYSON *looks scornfully down at* TOMKINSON. *He is flanked by two very large rather broken-faced schoolboys, sons of night club bouncers and joint holders of the Bradshaw Intimidation Trophy. They carry his books. There is a sudden silence as the area around them clears, everybody looks on.*

TOMKINSON: I say . . . sorry, Grayson.
GRAYSON: Call me 'School Bully' you miserable little tick!

GRAYSON *kicks* TOMKINSON *in the time-honoured School Bully fashion — A leisurely boot on the side of the head. Everyone laughs.* GRAYSON *and his henchmen move off.* TOMKINSON *is left nursing the side of his head and trying, despite being soundly trussed up, to pick up the books he has dropped in the mud.*

Five weeks after the start of term I had an amazing stroke of luck. I was accidentally shot in the stomach by Monsieur Lapointe during French translation.

A stretcher is carried out of a big door opening onto the quad: TOMKINSON *lies on it, bleeding profusely. Two boys carry it across the quad.*

SHOOTING.

THE FOLLOWING BOYS
HAVE BEEN SHOT.

K. Potter
N. Rutherford
J. D'A Smallpiece.

SCHOOL LECTURE 1913

On June 12th in big school
Rear Admiral Sir Vincent Smythe
Obleson, the polar explorer,
will address the school.
Attendance is compulsory.

*Beating the Headmaster was just one of those ghastly
chores that produced such depression in me . . .*

And I ended up in the school sanatorium.

Interior of the school sanatorium. There are four or five beds, in all of which boys are nursing quite serious injuries — heavily bandaged heads, both legs in plaster, entire bodies in splints.
A notice on the wall reads: "No screaming after 10 o' clock".

Now at last my parents would come to visit me and I could tell them of the horrors I was going through. I felt sure they would understand.

A door opens at the far end of the room. TOMKINSON *puts down his copy of "Healthy Hobbies for Boys", and looks towards the door with dawning pleasure.*

TOMKINSON: Hello Mummy . . !

MUMMY enters anxiously. She is a rather glamorous middle-aged lady, dressed expensively, in the latest Parisian style.

MUMMY: Hello Tomkinson . . . How are the wounds?
TOMKINSON: Oh, not bad.
MUMMY: Here, I brought you these . . .

She feels in her handbag and produces two articulated steel shoe trees.

TOMKINSON (*uncertainly*): What are they?
MUMMY: Shoe trees, dear.
TOMKINSON (*even more uncertainly*): Oh . . . super . . . Where's Daddy . . . ?
MUMMY (*dramatically casting her eyes downwards*): He's at the South Pole again dear.
TOMKINSON: Oh, lucky Daddy . . . Look, perhaps I could go and —
MUMMY (*as she turns away*): Tomkinson?
TOMKINSON: Yes, Mummy.
MUMMY (*tragically*): He may . . . he may not be back from the Pole . . .
TOMKINSON: You mean —
MUMMY: Yes . . . he's got a woman down there. . .
TOMKINSON (*incredulously*): Another woman . . . besides you . . .
MUMMY: Yes . . . I think so . . . He keeps going back there you know . . . this is his hundred and forty-sixth expedition.
TOMKINSON: Yes . . . I never realized . . . I thought he was —
MUMMY: Mapping the annual movement of the Polar Ice Shelf . . . yes so did we all.
TOMKINSON: Well perhaps I should come home and . . .
MUMMY (*quickly*): No . . . I'm afraid you must stay here Tomkinson. A kind man has agreed to pay your school fees for the next four years . . . and the Headmaster will let you stay on here free during the holidays.
TOMKINSON: But Mummy —

MUMMY: It's the only thing we can do, Tomkinson. I shall continue to send you cakes, of course . . .

TOMKINSON: But . . . ?

MUMMY: I must go now dear . . . I hope the wounds heal up.

TOMKINSON: Oh . . . they're nothing . . . but . . .

The head of a naked man appears round the door of the sanatorium. His hair is neatly centre-parted and he has a tidy moustache, and a pair of white woollen briefs, tightly gathered round his lower parts.

NAKED MAN: Are you coming Elspeth?

MUMMY: Yes Mr Rogers!

She turns back to TOMKINSON.

Bye bye Tomkinson . . .

TOMKINSON (*choking back his emotion*): Bye bye . . . Mummy.

She walks towards the door. TOMKINSON *looking pathetically after her. After one final, abstracted smile,* MUMMY *leaves. The door bangs shut. Silence. (As it's after 10 o'clock).*

I was shattered. I couldn't believe that my father would just go off like that with another woman. From that moment on I resolved to do everything in my power to escape from Graybridge at the first opportunity . . .

A rugby match is in progress. TOMKINSON *is playing. It is a cold day. On one side of the pitch a line of masters and boys are supporting miserably. The boys look chilly and clap occasionally. They all have chains attached to their ankles and hooked over stakes hammered into the ground. On the other side of the pitch is one lone master from the opposing team. A very keen housemaster (*MR ELLIS*) keeps cheering Graybridge on. He is conspicuously the only enthusiast.*

MR ELLIS: Up Graybridge! Go! Go! Go! Graybridge . . . Gr . . . ay . . . bridge!

The master next to him, MR LENDON, glowers a little, takes a long drag on a suspiciously fat cigarette and passes it on to the next master.

MR LENDON: Roach?

MR ROACH: Thanks, man — you're beautiful . . .

MR ROACH pulls on it slowly. His pupils dilate in more than purely nicotinal pleasure. He passes it back to MR LENDON.

MR ELLIS: Up . . . Stanners . . . Oh well taken.

TOMKINSON catches the ball at the full back position.

Well taken, Tomkinson!

TOMKINSON runs with the ball through the other team.

Oh played! Graybridge . . . *played!*

TOMKINSON whisks in great style past the other team and heads between the posts.

Well pl . . .

His voice trails off and his face drops . . . As he looks on in bewildered amazement, TOMKINSON keeps running through the posts, and off up the hill behind, still holding the ball.

MR ELLIS (*his face falling a little*): Tomkinson?

But TOMKINSON is speeding away towards the distant moors.

I was seventeen miles from Graybridge before I was caught by the school leopard.

The courtyard with the sanatorium in it — a stretcher appears round the corner. On it is TOMKINSON covered with a blood-stained blanket: two football boots stick out the end. A trail of blood drips down from the stretcher, as it is carried into the sanatorium.

Two weeks later I tried to get out disguised as a woman.

TOMKINSON, in a black housemaid's dress with white apron and a basket, is on his way towards the school gates. He passes the CHAPLAIN, digging hard in a

deep hole, surrounded by large sewage pipes.

TOMKINSON (*putting on a shrill voice*): Morning chaplain . . .
CHAPLAIN: Morning, cleaning lady . . .

TOMKINSON passes through the gates and starts off down the road.

. . . but I was caught by Mr Moodie, the Spanish master.

*As TOMKINSON gets out of the school gates and starts to walk more lightly,
a shape (MR MOODIE) emerges, fast and lecherous, from behind a bush. There
is a scuffle and a stifled scream, as he leaps on TOMKINSON, followed by
various grunts from MR MOODIE, who suddenly starts back with a cry of horror.*

MR MOODIE: Tomkinson!

From then on I was confined to indoor activities only.

*The Hobbies Hut, a sign on the wall reads — "Model Boat Club".
Two or three boys are earnestly at work on little balsa wood models. But
over this scene of quiet, dedicated application there is a loud noise of
rivetting, banging and welding. Suddenly MR ELLIS, who is supervising, stops
and looks up. He starts back in horror.*

MR ELLIS: What's that, Tomkinson?

MR ELLIS is looking up at the end of the classroom where there stands the prow of a fourteen-thousand-ton ice-breaker.
TOMKINSON is on the deck some forty feet up with welding equipment. He shouts down.

TOMKINSON: It's a model ice-breaker, sir.
MR ELLIS: It's a bit big for a model, isn't it, Tomkinson?
TOMKINSON: It's a full-scale model, sir . . .
MR ELLIS: It's not a model if it's full-scale, Tomkinson, it's an ice-breaker.
TOMKINSON: It's good isn't it, sir . . . it's got three engines and —
MR ELLIS: No . . . no . . . you miss the point, Tomkinson, this is not a model . . . there'll be a hell of a stink if this comes up at the Speech Day Exhibition.
TOMKINSON: Yes, sir . . .
MR ELLIS: You're a very stupid boy, Tomkinson, building ice-breakers like this.
TOMKINSON: Yes, sir . . .
MR ELLIS: Now, I won't say anything to the Headmaster provided you can get this down to a minimum of four foot . . .
TOMKINSON: But, *sir* . . . there's four thousand tons of steel . . .
MR ELLIS: D'you want to come and see the Headmaster with me?
TOMKINSON: No, sir.
MR ELLIS: All right . . . melt it down . . . this minute!
TOMKINSON: Yes sir . . . sorry sir.

Later that same term.
In a passageway outside the headmaster's study, TOMKINSON broods unhappily.

There seemed no way I could escape from this prison.

He goes across to the window and gazes out, longingly.

Daily my depression and misery mounted until one day . . .

He turns to look at the school notice board.

Amongst the usual games announcements on the school notice board, something caught my eye.

His eye passes quickly over the usual school notices:

FOOTBALL:
The following have been chosen
to represent the School against
St Elfinrudes:-
Botts A.
Botts T.
Botts F.
Botts C.D.E.
Botts N.
Botts K.
Botts L.
Botts F.
Botts E.D.A.
Botts R.H.K.
Revie

Signed: A. St J. Botts
(Headmaster)

FOR SALE:
2 pieces of blotting-paper
1 dead hamster
Oil
Apply J. Getty (Shell b)

TABLE TENNIS:
v. St. Gonads —

Botts F.O.
Botts R.
Botts C.
Botts O.Q.

RUGBY:
J.D.C. Botts and L. Botts have
been awarded their school colours.

SHOOTING:
The following boys have been
shot:-

K. Potter
N. Rutherford
J. D'a Smallpiece

CAMP
School Camp this year will be on
Krakatoa, east of Java. Please
bring light summer shirts, and
change of underwear.

But TOMKINSON'S *eye lights on one particular announcement:-*

SCHOOL LECTURE: 1913

On June 12th in Big School,
Rear-Admiral Sir Vincent-Smythe Obleson,
the polar explorer, will address the School.
Attendance is compulsory.

I wondered . . . could this be my chance? . . .

The scene shifts to the School Hall on lecture day: The HEADMASTER *is up at the lectern again.*

HEADMASTER   (*eyes clenched in prayer*): And finally, O Lord, we beseech thee at this time to show us the virtues of severity and to instil in each and every one of us a proper and due regard for our own worthlessness; excepting at this time, of course, the masters. Furthermore, we ask thee for soft going at

Redcar and a full house or three aces for Mr Motson in the staff common room. And may thy just and awful wrath descend, for the second week running upon . . . (*And here he opens his eyes and consults a folded piece of paper on the lectern.*) Tibbs, Potter, A., Potter, S., Higham, Dibley, Norman and Yewthrop Minor . . . Amen. Amen. Now for the school lecture this year, we are extremely fortunate to have secured the services of one of our most distinguished old boys, the Polar Explorer — Rear-Admiral Sir Vincent Smythe-Obleson. Applause! Applause!

Applause breaks out obediently. The HEAD, *satisfied, sits down on a chair at the side of the stage.* SIR VINCENT *in full polar gear, mounts the stage cumbersomely. He has a thick knitted balaclava all over his face, with just a couple of eye-holes. He speaks in a rather muffled upper-class voice. He fumbles with some notes, which he tries to arrange on the lectern, with great difficulty, owing to a large and clumsy pair of woollen mittens.*

EXPLORER (*muffled*): Hello, boys . . . How nice it is to be . . .

VOICE FROM THE BACK
OF THE SCHOOL HALL: Speak up!

The HEADMASTER, *outraged, leaps out of his chair and comes to the front of the stage.*

HEADMASTER: Who said that?

EXPLORER: I would like to say . . .

HEADMASTER (*to* EXPLORER): Shut up. Who was it . . . ?

Silence from the Hall.

Right, the entire back three rows will come and beat me this evening . . .

Stunned silence. He turns to EXPLORER.

Carry on . . .

EXPLORER: Thank you . . . You know it's very fashionable nowadays to scoff and to . . . (*He fumbles with his notes.*) . . . people say to me what are the . . . ? (*And drops a bit of paper.*) Why are you such and such? (*Before at last finding his place.*) Well I've just returned from exploring one of the enormously interesting Polar Ice Caps . . . I explored for over three months, eight hours a day . . . I got up at nine and explored till six, with a one-hour non-exploring break for lunch, and during that time I can safely say I have explored in His Majesty's name an area the size of Yorkshire . . .

Desultory applause. The HEADMASTER *narrows his eyes.*

This area . . .

HEADMASTER *leaps up and strides to the front of the stage.*

HEADMASTER: Stop it! If the school refuses to show its appreciation spontaneously, I shall be forced to close it down instantly and burn selected boys.

EXPLORER: This area —

HEADMASTER *(to* EXPLORER*)*: Wait! *(To the School.)* Is that clear?

Surly silence. He turns back to the EXPLORER.

Right . . . carry on . . .

EXPLORER: This area of Polar ice-cap I have called Graybridge-Land

A vast surge of applause greets this.

HEADMASTER: That's better!

EXPLORER: And the little settlement there which may one day grow into a great city, I have called Headmasterville.

Cheers and roars of applause from the School.

HEADMASTER *(yelling above the din)*: That's *too much!*

EXPLORER: Now people say to me, what are the qualities which go to make a great nation? Well they are the same as those which go to make a great school — Love of one's country . . .

He pauses for effect — Absolutely no response.

HEADMASTER *(yells)*: Applause!

Sudden voluminous applause. SIR VINCENT *continues.*

EXPLORER: Love of one's King.

Applause.

Love of . . . *(The heavy sub-polar gloves he's wearing are giving him more trouble with his notes.)* . . . love of one's fellow men . . .

Applause.

Love of . . . *(He has lost his place totally.)* . . . and other things.

Applause. He tries to improvise frantically.

Love of er . . . apples.

Applause.

Love of . . . kidney beans.

Applause.

TOMKINSON *looks around him.*

This was my chance . . .

Quickly, furtively, he slips out along the row of boys.

EXPLORER: You know, boys, there is nothing worse than seeing the human body abused . . .
VOICE FROM BACK: Rubbish!
HEADMASTER *(leaping to his feet)*: Who said that?
ANOTHER VOICE: Mr Roach, sir!
HEADMASTER: I see . . . sorry . . . I thought it was one of the boys.

He sits down again.

Carry on . . .

As SIR VINCENT *drones on* TOMKINSON *makes good his escape into a small backstage room. A number of pieces of exploring equipment lie around, including a large old trunk marked:* REAR ADMIRAL SMYTHE-OBLESON BRITISH ANTARCTIC EXPEDITION 1910. TOMKINSON *looks around, lifts the lid and slips into the trunk.*
Back in the hall the lecture is still in progress. SIR VINCENT, *having lost all his notes, is improvising wildly.*

EXPLORER: And indeed the future of our children and their children, and their children's children . . . I say to you all . . . long live Britain . . . And long live the very reasonably priced Graybridge. Let us all stand together now and sing the School Song.

The boys stand. Some of them look at each other a bit uncertainly. A piano starts boldly, but no one knows the words or the tune. An awful flat cacophony results.
TOMKINSON *hears it from inside the box. After a while it stops.*

The lecture had finished. Soon I felt myself being lifted up.

The trunk is yanked into the air.

It had worked. At last I was on my way out of Graybridge.

As the trunk is carried, downstairs and round corners, TOMKINSON *nods happily off to sleep. Suddenly he awakes with a jolt.*

I seemed to have lost all sense of time, when my journey finally came to an end. Where on earth was I? At the docks? In the dark hold of some creaking cargo boat . . . hell bent for the Falkland Islands? Hardly daring to breathe — I looked out on a new world outside.

As the lid is slowly raised TOMKINSON *peers out and blinks. He hears the sound of the* HEADMASTER'S *voice.*

HEADMASTER: That was very good, Ellis . . . very good indeed.

Through the gap of the lid of the trunk, TOMKINSON *sees he is in the headmaster's study yet again. The* EXPLORER *is busy pulling off his gear, he pulls the big woollen balaclava off his head to reveal he is none other than the housemaster,* MR ELLIS.

HEADMASTER: But why . . . *why* the school song, Ellis? You know no-one knows it.
MR ELLIS: I'm sorry, sir, I thought it was a jolly good wheeze for ending up, sir. It just came to me.

HEADMASTER: Well stick to the script in future.
MR ELLIS: Yes sir, sorry sir, but . . .

TOMKINSON *drops the trunk lid, with an uncontrollable cry of disappointment, the* HEAD *and* ELLIS *turn sharply to the sound.*
Later that day: the school grounds. It's dusk — the CHAPLAIN *wheeling a barrow with a huge load of earth and a spade stuck in the top, passes a filthy refuse pit. There is a sack in the middle of it, which moves occasionally.*

After the incident with the trunk, things became really hard for me. My ears were sewn back and I had to do three weeks' detention in a sack on the school maggot pit. But for the first time, I became the centre of some attention at Graybridge, and to my surprise I found myself once again in the presence of Grayson, the School Bully.

Two boys approach the maggot pit and start to pick up the sack. The sack is dragged up a school stairway, and along a faceless corridor. The two boys stop outside a door. One knocks.

GRAYSON'S VOICE   (*from within*): Come!

Inside the room GRAYSON *lies stretched out on a sofa, in a study hung with luxurious trappings and expensive ornaments. A dusky oriental girl is gently massaging his temples. At a desk at one side, a fag is cleaning a pair of immaculate and expensive shoes, the end of a long line of four hundred similarly immaculate and expensive shoes, another is buttering a huge pile of toast.*

In return for not hitting any of the masters, the Head had allowed Grayson certain privileges, such as having unmarried Filipino women in his room, smoking opium and having a sauna instead of prayers. He had just returned from a winter term cruise to South America and looked fit and well.

TOMKINSON *has been dragged in and released from the sack. He is trussed up, his face is covered in mud and filth, and a few houseflies still buzz angrily around him . . .*

GRAYSON: Tomkinson, you appalling little tick — you really are as ugly and unpleasant a little piece of vermin as it's ever been my misfortune to encounter.

I breathed a sigh of relief . . . at least he liked me.

GRAYSON: Some filthy little creeps in the Lower School have been telling me about your escaping tricks . . .
TOMKINSON: That's right . . . you —
GRAYSON: Don't answer back you snotty little oik.
TOMKINSON   (*under his breath*): Sorry . . .
GRAYSON: You know that all the escape routes from this school are run by myself and the Chaplain? Eh? Don't you?
TOMKINSON: No . . .
GRAYSON: Why do you think the Chaplain's always laying gas mains and doing sewage work . . . ?
TOMKINSON: I thought he liked it.
GRAYSON: Shut up! . . . I'm talking. Of course he doesn't like it. He does it because I tell him to and because I'm the only person he knows who's ever likely to get him an archbishopric . . .
TOMKINSON   (*incredulously*): Is Mr Hoskins going to be an Archbishop?
GRAYSON: When he's finished digging. (*Reflectively.*) Trouble is he thinks it's York or Canterbury . . . which is sad really.
TOMKINSON: Where . . . is it?

GRAYSON: Soligorsk . . . it's in the Ukraine, bitterly cold, and the food's appalling, but I can't help that . . . The point is the Chaplain has nearly completed a network of tunnels over twelve miles long . . . and the last thing we want is for spotty little twerps like you to spoil —

A phone rings beside his chaise longue.

GRAYSON (*picking up the phone*): School Bully. What? Ah! We were just talking about you . . . no, no . . . it hasn't arrived yet . . . (*He covers the receiver.*) He wants to know about the hat . . . the archbishop's hat . . . (*His minions all shake their heads, one or two giggle.*) No it's not here . . . no you can't start at the weekend . . . what? . . . because the old one has to die for a start . . . no I couldn't do that . . . anyway, why the big hurry? . . . you *what?* . . . oh no! . . . listen . . . (*Slamming the phone down.*) The idiot!

TOMKINSON: What's the matter?

GRAYSON (*he is about to be very angry, but on seeing* TOMKINSON'S *look of eager innocence, his expression slowly changes*): Nothing, nothing at all. (*An idea occurs to him.*) Listen Tomkinson . . . you're pretty keen to get out of this place, aren't you? . . .

TOMKINSON: *Rather!*

GRAYSON: Well, though I detest and loathe the sight of your odious little face . . . I'm prepared to let you be the first to try out the Chaplain's new tunnels.

TOMKINSON: Oh, thank you, Bully!

GRAYSON: You like girls . . . ?

TOMKINSON: Who?

GRAYSON (*beckoning to the* NUBILE ORIENTAL *behind him*): Suki?

GIRL: Yes . . . School Bully?

GRAYSON: I thought perhaps you'd like to show Tomkinson the tunnels . . . keep him company, eh . . .

The delectable SUKI, *a third generation Sumatran, snakes up to* TOMKINSON *and puts her tongue gently in his ear.*

TOMKINSON: Gosh . . .

GRAYSON: Cigarettes . . . ?

TOMKINSON: Oh gosh . . . I . . . I don't really.

GRAYSON: Go on. I've got hundreds.

GRAYSON throws him a pack of 200 Capstan Full Strength (13.8%). SUKI puts a cigarette in his mouth and lights it. A fag hands GRAYSON a drink, he pours an extra slug and hands it to TOMKINSON, while SUKI is kissing him and ruffling his hair. GRAYSON pours another for himself and raises his glass.

GRAYSON: Well . . . here you go . . . let's drink to it . . . here's to the end of the tunnel.

TOMKINSON: Oh gosh . . .

He drinks the whisky. GRAYSON *immediately pours him some more.*
Jollity all round.

So it was that four hours later, carrying two hundred cigarettes, completely
drunk and with a half-naked, unmarried Filipino lady, I emerged, behind
the writing desk in the Headmaster's study — simultaneously breaking a
hundred and twenty-seven school rules. The Chaplain, now seventy-four
and impatient to get his Archbishopric, had finished the tunnel just a
hundred yards too early.

From the door of the Head's house, two boys emerge carrying TOMKINSON
*on the inevitable stretcher. There is a blanket over him, but his arm is
hanging down outside of the stretcher still clutching a bottle of whisky,
three quarters drunk: the stretcher goes into the sanatorium as before,
with* TOMKINSON *singing bawdily.*

I was found guilty of smoking, drinking, lying, thieving, breaking the
Headmaster's writing desk, and escaping without permission. And I was
sentenced to the most awful penalty the school could provide — the
Thirty Mile Hop against St Anthony's. Training for the hop was a night-
mare . . .

The boys in the hopping team, TOMKINSON *leading, are hopping in increasing
desperation, up a never-ending hillside.* TOMKINSON *looks up and straight
ahead of him is a blood-stained skeleton, swinging crazily from a tree.*
TOMKINSON *screams and wakes up. He is in his bed in the dormitory, eyes
staring and face sweaty with fear.*

And after three weeks of these nightmares we had a hopping team second
to none . . .

A desolate hillside, TOMKINSON *and the boys of Graybridge are trailing
unhappily up to the start.*

I'll never forget the day of the hop . . . the whole school was in a fever . . .
mostly dysentery and beri-beri, but with a few cases of blackwater fever
and scurvy amongst the older boys.

A starting line with flags. It is cold and windy. The St Anthony's team (six strapping athletes all over six foot two and blond) run in at the double, fearsomely well-drilled: making the Hitler Youth look like an old folks' outing.

Our opponents, St Anthony's, a Buddhist public school in Yorkshire, were legendary hoppers . . .

MR ELLIS   (*rubbing his hands in the bitterly cold weather, as he lines them up at the start*): Right! Good hopping, Graybridge. Keep that leg up, remember what W.G. Grace said, "Don't play the ball, unless the what-not's . . . something or other on the . . . whatsit . . . thingummy . . ." and you can't go far wrong.

MR ELLIS stands to one side . . . beside him is MR CRAFFIT, the maths master, in black velvet jacket, long khaki shorts, army boots and a three-cornered hat with a knobkerry.

As soon as we were in line . . . Mr Craffit who was Gundy for the day, gave us each a Palfreys, and we were ready to start . . .

Walking rather eccentrically, the oddly-attired MR CRAFFIT, head to one side and bending forward, goes up the line and confronts the first boy.

MR CRAFFIT: First wee laddie for a Palfrey . . . hit!

He strikes the boy hard on the side of the head with his knobkerry, and moves on to the next one . . .

Second wee laddie for a Palfrey . . . hit!

He repeats the action and moves on.

Medium-sized laddie for a great big Palfrey . . . . hit!

He strikes him sharply. And moves on. Having hit all the boys, MR CRAFFIT, walks to one side and assumes a strange posture. MR ELLIS picks up a starting pistol and stands poised.

MR ELLIS: Boys of St Anthony's and Graybridge School . . . Hop ye! And hop ye good this day! On your marks . . . get set . . .

ELLIS fires. No-one moves. Total silence.

MR ELLIS   (*to boys*): Well . . . go on!

They stream off across the mountain. The six foot two boys from St Anthony's go into an immediate lead.

GRAYBRIDGE WELCOMES TOMKINSON

You just . . . sniff it.

MR ELLIS   (*shouting after them*): Hop, Graybridge! Hop up! Hop up!

We all did our best, God knows, but we were severely weakened by our training and were no match for the St Anthony's boys, many of whom had hopped internationally. The terrain soon began to take its toll of young bodies ravaged by two terms of athlete's foot and Dhobi's itch.

There is a long line of white-vested, blue-shorted, gymshoed figures straggling up a three-in-one cliffside. One of them falls.

After twelve and a half miles, I saw Venner of 5A fall and die of exhaustion, and after seventeen miles he was joined by Apsley, Credworth P.E., Spitwell, Emerson and Zappa Major.

TOMKINSON himself is sweating and fearful, desperately hauling his body along.

. . . and I knew that my own time would soon be up.

Finally his non-hopping leg begins to sag. He staggers and sways in the last throes of exhaustion.

On the twenty-first mile a wave of darkness swept over me. I could go no further. This was it.

TOMKINSON collapses. Around him all seems to be blackness. Suddenly a voice comes from nowhere.

GRAYSON: Hello, you snivelling little creep.

TOMKINSON looks up. There, silhouetted against the rays of a dying sun, is GRAYSON the School Bully in a sedan chair borne by two fags.

TOMKINSON   (*with his last breath*): Hello, School Bully.
GRAYSON: Listen, you little toad, I'm sorry about getting you — (*He lowers his voice.*) — into this spot . . .

TOMKINSON: Oh, the hop . . . it'll be all right . . .

GRAYSON: Of course it won't, you pathetic twerp, you'll never last the course, no-one from Graybridge ever has . . .

TOMKINSON's head drops in dismay.

. . . still, I've got something that may help.

He feels in his pocket and pulls out a bottle of strange white substance.

Just sniff this.

TOMKINSON: What is it?

GRAYSON tips out a little of the white powder on to the back of his fist.

GRAYSON: Just sort of smelling salts — come on.

TOMKINSON: And I just . . . ?

GRAYSON: Hurry.

TOMKINSON (*he sniffs*): Gosh!

GRAYSON: Well good luck, you dismally untalented little creep. That should keep you going a bit longer . . .

GRAYSON smiles enigmatically, nods his head and the two fags pick him up and bear him away down the hill.
A strange look has come over TOMKINSON's face, a dawning omnipotence, a slowly spreading smile of triumph. He rises majestically to his feet, raises his leg crisply into the correct hopping position, and starts off at tremendous speed. Within seconds, TOMKINSON has disappeared up and over the hill. . .

I didn't know what Grayson had given me but the mountains looked wonderful that day . . . Huge grey-green monsters that grappled with the Satan-like demons of the cliffs and crags . . . I could hear sheep talking and the grass reciting poetry. My father always said Nansen was "on something" when he explored Greenland and now I could understand it. I felt I could hop for ever, anywhere . . .

TOMKINSON rounds the side of a mountain ridge, past a group of St Anthony's hoppers — they are still looking grimly fit, but just beginning to show signs of fatigue. TOMKINSON passes them with arrogant ease and hops off towards the horizon.
TOMKINSON hops round the corner of a deserted country lane, and turns into the gates of a modest early Georgian manor house. A maid (a shy quiet girl) is beating a doormat . . . he hops up to her.

TOMKINSON: (*hopping on the spot*): My mother? . . . is she in? . . . I must see her.

MAID: I'm afraid she's . . . busy, sir . . .

TOMKINSON: I don't care, I must see her . . .

MAID: She's . . . playing tennis, I think, sir . . .

TOMKINSON: Thank you.

As he turns to hop off, the MAID *rather resignedly starts to unbutton her blouse . . .*

MAID: D'you want a bit of —

TOMKINSON (*colouring*): No . . . no . . . thank you . . .

He hops away, leaving the MAID *a little disappointed, and crosses the exquisitely-kept lawns, in the direction of the tennis court. He hears the sound of a game in progress. He hops round a greenhouse, up a little path, and ahead of him sees the tennis court. But there is no game in progress. Instead* MUMMY *and a* MAN *in long white shorts, socks and shoes, but no shirt, are rolling on the court together. At the edge of the court a rather crackly old record of a tennis game is playing on a horn gramophone.* MUMMY *shrieks and moans in delight.*

TOMKINSON: Mummy!

MUMMY *and the* SEMI-NUDE MAN *look up.*

MUMMY (*taken aback*): Tomkinson! . . . (*She quickly regains control of the situation and starts to push the* MAN *away.*) Good Lord. Mr Bradman! What a service!

The MAN *leaps up, snatches his clothes and backs away in undisguised confusion. He disappears into the bushes on the far side of the court.* TOMKINSON *joins his mother innocently and joyfully, and they walk through the country house garden, away from the tennis court. She brushes herself down and smooths out her clothing, trying to look dignified in spite of it all . . . They are talking, and* TOMKINSON *is trying to persuade her to let him leave Graybridge . . .*

MUMMY: No! . . . I'm afraid . . . you can't just let your schooling go Tomkinson, you owe it to me and you owe it to your father . . .

At this point a NUDE MAN, *with only socks and shoes on, darts from behind an ornamental hedge, grabs a piece of clothing and vanishes behind another hedge. But* TOMKINSON *is talking far too earnestly to notice this, or any other manifestations of* MUMMY'S *prolific promiscuity.*

TOMKINSON: You can't send me back to that prison.

Another couple of NUDE MEN *dive for cover behind an immaculately-clipped privet.*

MUMMY: Now don't be silly dear.

TOMKINSON: Oh you don't know what it's like . . . they torture you and beat you and humiliate you.

MUMMY: It sounds *very* nice, dear.

A NUDE MAN *drops from a yew tree and scrambles off, clutching a bundle of clothes.*

TOMKINSON: Mother, I'm never, *ever* going back.

MUMMY: Listen . . .

She stops short, seeing a MAN *pop up from behind an ornamental urn.* MUMMY *deftly turns and steers* TOMKINSON *along another path, which leads to the French windows.*

MUMMY (*with well-organized tears in her eyes*): When your father set off on his last, fateful polar journey, I made a solemn vow that I would always, always keep you at school.

TOMKINSON: Let me go and talk to him . . . he'll understand.

MUMMY: Don't be a fool, dear. He's at the other end of the earth, surrounded by five million square miles of uncharted ice and snow . . . how on earth d'you think you'd find him?

TOMKINSON: Well, you've got his address.

MUMMY: Yes . . . but I can't give it to you.

TOMKINSON: Mother I . . .

MUMMY: He made me promise never to reveal his whereabouts to a member of the press.

TOMKINSON: But I'm not . . .

MUMMY (*with a world-weary sigh, striking a thirties pose by the French windows*): No! You must go back to Graybridge, as *he* would have wanted it, and I must get on with the gardening.

Four NUDE MEN *behind the rhododendrons smile happily as they hear this.*

TOMKINSON: But . . .

MUMMY: Take my bicycle . . . And here's some rhubarb for the journey.

TOMKINSON (*faintly*): Oh thank you.

MUMMY (*kissing him*): Goodbye Thomson.
TOMKINSON: Tomkinson . . .
MUMMY: I'm sorry . . . Tomkinson . . .
TOMKINSON: Bye, bye, mother.

TOMKINSON is about to turn away downcast when an UNDRESSED MAN, unable to contain himself any longer, suddenly drops onto MUMMY from above the French windows. He starts grappling with her on the ground in wild embraces.

TOMKINSON: Mummy! Who is this?

MUMMY'S head sticks out from the mêlée.

MUMMY: Who is *what*, dear?
TOMKINSON: This man?
MUMMY: What man? (*Then, as if noticing her randy assailant for the first time.*) Oh good Lord! Get off!! Get off!

TOMKINSON steps fowards to prise the MAN from his mother.

TOMKINSON: Take your hands off her! You —

The MAN turns to remonstrate, but on seeing TOMKINSON, his mouth drops open.

UNDRESSED MAN: Tomkinson!
TOMKINSON (*even more shattered*): Daddy!

Back at Graybridge, the HEADMASTER is hurrying along the corridor towards the School Bully's study. He knocks at the door, a trifle breathlessly.

GRAYSON (*voice from within*): Enter . . .!

In the study, the SCHOOL BULLY is being dressed by two boys. All his cases are packed, champagne bottles litter the room. He's clearly about to leave.

HEADMASTER: I'm sorry I'm late, School Bully, I was detained at Prayers . . . you've heard the good news — Tomkinson won the Hop . . . ?

GRAYSON: Yes . . . yes . . . yes . . . jolly good.

HEADMASTER: Yes . . . certainly is jolly good . . .

He looks round the bare study with puzzlement.

GRAYSON: Jolly good.

HEADMASTER: Yes . . . it was a record . . . amazing . . . er . . . (*Laughs uneasily.*) . . . are you . . . er . . . going anywhere . . . Bully?

GRAYSON: Yes . . . I've been offered a job at Eton . . .

The HEAD's jaw drops.

HEADMASTER: At Eton!

GRAYSON: Yes, Eton . . . you've heard of it, haven't you . . . you silly little headmaster . . .

GRAYSON: Oh yes of course, Bully . . .

GRAYSON: Their School Bully's left to join the Government, they've offered me the job . . . a thousand pounds a year, meals sent up from London, house in France during Prep and full insurance on all boys damaged . . .

HEADMASTER: Well look, er . . . School Bully . . . you really can't leave just like that, you know . . . I mean parents send their boys to Graybridge just to be bullied by you . . .

GRAYSON: That's your problem, you shabby creature.

The BULLY pushes the HEADMASTER to one side as he checks his appearance in the mirror.

HEADMASTER: Look . . . think this over, Grayson . . . let's not be hasty. I mean Graybridge has got such a good name for bullying . . .

GRAYSON: You can appoint someone else.

HEADMASTER: Bully, you can't do this to me . . . you know there's no one on the school with your strength, your effortless, almost superhuman . . .

The BULLY adjusts his immaculate white gloves and takes a last sip of champagne.

GRAYSON: What about Tomkinson?

HEADMASTER: Tomkinson?

GRAYSON: First ever winner of the Hop . . .

HEADMASTER: Oh yes . . . but I was going to make him Head of School.

GRAYSON: Oh come on! He deserves more than that.
Bye Suki . . .

The BULLY gives SUKI a long, rather sophisticated kiss. The HEAD is slightly embarrassed, and looks away. After what he feels is a decent length of time. for an embrace he turns back to the BULLY, but finds he is still deep in a clinch with SUKI

HEADMASTER: Yes, he won the Hop . . . certainly, but bullying — d'you really think he's up to it?

Some miles away, across the other side of the county, TOMKINSON is walking disconsolately down the drive away from his mother's house. He is wheeling a lady's bicycle.

So now I knew the truth. Daddy was no more an Antarctic explorer than Mr Amundsen at the post office and I had just been sent to Graybridge to keep me out of the way. My little world of schoolboy illusions was shattered for ever. Graybridge was now the only home I knew — there was to be no refuge from the tyranny and oppression it stood for . . .

As he reaches the gates of the drive, an open car full of laughing, shouting NUDE MEN turns past him and up the drive to the house.
Back at Graybridge the BULLY and SUKI are still in a clinch. The HEAD stands there awkwardly.

HEADMASTER: Yes . . . yes . . . on thinking about it . . . er . . . Bully . . . I think you could be right . . . I think Tomkinson could make a very fine bully indeed . . .

He looks up. They are still in a clinch.

HEADMASTER: Well . . . jolly . . . good.

GRAYSON finishes his long, lingering kiss, picks up his bags and pushes past.

GRAYSON: Well, there's your problem solved, you dreadfully indecisive little squirt . . .
HEADMASTER (*following him out*): Oh, thank you, Bully, thank you, for everything . . .

The BULLY goes out, with fags carrying his cases. The HEAD shouts after them, down the corridor:

HEADMASTER: Beggins! Foster! When you've been kicked, come straight back here and repaint the study. Watkins, take your hands out of Gilbert's pockets and go and get the opium from Matron. Hawker, Bulstrode and Neames, go and find the Art Master . . . I want a banner eight foot by twenty foot . . . right across the school buildings. . .

Meanwhile TOMKINSON is cycling wearily, resignedly back to the school.

As I cycled back through the leafy English countryside towards Graybridge, a thousand memories crowded into my mind . . . of the horrors that had blighted my life there and the lives of so many of my companions . . . and were to ruin my life for three more years. How could a system like that ever change? There was no hope left . . .

He remembers Graybridge in its full awfulness — the maggot pit, the fight with the grizzly bear, boys being nailed to the wall, MR MOODIE, *the Spanish master, goosing him. Boys' ankles in irons as they watch rugby. The leering face of the* HEADMASTER. *The leering face of the* BULLY. *At these memories his eyes water, and he hangs his head hopelessly, helplessly, and cycles on.*

Meanwhile, back at Graybridge: in the main quad a dais has been hastily and insecurely erected. On it are arrayed the members of staff, two of whom are clearly still in a psychedelic seventh heaven. The HEAD *stands, looking anxiously at his watch. He is waiting for* TOMKINSON'S *arrival. Above him is draped a banner which reads:*

"GRAYBRIDGE WELCOMES TOMKINSON"
Another, across the front of the dais reads:
"WELCOME HOME TOMKINSON! OUR VERY OWN BULLY!"
And another:
"TOMKINSON — OUR NEW BULLY".

The whole school has been assembled in the quad. The school brass band are murdering some popular melodies, MR ELLIS *is obviously dying to sing the School Song, and behind the senior boys, at the back of the crowd is a small group of fags, who are looking towards the school gate hopefully. They surreptitiously clutch makeshift signs like:*

"TOMKINSON, FAGS' HERO" "FAIR PLAY FOR FOURTH FORMERS"
"TOMKINSON TAMES THE TOUGHS" "UNSHACKLE THE SHELL"
"NO MORE FLOGGING"

Outside the school: TOMKINSON *starts his long and weary, hopeless approach up the school drive. He passes the War Memorial, which commemorates the ninety-four boys killed during the war between the lower sixth and the third form in 1909. He passes the statue of the school's most famous*

*old boy — Albert Bexall, the Nottingham Rapist (Stoddart's 1902-05).
Then all at once he hears the band. He stops. he looks up in astonishment
at the banner across the main entrance:*
"TOMKINSON — BULLY FOR US".
A tiny boy, deputed by the HEAD *to alert the School, sees* TOMKINSON *and
gives a shrill shout.*

TINY BOY: He's here!

TOMKINSON dismounts and slowly approaches the gate.

At first, I couldn't believe what was happening . . .

*A huge cheer goes up as soon as he is seen. The band strike up an horrific
version of "For He's a Jolly Good Fellow". The* HEAD *beams and leads the
applause. The third- and fourth-formers joyfully waggle their little banners.*
TOMKINSON wheels his bike slowly across the quad towards the crowd.

**Then I realized. Perhaps there *was* a chance to change Graybridge — and
it was suddenly, amazingly being offered to me.**

*Suddenly a small, spotty, runny-nosed snivelling little junior is pushed
out, and falls in front of TOMKINSON.*

SNIVELLING JUNIOR (*summoning up all his courage*): Jolly good show, Tomkinson!

*At this there is a sudden silence, a sharp intake of breath. The disastrous
band grinds to a halt. Everyone waits. The* HEADMASTER *frowns slightly
and looks to* TOMKINSON *for his reaction to the* BOY. *The snivelling* BOY
looks up at TOMKINSON *looking down. Slowly a look of compassion comes
across* TOMKINSON'S *face as he shakes his head sadly.*

But of course, I knew I would have to do it in easy stages.

TOMKINSON: Call me "School Bully", you ghastly little toad!

TOMKINSON kicks the snivelling BOY *on the side of the head in the time-honoured School-Bully fashion. As the* BOY *crawls back into the crowd, the atmosphere relaxes, everyone cheers. The* HEADMASTER *beams, and all the masters look relieved.* TOMKINSON, *with a new-found swagger, goes up to the* HEADMASTER *and shakes his hand.*

HEADMASTER (*beaming*): I knew you'd make a go of it, Thomson.
TOMKINSON (*reacting sharply*): *Tomkinson, cloth-ears!*
HEADMASTER: Oh sorry, School Bully.
MR ELLIS: Let's sing the School Song.
HEADMASTER: No! no! Ellis, please . . .

The band starts up hopelessly on one side of the crowd. The banners of the disappointed fags and first-formers are being broken up by senior boys. All the masters shake TOMKINSON'S *hand. The tuneless School Song led by the tone-deaf* MR ELLIS *fills the ancient quadrangle and the old school of Graybridge (motto: "Pecuniam habere nobis necesse est." — we need the money) returns to its old self once again.*

ACROSS
THE ANDES
BY
FROG

Captain Walter Snetterton

Captain Peary

Roald Amundsen

El Misti

ACROSS THE ANDES BY FROG

In the late nineteenth century and early twentieth century, Man's Knowledge of the World was expanding rapidly. He reached the North and South Poles, made journeys across deserts and through mountain ranges hitherto thought impassable. There seemed no limits to the courage of intrepid and resourceful men, prepared to test the barriers of physical endurance, to accept the ultimate challenge of unknown dangers in the unceasing search for knowledge.

One of this new breed was Captain Walter Snetterton, who, in 1927, against all the best advice of friends and colleagues, decided to embark on a truly awesome quest — to go Across the Andes By Frog!

High Altitude Amphibian Exploration was still the poor sister of Zoological Experiment, but Captain Snetterton was obsessed by what he felt was the underestimation of the species Anuriae. At the Royal Zoological Institute, in Kensington, he spent years in the laboratory detailing and observing frog behaviour, and in particular their adaptability to hostile environments. After six years of research, Snetterton decided to test his frogs on one of the most inhospitable mountain ranges on earth. It was in the Southern Cordilleras of Peru that, in May 1927, he made the first All-Frog assault on any mountain . . .

Quequeña, Peru. May 1927

An old battered radio of the period stands on a table in the dusty main square of a sleepy Peruvian village. It has an enormously long short wave aerial. In front of it is slumped a Peruvian in a wide-brimmed sombrero. The only sounds are the buzz of flies in the pitilessly hot midday sun and the crackling but excited voice coming from the radio . . . A very fruity British voice it is too.

BBC COMMENTATOR
ON RADIO: And it's Denis for Cardiff now . . . pushes the ball inside to Glover . . . Glover outside to Wadworth and Wadworth takes it round Hillaby . . . round Dodgson, but he can't get past Braithwaite . . . and this burly

Arsenal centre-half clears the ball and boots it way upfield . . . still no score, but the pressure is increasing now on Arsenal and this is Cliff Boles for Cardiff City . . . to Afron Carter inside to Griffiths . . . and . . . (*The radio sound fades totally for a moment.*) . . . and Ferguson has scored! A memorable shot from twenty-five yards into the top left-hand corner, leaving Halliwell no chance at all. So Cardiff City, beaten here only two years ago, now lead Arsenal one goal to nil, with just nineteen minutes of this 1927 Cup Final left . . . and the crowd are erupting here at Wembley . . .

Above the sound of the radio we hear the distant tramp of marching feet. A BRITISH RSM's *voice is shouting orders. Into the square marches a squad led by the* RSM *and* CAPTAIN SNETTERTON *in a solar topee and slightly too long khaki shorts, who marches at the head of his little expedition. They pass under a crudely drawn banner which reads:* "PERU WELCOM OUR GERMAN FREINDS" *and come to a halt in the middle of the square. The squad comprises: two English soldiers with packs on backs, sweating profusely; two native bearers behind with a small box slung on a pole between them . . . It is marked:* "FROGS. THIS WAY UP". *Then behind them come two more native bearers carrying a similar box on a pole, labelled:* "FROGS – KEEP MOIST." *An English Corporal brings up the rear. The football commentary on the radio is still going on excitedly.*

ENGLISH

RADIO: . . . Glover now . . . to Ferguson, the hero of the hour, who picks it up, pushes it out to Vernon . . . Vernon to Waddilove . . .

SNETTERTON *looks around. He pushes back his topee and mops his brow.*

SNETTERTON: Get the frogs in the shade, Sergeant-Major . . . and give them plenty of slime.

RSM (*he turns to the squad*): Company! . . . Company . . . right . . . turn! . . . Bearers . . . fall . . . out . . . Get your boxes over there.

The RSM *indicates some shade under the awning of a well in the centre of the square.* SNETTERTON *takes in the square which, apart from the banner and a few flags, shows no sign that they are expected.* SNETTERTON *registers disappointment.*

SNETTERTON: Well, doesn't seem to be any official welcome of any kind . . .

RSM: No sah . . . I noticed that, sah . . . remarkable absence of any official welcome. (*He gets out cigarette and offers it to* SNETTERTON.) Oily rag, sah?

SNETTERTON: What?

RSM (*proffering the cigarette*): *Fag,* sah?

SNETTERTON: No . . . no, thank you . . .

RSM (*mopping his brow*): Phew . . . isn't 'arf peasy.

SNETTERTON, *obviously pained by the* RSM's *noisy chumminess, goes across to the* PERUVIAN *listening to the radio. The* PERUVIAN *doesn't budge. The football commentary goes on even more excitedly.*

RADIO: And now Arsenal are throwing everything at this Cardiff goal . . . and it's Lambert now who goes up that corner and oh! Only inches wide . . . of the post . . .

SNETTERTON: Hello!

RADIO: And it's another corner for Arsenal now . . . I make it a little over a quarter of an hour of this Cup Final still remaining, and surely Arsenal *must* pull back this Cardiff lead as James now lofts over a beautiful centre and . . .

SNETTERTON *turns the radio off. The* PERUVIAN *suddenly jerks up. Awake.*

PERUVIAN: Hey! What are you doing? Ees the Cup Final . . .

SNETTERTON: We are the expedition from England . . . I'm Captain Snetterton.

PERUVIAN: Please . . . there's only fifteen minutes . . . Cardiff one-nil . . . It's a great final.

SNETTERTON: We are the English expedition to cross the Andes . . . we were expecting to be met here . . . *please! (Incomprehension.* SNETTERTON *repeats slowly, deliberately.)* We . . . have . . . come . . . to . . . cross . . . the Andes.

PERUVIAN *(looking blank)*: I don't know . . .

RSM: D'you want me to clout him, sir? Fetch him one around the face!

SNETTERTON: No, Sergeant . . . I don't think that'll do any good.

Suddenly a British voice rings across the square.

GREGORY: Hello!

A man in rather sweaty tropical clothes appears on the balcony of a house opposite, doing up his flies.

GREGORY: Hello! Captain Snetterton?

SNETTERTON: That's right.

GREGORY *finishes doing up his flies and puts an arm out, after wiping his hands heavily on his shirt. The* PERUVIAN *peasant switches the radio on again.*

GREGORY: My name's Gregory . . . I'm the Vice-Consul here . . . come and have a woman . . . er . . . a drink.

SNETTERTON *(briskly)*: I'd rather not, thank you. I have to get the frogs housed, and I'd like to do a quick recce of the approach slopes of the Cordillera before nightfall . . .

GREGORY: Ah! I see . . . only got the telegram yesterday . . . that's why the place isn't quite . . . there was going to be a band to meet you . . . Political Prisoners' Band from Lima . . . excellent . . .

SNETTERTON: What you can do for me is to get a couple of guides.

GREGORY (*his eyes lighting up*): Girl Guides?

SNETTERTON: No, guides . . . for the mountains . . .

GREGORY (*disappointed*): Ah . . .

SNETTERTON: I want men who know the mountains backwards, every ravine, every track, every rock . . .

GREGORY: Ah well . . . I'm afraid you won't be able to get any tonight . . .

SNETTERTON: What d'you mean?

GREGORY: Well it's the Cup Final . . . Specially if Cardiff win . . .

SNETTERTON: Look . . . man . . . if we can walk a hundred and four miles in five days, the least you can do is find us a couple of guides. I want them here by six.

GREGORY: Not on Cup Final Night . . . Captain . . . it's their big celebration of the year.

SNETTERTON: But . . . all right . . . all right . . . tomorrow at first light.

GREGORY: Ah no! Wimbledon fortnight.

SNETTERTON: *Wimbledon fortnight?*

GREGORY: Yes . . . They won't miss Wimbledon.

SNETTERTON: But the rainy season starts in two days . . . we must be ready for the first assault by then or the whole expedition might as well pack up.

GREGORY: Well . . . I suppose I may get someone . . . not all of them are so interested in the early rounds . . . but I can't promise the best . . .

SNETTERTON: I don't care how you do it, Gregory . . . but I want guides who know those . . . (*He looks up at the mountains.*) those *brutes* . . . and I want them soon . . .

GREGORY: Yes . . . of course, Captain.

SNETTERTON turns on his heel and walks away.
GREGORY turns, makes for the door of the Consulate, pausing by the NATIVE with the radio.

GREGORY: Score?

PERUVIAN: Cardiff! One-nil.

GREGORY shakes his head in disbelief and scuttles indoors.
Next morning: the expedition has set up camp in a nearby field.
SNETTERTON is outside his tent, shaving. GREGORY his hair awry and trousers creased horizontally, as usual, appears behind him.

GREGORY: Captain Snetterton!

SNETTERTON: Good morning, Gregory.

D'you want me to clout him, sir?

GREGORY: I've managed to find you a guide.

SNETTERTON: Ah . . . good man.

GREGORY *(turning to shout)*: Manata . . . atawa . . . manata . . . si . . . appredo.

There is a slight pause. Then a very small, very wrinkled OLD LADY, *in her late eighties, comes running up. She grins and giggles toothlessly up at* SNETTERTON, *who looks utterly disbelieving.*

GREGORY: She knows the mountains like the back of her hand.

More giggles from the GUIDE.

GREGORY: Both her sons were mountain guides.

SNETTERTON *(with scarcely concealed irritation)*: Well why aren't *they* here?

GREGORY: Both dead. I'm afraid . . . fell down a ravine.

SNETTERTON: Look . . . surely she's not the . . .

GREGORY: Best you'll get in Wimbledon fortnight.

SNETTERTON *seems about to protest but just shakes his head wearily. The* OLD LADY *suddenly breaks into a rapid little oration, delivered in a shrill high-pitched screech with much head nodding, in* SNETTERTON'S *direction.* SNETTERTON *backs off, a little apprehensively.*

SNETTERTON: What does she say?

GREGORY *(slightly apologetically)*: She says . . . er . . . great win for Cardiff . . .

SNETTERTON: Oh . . . yes . . .

On May the ninth, 1927, shortly after midday, Snetterton and RSM Byng made the first reconnaissance with their new mountain guide.

The RSM *and* SNETTERTON *are clambering up a rocky, rather perilous mountainside strewn with boulders. They are out of breath and sweating profusely. The* RSM *looks fed up, shakes his head wearily at* SNETTERTON, *and raises his eyes heavenward. They both look up. There, high above them, scrambling with the agility of a mountain goat, leaping from rock to rock and across ravines, is the* LITTLE OLD LADY.

SNETTERTON: These boulders are too sharp and smooth for a frog assault, Sergeant-Major . . . we need a gravel or sand-based approach so the frogs can grip.

RSM: Yes, sah.

SNETTERTON: I think the North-West face'll be better.

RSM: Yes, sah. North-West face, sah.

SNETTERTON: There's much higher precipitation on the Western slope . . . plenty of soil movement . . . ideal frog conditions . . . (*He shouts up to the* OLD LADY.) Hey! Er . . . Ahoy! . . . (*To* RSM.) Look, can't you tell her to stop?

RSM: I don't know what "stop" is, sah.

SNETTERTON: Well it's just "stop" in Spanish, isn't . . . er . . . Stoppo! . . . Arresto . . .?

RSM (*proudly*): I know "stop" in Norwegian, sah . . . . (*He shouts.*) Stanse!

SNETTERTON: She won't understand Norwegian . . . they're all Spanish here. (*He tries shouting.*) Er stop, please! . . .

RSM: No she's not Spanish . . . She's Indian.

SNETTERTON: Well, say something in Indian for God's sake, she'll be in Brazil in twenty minutes.

RSM (*doubtfully*): I only know one word in Indian, sir.

SNETTERTON: Well go on . . . we don't want to be stuck here for life.

RSM: Right . . . er . . . what was it? . . . Oh yeah . . . Damassi . . . that's it . . . (*He shouts.*) Damassi!

The OLD LADY *stops this time, turns, and breaks into a toothless grin.*

OLD LADY: Damassi! Oh! Si! Si! Compreno . . . Damassi!

She giggles and starts to come down, grinning broadly.

SNETTERTON: Oh . . . well done, Sergeant-Major . . . that did the trick. Come on.

The RSM *looks slightly worried but* SNETTERTON *confidently turns and starts down.*
Some time later we find them in the square embroiled in a lively argument. The LITTLE OLD LADY *is screaming and shouting and getting very angry. Two rather dishy Indian girls, hastily dressed for the occasion in Roedean-style blazers, stockings and straw hats and satchels stand at the doorway of a house.* SNETTERTON *is getting the full wrath of the* OLD LADY. *The* RSM *is looking embarrassed,* GREGORY *faintly amused.*

SNETTERTON: No . . . no . . . we did *not* ask for schoolgirls.

OLD LADY: E pudido Damassi. (*She jabs a finger at the* RSM.) Silvato . . . noyenya . . . damassi . . .

GREGORY: Ah . . . she says the fat one asked specifically for schoolgirls.

SNETTERTON: No . . . listen! Please! (*He silences the noise, then turns to the* LADY *and says slowly in his best ruling class voice.*) We . . . were . . . asking . . . you . . . not to go any further . . . We wanted . . . you to stop . . . d'you understand . . . (*Very positively.*) Damassi!

OLD LADY: Si! Si! Damassi! (*Indicates girls.*) Buene . . . settanta peseta . . .

GREGORY (*looking at* SNETTERTON *with regret but a certain renewed interest*): Ah you *did* want schoolgirls . . . well if you'd asked, old chap, we could've . . .

SNETTERTON: Look, I wanted this . . . so-called guide to stop rushing around all over the Andes . . . we never said anything about schoolgirls . . . we just asked her to stop . . .

GREGORY: "Damassi" means "schoolgirls".

SNETTERTON: . . . charging up . . . (*His voice trails off.*) . . . What? (*His eyes turn slowly to the* RSM.) Sergeant-Major . . . I'd like to see you back at the tent immediately please.

He walks away.

RSM: Shall I bring the schoolgirls, sah?

SNETTERTON (*with bitter distaste*): Oh! Shut up!

The scene fades.
That night, all is quiet in the expedition's camp, lights burn warmly in the tents, and only the sound of frogs croaking is borne on the still night air. SNETTERTON *is standing outside his tent, looking out towards the frog boxes which are still gathered around the well in the middle of the village square. Suddenly a rumble of distant thunder makes him look up towards the mountains. The* RSM *joins him.*

SNETTERTON: The frogs are restless tonight, Sergeant-Major.

RSM: Oh yes, sah. It's nerves . . . they can hear the thunder . . . they know the rain's coming sir . . . it's like the first night on the stage, sah . . . they want to get going . . . just like if you was playing Hamlet, sah . . . you'd want to get out there and get a few belters . . . and then you're all right. That's what the frogs are feeling, sir. They're getting in a right old two-and-eight.

Then there is another rumble of thunder, mixing now with the sound of natives jabbering excitedly in the distance. SNETTERTON *and the* RSM *both peer into the darkness, trying to make out what is going on.*

SNETTERTON: Fascinating thing — the frog mind, isn't it?

RSM: Oh yes, sah . . . it's like the night before an important business meeting, sah . . . they get . . .

SNETTERTON: Did you know you could carry on a conversation with a frog, Sergeant-Major?

RSM: (*with a hint of a "here we go again" expression*): Yes sah . . . so they say . . .

SNETTERTON (*still looking off into the distance but becoming more abstracted*): Oh yes . . . I've often chatted to them, you know . . .

There is a very strong rumble of thunder. The noise of an excited crowd of natives grows slightly stronger. As SNETTERTON *drifts off into his own private reverie the* RSM *becomes more engrossed in trying to see what's going on.*

They have a surprisingly wide vocabulary. You see each croak has thousands of little resonances within it . . . a complex system of modulations and variations which can express dozens of thoughts, concepts, ideas. D'you know, Sergeant-Major, that in each inflation of the vocal sac — (SNETTERTON *gives a large "Oink"* — *the* RSM *looks at him long-sufferingly.*) — he is expressing a whole complex theory of amphibian social organization. "Oink!" — "This particular piece of vegetation is my own" . . . "Oink!" "This piece of — "

RSM: I like watching 'em mate, sir.

SNETTERTON (*with irritated disgust*): Yes . . . well . . . you would . . . .

The native voices are louder now.

RSM: They get in each other's mouths . . .

SNETTERTON: Of course they don't.

SNETTERTON *has now refocussed his attention on the disturbance which seems to be coming from the direction of the square and the boxes. Then a strong rumble of thunder.* SNETTERTON *peers into the darkness.*

RSM: They got no organs you see . . . imagine what life would be like if you had nothing in yer trousers!

I'd better shoot a couple of them, Sah!

Suddenly a gunshot shatters the night.

SNETTERTON: What the devil's going on out there?

A breathless CORPORAL MILLER rushes up.

CORPORAL: You'd better come quickly, Captain. Spot of bother with the frogs.
SNETTERTON: Oh My God!

They run towards the square. There is an excited group of natives around the frog boxes. CORPORAL JOHNSON is trying to keep them off by firing shots over their heads, but they already have hold of one box and are holding it high up in the air, amidst much noise and confusion.

SNETTERTON: By Jove! They've got one of the boxes!
RSM: (*raising his rifle*): Shall I let 'em have it, sah?
SNETTERTON: No! Just fire above their heads.
RSM: How about above their *knees*, sah?
SNETTERTON: Above their *heads*, Sergeant-Major. We don't want to lose their goodwill by killing them.
RSM: As you say, sah.

The RSM fires above their heads. But though they turn for a moment to see who it is, they all turn back again and carry on as before.

RSM: I'd better shoot a couple of them, sah.
SNETTERTON: No, hold on. I'll speak to them.
RSM: Remember they don't speak English, sah.
SNETTERTON: That doesn't matter, it's the attitude they respect, Sergeant-Major.

SNETTERTON walks bravely forwards, adopting his impeccable Head Prefect manner.

Now what's going on here?

The mob subsides obediently at the unmistakable tones of command. He points at the frog box which is still being held aloft.

Put that down at once, d'you hear?

The box is replaced on the well. SNETTERTON walks into the midst of them and they fall back. He walks up to the boxes and opens them, checking that the frogs are undisturbed. The natives look on, silent and rather shame-faced. Having satisfied himself that the frogs are safe, SNETTERTON turns on the mob.

Who's in charge here?

There is no answer — the natives look at each other.

Come on! Who organised this?

There is much jostling and pointing and arguing amongst the Indians.
Each one denying responsibility and pointing to someone else. Eventually
by mutual elimination they select amongst themselves the most
insignificant, weedy and generally wretched specimen. He is thrust forward
to bear the full brunt of SNETTERTON'S *wrath. The rest close ranks. The*
WEEDY NATIVE *hesitates for a moment but then realises there is no escape.*

Well? What's the meaning of this? Eh?

WEEDY WHINING NATIVE: Senhor non . . . posso dirigarle poteo donde esta muy boroco ande
picayhuna tendativeho chuaco masa tichuanaka assimpaca meyo sempego
chiqua chiqua juanamentaque juande juande — (*The* WHINING NATIVE *is all*
the time growing steadily more demagogic . . .) — e quasa grande quasa
o . . . ka . . . ma! (*He leaps onto the side of the well and starts gesticulating.*)
Ah! Katacha! immediamente glorioso muchachas vidiero esquator
dirintinho . . . aguava . . . oh mache . . . e de limero . . . e dehiradargo . . .
e de fundalmente organisante diverso . . . noche . . . vachas . . . los vachas
maguava!

He brings his oration to a powerful climax and there is a spontaneous
outburst of applause.
GREGORY *suddenly appears at a dimly-lit doorway. His hair is awry and as*
usual he is doing up his flies. He shouts at the native who has just
delivered the speech.

GREGORY: Pedro . . . Aguate! Aguate . . . instante!

The NATIVE *glowers rather grumpily and retreats back into the crowd.*
GREGORY *wanders up to see what's going on.*

SNETTERTON: What's the matter?

GREGORY (*dismissively*): Oh don't worry about him . . . he wants a three-chamber national assembly with universal adult suffrage, land reforms, abolition of censorship and all sorts of nonsense — half the stuff's not been done in Europe yet, let alone here.

He shouts sharply at the MAN *again and indicates* SNETTERTON.

Aguate!

MAN *cowers away.*

Now what's going on?

All the natives start to jabber away at him and point at the boxes and elsewhere.

NATIVES: Siquato . . . El Misti . . . Equo . . . Catarat.
SNETTERTON: The frogs! Please! You're alarming the frogs!
GREGORY: E equanda davorco . . . aguate!

The noise subsides.

Ah . . . trouble, I'm afraid . . .
SNETTERTON: Why?

There is an ominous roll of thunder over the mountains. They all look up . . . fear is written over the faces of the native crowd. GREGORY *turns to* SNETTERTON.

GREGORY (*indicating thunder*): They think that's because of you, I'm afraid . . .
SNETTERTON: What — the thunder?
GREGORY: No . . . that's not thunder, old boy. I only wish it were . . . that's El Misti — the volcano.
NATIVE: Etali emanati el Misti . . . titiqua . . . dos omeros . . . quercos . . . (*Indicating the frogs.*) Titiqua.
GREGORY: I'm afraid they say the frogs are bringing bad luck on the village . . . they are making El Misti restless . . . he will rain down fire and ashes on all sides . . .
NATIVE (*prompting*): E titiqua.
GREGORY: And molten lava as well.
NATIVE: E titiqua . . . qua.
GREGORY: And small pieces of . . . (*Even* GREGORY *can't follow this.*) . . . What?
NATIVE: Qua . . . titiqua . . . insindero.
GREGORY: Pieces of lava-based . . .
NATIVE (*shakes his head vigorously*): Nono! Nono! Qua . . . (*He enunciates enormously clearly.*) Qua . . . titiqua . . .
GREGORY: Rocks . . .

NATIVE (*does little gesture*): Nono. *Titiqua . . . Tit . . . i . . . qua . . .*
GREGORY: Fragments . . .
NATIVE: *Si si!* . . . Titi*qua . . . qua . . .*
GREGORY: Fragments of oolite?
NATIVE: *Nono . . . insindero menamente . . . titqua . . . qua!*
GREGORY: Small fragments of silurian . . .
NATIVE: *Si! Si!* (*Encouraging him.*) *Titiqua . . . titiqua . . .*
GREGORY: Silurian . . . basalt . . . ?
NATIVE (*very pleased and relieved*): *Si. Titqua . . . si!*
GREGORY: Small pieces of silurian basalt will fly into the air.
NATIVE: *E titiqua . . . aaaaaar gggghh.*
GREGORY: And it's ruining the radio reception.

He points at some natives holding the crackling radio.

NATIVE: *Si!! Si!*
GREGORY: The frogs are imprisoned, you see . . . their souls are appealing to the Gods . . .
SNETTERTON: Well I'm sorry to hear that, but I'm certainly not going to let a lot of superstitious clap-trap get in the way of a scientific expedition . . .

There is a huge crash of thunder from El Misti, the natives look up with fear. So does GREGORY. *Even* SNETTERTON *looks up in the direction of the volcano. The natives move towards the boxes and start picking them up again.*

SNETTERTON: Get away from those boxes, d'you hear!

SNETTERTON *is becoming more threatening.*

GREGORY: Aquate! Inbebe!

The natives murmur amongst themselves rebelliously.

SNETTERTON: Mr Gregory, will you please tell these people to return to their homes at once.
GREGORY: Well, I'll try . . .

GREGORY *turns to the natives and starts haranguing them in their own tongue. Pointing at* SNETTERTON *and the others. The natives eventually look chastened and finally turn back to their houses still muttering.* SNETTERTON *meanwhile turns to the* RSM.

SNETTERTON: Sergeant-Major. Mount a twenty-four hour guard on the frog boxes.
RSM: Sah!
SNETTERTON: I'm holding you responsible for the safety of those frogs.
RSM: Don't worry, sah . . . if anyone so much as looks at the boxes I'll let

'em have it right in the orchestras.

SNETTERTON (*closing his eyes with distaste*): Just guard the boxes, Sergeant-Major, you don't have to shoot anybody.

RSM: You got to shoot somebody, if you're guarding.

SNETTERTON: You don't *have* to . . . you only have to look as though you *would* if you *had* to.

RSM: Ah, but you've got to be *prepared* to, if you *do* have to . . .

SNETTERTON: All right! All right!

RSM: Right . . . then I've got your permission to kill someone, sah.

SNETTERTON: No! . . . I'm not giving you a carte blanche to kill someone, sah.

RSM: Oh *no*, sah — only if I have to.

SNETTERTON: That's right. (*Turns to* GREGORY *who is still shooing off natives.*)

RSM: So if they so much as *glance* at the boxes . . .

SNETTERTON *stops and turns back to the* RSM.

SNETTERTON: Sergeant Major . . . *if* they come up to the boxes and attempt to free the frogs, and *if* they ignore all your reasonable warnings, then, and only then . . . you may be forced to . . . to use your weapons . . .

RSM: And kill 'em sah.

SNETTERTON: All right! All right! Just don't go on about it!

RSM: No, sir, Don't worry, sah . . . you leave it to me, sah . . . I'll give 'em a warning shot, sah . . . between the eyes . . . or in the stomach . . .

SNETTERTON, *whose regard for the* RSM *reaches lower levels by the hour, shakes his head and turns. The crowd of natives has dispersed, though one or two stragglers still linger on.* GREGORY *stands by the well smoking a cigar, and occasionally dropping a length of ash into one of the frog boxes.*

GREGORY: I say old boy . . . want a bit of advice? Get out while the going's good . . .

SNETTERTON: I'm afraid I'm not used to the word "failure", Mr Gregory.

GREGORY: These people have been living with that volcano for centuries — you can't just walk in and tell them it's all superstitious phooey.

SNETTERTON: The expedition will go ahead as planned, and Quequeña will remain our headquarters.

GREGORY: Well, don't say I didn't warn you — there's going to be trouble.

SNETTERTON: Thank you, Mr Gregory.

GREGORY *shakes his head, shrugs, and walks off, unbuttoning his trousers.* SNETTERTON *watches him go, lost in his own thoughts. Suddenly an ominous rumble from the volcano makes* SNETTERTON'S *eyes flick up towards it.*
Elsewhere in the camp, other members of the expedition hear the volcano and look up anxiously. SNETTERTON *rouses himself to action.*

Double the guard on the frogs Sergeant-Major — we won't take any chances.

RSM: Sah!

SNETTERTON makes his way back to his tent.
Later that night: dawn breaks over the volcano. A single lamp burns in
SNETTERTON's tent. The volcano rumbles ominously.

Captain Snetterton spent a sleepless night. By the morning he had decided
to forego another recce and set off as soon as it was light. Two frogs were
to lead off up the North-West Face of Mount Aguare. The European Tree
Frog (*Hyla arborea*) striking out west towards the Kinaca Pass and the
Italian Agile Frog (*Rana latastei*) going for the summit. The remaining
two Edible Frogs and the two European Marsh Frogs were to remain at
base camp at Quequeña, with the Himalayan Sleeping Frog, to be held in
reserve for the difficult crossing of the Nivana Glacier. The expedition
would re-unite at Uhinas for the final two hundred-mile push towards the
borders of Brazil, and if there was any time left, they would go on to look
for the source of the Amazon, and the so-called "silly" route to India* . . .
But all the time the distant rumble of the volcano reminded him that time
was running out, and that he was confronted by forces as strong and
elemental as Nature itself.

SNETTERTON is in his tent poring over a map on his desk and making
calculations. The atmosphere is brooding and tense. There is yet another
rumble from the volcano. Suddenly he hears a twig break — instinctively

* Via Scotland, Johannesburg, Siberia, Hong Kong and Paris.

*his hand reaches out for his gun . . . Meanwhile back at the well in the village square,*PRIVATE JOHNSON, *one of the guards, has nodded off. He suddenly jerks himself awake and rubs his eyes.*

JOHNSON: Blimey . . . nearly fell asleep then, Sergeant-Major . . . (*He looks around him.*) . . . Sergeant-Major? . . .

The RSM's *gun lies on the ground, and his empty blanket is still spread out for him, but the* RSM *has vanished.* JOHNSON *looks around himself with the creepy realisation that he is all alone. His hands tighten on his rifle. Suddenly he catches sight of something.*

Corporal Miller?

He sees a couple of dark eyes peering intently at him from behind some low bushes.

Who's that?

The eyes slip back into the shadows.

Is that you Miller?

JOHNSON *keeps a stiff upper and lower lip, and taking tight hold of his rifle, starts to walk cautiously towards the bushes.*
SNETTERTON *is still writing. Suddenly he hears something moving about outside. There is a rustle of bushes . . . a footfall . . . instinctively he drops his pen and goes for his gun. Another sound draws him to the opening of his tent. He looks out. Dawn has not yet dispersed the gloom. Cautiously, firmly grasping his rifle, he emerges from the tent, and screws his eyes up, peering into the gloom. Suddenly behind him a figure looms up in silhouette against the sky.* SNETTERTON *jumps round and raises his rifle . . . it is the* RSM.

RSM: Cor! Thought you was one of the nig-nogs sah.
SNETTERTON: I wish you wouldn't call them "nig-nogs", Sergeant-Major. They are rational human beings with an indigenous culture as worthy of respect as our own.
RSM: Just been having a bash with one, sah. Right little piece of stuff she was!
SNETTERTON (*outraged*): You mean you've been fraternising with a native?
RSM: Well it was a bit more than just fraternising, sah.
SNETTERTON: You're meant to be guarding the boxes!
RSM: Couldn't get away, sah. (*Warming to his theme.*) Everytime I pulled me round-the-houses up she pulls 'em down again . . . Then she has an idea, see, sah. In one corner of the room there's this . . .
SNETTERTON: I don't want to hear any more Sergeant-Major. (*He turns and disappears into the tent.*)

RSM: No, sah. (*He follows* SNETTERTON.)

SNETTERTON: It's disgusting — I leave you in charge of guarding the frogs — at a very critical time — and you go off hob-nobbing with a native girl.

RSM: Sorry sah.

There is an uncomfortable silence. In the distance they hear the rumble of the volcano.

SNETTERTON: Well, we can't waste any more time over that, I've decided we should set off today.

RSM (*rather more quietly*): I think its the real thing this time, sah!

SNETTERTON: What?

RSM: Love, I mean, sah . . .

SNETTERTON: Sergeant-Major, this is a scientific expedition . . . you must *not*, I repeat *not* in any way, fraternise with the natives . . . valid though their culture is.

RSM: I want to marry her, sah.

SNETTERTON: You *what?*

RSM: Marry her . . . I want to marry her.

SNETTERTON: Sergeant-Major, I don't think you realize the gravity of your situation . . . You desert your post, and then expect me to give you permission for some squalid liaison with a local girl. You know what the King's Regulations say about mixed marriages in the forces.

RSM: Yes sir. That's why I'm resigning, sah.

The RSM takes his hat off and hands it over to SNETTERTON, he rips the badge and medal ribbon from his tunic. SNETTERTON doesn't take them. His jaw drops in stunned disbelief. He stares at the RSM and has to sit down on a convenient camping stool.

RSM (*gently*): I felt I ought to come and tell you, sah. I'm not coming with the expedition now . . . I'm . . . I'm staying here with Barbara, sah . . . we're going to farm guano . . . sah.

SNETTERTON: I don't believe it.

RSM: It's bird-shit sah.

Another pregnant pause is punctuated only by the distant rumble of the volcano.

SNETTERTON: I just don't know what to say, Sergeant-Major.

RSM: It's funny, sah . . . I suddenly see their way of life here is a lot richer and more individually satisfying than ours, sah . . . and . . . and . . . they don't half go, sah! They don't half go . . .

SNETTERTON: But after all these years of preparation that we've put into this expedition . . . the very morning we're about to set off . . .

RSM: If you knew the little woman, sah . . . you'd understand. She's got no . . . she's got no trace of sardonicism about her, sah . . . she's intellectually very sharp too, sah. She's considerate without being in any way self . . .

SNETTERTON: Oh shut up!

There is another rumble from El Misti. The RSM lays his hat and badges down on the table, and is about to go, when he stops, obviously with something on his mind.

RSM: By the way, sah, Barbara said to tell you, sah . . . that . . . well, I don't know how to say it, sah . . . but she's got a friend . . . who . . . well . . . who's taken a bit of a shine to you, sah. She's a little darling, sah . . . and if you wanted to come in with us on the guano business.

SNETTERTON: Oh, go away! You dirty man . . .

RSM: Yes, sah . . . goodbye, sah.

The RSM proffers his hand, but SNETTERTON won't even look at him. The RSM goes, and SNETTERTON, like a man in a dream, walks back to his desk and buries his head in his hands. Then suddenly a thought crosses his mind. In a second he is on his feet and racing out of the tent.

SNETTERTON: Corporal Miller!

SNETTERTON runs through the still sleeping camp towards Corporal Miller's tent.

Corporal Miller! Could I see you at once please . . .

He yanks back the tent flap ahd peers in . . .

I want you to — oh dear, I'm sorry.

SNETTERTON replaces the flap of the tent as sharply as he can and stands with his back to the door, very embarrassed.

Corporal Miller . . . when you've finished could you come and see me, please.

There is a smothered "Sir!" from inside the tent and a naughty lady's giggle. SNETTERTON grits his teeth and shakes his head.

SNETTERTON   (*to himself*): Miller . . . Miller as well . . . I can't . . .

Suddenly he stops short and his eyes take on a look of horror.

The frogs! Miller! The *frogs* . . . who's guarding the frogs! . . . ?

SNETTERTON breaks into a frantic run towards the square where the frog boxes are.

SNETTERTON: The frogs!

He stumbles and falls head first over some obstacle. There is a gruff complaint . . . We see it is none other than PRIVATE JOHNSON, shirt off, in flagrante with a dark-eyed native girl.

Johnson! What are you doing down there? What about the frogs . . . I'll have you court-martialled, . . . whipped . . .

NATIVE GIRL   (*appreciatively*): Mm . . .

SNETTERTON races on into the square . . . The boxes lie open, strewn around the well.

But he was too late. The frogs had gone.

SNETTERTON picks up one of the boxes and cradles it in his arms. He takes it over to a hurricane lamp which hangs from a veranda and stares down lovingly at it.

Only the Himalayan Sleeping Frog — going about its normal habit of sleeping — remained.

SNETTERTON'S eyes take on a look of grim determination. He looks round at the sheepish faces of the dishevelled guards. El Misti has stopped rumbling . . .

Later that morning, in the village square: the square is filled with a long line of locals combing the village for any trace of frogs. They are doing it, however, only because SNETTERTON, *shouting orders, toting a pistol, in a new, fierce determined way, has the other two* SOLDIERS *pointing guns at them. Everyone is looking under chairs, in window boxes, beneath tables, behind pillars . . . in all sorts of nooks and crannies. They are doing this in a very resentful fashion — like a very half-hearted game of hide-and-seek.* SNETTERTON *has a look of bitter anger on his face.*

SNETTERTON: Come on! Come on! Findo! Findo!

He catches sight of a beautiful dusky lady, presumably the one the RSM *has mentioned, who gives him a flashing smile.* SNETTERTON *looks away very embarrassed, hoping none of the men have seen, although it is painfully obvious that they each of them have their own amours hanging around waiting for them to finish.*
GREGORY *strides up, sexually dishevelled as usual.*

GREGORY: Sorry to hear about the trouble in the night.
SNETTERTON: (*heavily*): Oh nothing to worry about . . . only six years of research gone.
GREGORY: I hear a couple of your chaps . . . are going to stay here . . . going into the guano business . . .
SNETTERTON: Absolute nonsense! Bit of trouble with Sergeant-Major Byng that's all . . . mentally unstable . . . couldn't take the pace . . .
GREGORY: Young Miller came to see me this morning with his new wife . . .
SNETTERTON: Wife? Miller! He's in the bloody army . . . where is he . . . ?
GREGORY: Gone off to the Building Society in Iquique . . . I gave him the address.
SNETTERTON: He what? . . . he'll be court-martialled! I'll tear his bowels out with my own hands.
GREGORY: I told you, old boy, you can't fight these people . . . you might as well go or stay . . .
SNETTERTON: (*slowly, spelling out his philosophy, such as it is*): You don't seem to realise, Mr Gregory, I'm going through with it . . . I will not move from here until this frog expedition has achieved *everything* it set out to achieve, and that is final, do you understand . . . ?

GREGORY *drops his eyes knowingly . . . a little sadly. In a corner of the square one of the natives switches on the radio. Immediately, the distinctive sounds of a Wimbledon commentary, the thwap of tennis ball and the rich commentator's voice, fill the square.*

RADIO: Perry a backhand . . . Rodrigues a forehand lob down the back court . . .

The locals stop and break into nervous smiles. SNETTERTON *rounds on the man with the radio.*

SNETTERTON: Turn that off!
RADIO: Perry a backhand, and a beauty down the line . . . thirty — forty . . .

SNETTERTON *marches up to the peasant beside the radio, white with anger.*

SNETTERTON: Turn that off!

The man doesn't move. Tension on all the faces. The radio chortles on about Fred Perry while faces smile no longer but look from SNETTERTON *to the peasant and back.*

RADIO: Perry now serving for this fourth set . . . forty — thirty, if he wins today he meets Olvares of Spain in the semi-final. So here's Perry . . .
SNETTERTON: *Turn* it off!
RADIO: This lean figure . . .

SNETTERTON, *now almost psychopathically angry, aims his service revolver.*

RADIO: . . . with that familiar lock of hair falling in front of . . .

SNETTERTON *fires at the radio repeatedly, savagely, as if venting all his pent-up fury and frustration. There is a silence. All activity in the square freezes. The natives turn. All eyes are on him.*

GREGORY: You shouldn't have done that old boy.

SNETTERTON *tries to look tough, but as he looks around the faces in the square he sees he has made the big mistake . . . the Big One. Apathy has been replaced by a new sinister anger as slowly the natives move into a semi-circle around him, arming themselves with odd bits of wood, stones, etc. Quite obviously they aren't looking for his autograph.*

SNETTERTON (*to his men*): Go on! Fire!

JOHNSON *reluctantly fires a couple of shots in the air.*

Not above their heads!

Suddenly the natives charge. JOHNSON *etc. are quickly disarmed.*
SNETTERTON *looks around for help.* GREGORY *does nothing so* SNETTERTON
*picks up the remaining frog box and flees. They chase him . . . shouting
and yelling, brandishing their improvised weapons.* SNETTERTON *runs
blindly but determinedly out of the village and up into the foothills and
then the mountains, until he becomes a tiny, desperate figure, lost in the
vastnesses of the mighty Andes.*

Clutching only the Himalayan Sleeping Frog, Snetterton took to the
mountains . . .

After three weeks of wandering through the Cordillera, his failure seemed
complete . . . On June the fourth, nineteen twenty-seven, three and a half
months after leaving England . . . he ate the Himalayan Sleeping Frog . . .
In a final note, found in a Final Note box, erected by the Peruvian
Government high on the slopes of El Misti, Snetterton wrote:
"Today I ate the last of the Sleeping Frog. The plucky little fellow had
saved my life without waking up once . . . I ate him with a sort of berry
sauce . . . and a very acceptable lichen and moss soufflé brought out the
delicate flavours of the . . . "

Nothing more was heard or seen of Captain Walter Snetterton . . . the
man who set out with such high hopes to conquer the most unforgiving
mountains of all . . . But the six frogs who were released in Quequeña that
fateful morning hopped into Mexico City, six thousand three hundred

Today I ate the last of the Sleeping Frog. The plucky little fellow had saved my life without waking up once. I ate him with a sort of lichen and moss soufflé and a very acceptable sauce, and brought out the delicate flavours of

miles north, on the twenty-second of September nineteen twenty-seven . . .
Captain Snetterton's belief in High Altitude Amphibian exploration had
been justified after all . . . his observations, research and training
techniques, for which he gave his life, at last bore fruit.

Once again, Science proved that there are no limits to what Man can
achieve. Without such men of courage and determination, as Captain
Walter Snetterton the Progress of Human Knowledge would be an empty
myth, and the World would never have had the Teflon non-stick saucepan,
self-opening doors nor any of the other wonders of Modern Technology.

A rocket soars into space over a triumphal and hopeful climax of music. *

No: 6 DUDLEY

GREAT BRITISH FROGS

No: 4 AMOS

GREAT BRITISH FROGS

No: 18 ROVER

GREAT BRITISH FROGS

* Recorded on the Mellotron — another frog-based Wonder of Modern Technology.

MURDER
AT
MOORSTONES
MANOR

MURDER AT MOORSTONES MANOR

Somewhere in Scotland, the year: 1926.

A wild craggy moorland. A car approaches along a lonely road . . . it is a new A.C. In it, wearing a rather delicate light summer frock and straw hat and scarf is a girl in her middle twenties: DORA. Alongside her in a college scarf and tweed jacket is boyish, twenty-nine-year-old HUGO CHIDDINGFOLD, eldest son of Sir Clive and Lady Chiddingfold of Moorstones Manor. He is obviously very happy.

HUGO: The old A.C.'s going well.

DORA: Yes darling . . . it seems to be.

HUGO: The old trick worked you see . . .changing the stroke ratio on the crank-case mountings . . . you get a lower rev rate with more horsepower . . .

DORA (*romantically*): Oh . . . it's so wild and lonely up here.

HUGO: Buffy Andrews tried to uprate his Talbot . . . used a two-stroke alternator . . . split the bloody crankcase . . . Ha! Ha! Ha! Ha!

He literally snorts with laughter.

DORA: Do your parents live all on their own out here?

HUGO: No . . . They've got a couple of Davenport 257s . . . bought them cheap in the war, had both the engines re-bored, put in a Farrars-Knighton dual piston screen converter, cleaned up the old Lucas 206 distributor, and banged in four more carburettors. Went like a bullet Ha! Ha! Ha! Ha!

DORA: It's not any better . . . is it darling? . . . The problem I mean . . .

HUGO (*suddenly serious*): No . . .

DORA: I think you ought to give up driving . . . obviously if you're in a car, it's not going to help.

HUGO: I'm not giving up driving, Dora . . . Who'd look after the Talbot? . . . Those adjustments on the pistons need oiling every week, and there's the tappet clearance, which needs constant . . .

DORA: Stop it Hugo!

HUGO: I'm sorry . . . I'm sorry . . .

DORA: Hugo . . . you must decide between me or the car . . .

HUGO: All right, I'll take the car . . .

DORA: Oh . . .

HUGO: I love her, Dora . . . I love the way I can get twice the speed at less revs by a simple adjustment to the timing ratio in a fan-scavenged engine, so that the cylinder leads on the alternator . . .

DORA: Stop here Hugo!

HUGO: Emergency stop . . . jolly good!

He stands on the pedals and the car grinds to a sudden, slithering halt.

You see that — no locking! . . . that's using the new friction-liner plates I fitted down at Tony's . . .

DORA gets out in desperation.

DORA: Goodbye Hugo . . .

She looks at him for a moment, then with a dramatic flourish slams the car door.

HUGO: Goodbye old love . . !

Then, quite blithely, without another thought, he drives away. DORA is left by the roadside, crestfallen and stunned, looking helplessly after the vanishing A.C.

DORA: Hugo . . . ?

The wind whips at the hem of her light summer dress . . . There is the distant rumble of an approaching storm . . . HUGO disappears into the distance.

Hugo!

The road outside Moorstones Manor: half-an-hour later. HUGO is driving happily along. He turns the car into the long and elegant driveway of a country manor. His MOTHER comes out to greet him. She is a good-looking woman in her early fifties. She is rather fragilely built, and looks anxious.

MOTHER: Hello Hugo darling . . . how are you?

HUGO: How about that mother, from Darkstones Moor to here in forty-one point seven minutes . . . that's an average of . . . fifty-two . . . and a half! Damn good old tub . . .

MOTHER: Where's Dora?

HUGO: That's the first time Ma, I've used the re-bored cylinder . . . with the injector feed I told you about.

MOTHER: Where's Dora?

HUGO: She got out on Darkstones Moor.

MOTHER: *She got out* on Darkstones Moor?

HUGO: Yes . . . I think that's what made all the difference to the average . . . I remember once trying the Morgan out on the Brooklands track with "Tiny" Townsend and only made fifty-five and that was with a twin exhaust!

Hugo's father, SIR CLIVE CHIDDINGFOLD, *a crusty man with a stick, appears looking cantankerously quizzical at the doorway.*

MOTHER (*quietly*): Yes dear how interesting. (*She turns to* FATHER, *explaining.*) Dora's out on Darkstones Moor alone, Clive.

FATHER: What! (*He glares violently at his car-tinkering son.*) I'll kill him!

MOTHER (*softly, patiently*): No, he is very bad today, Dada, we'd better call a doctor.

HUGO (*cheerily*): Hello Father . . . Come and have a look at this manifold now I've cleaned it all up.

FATHER: Call the *doctor!* . . . What he needs is a damn good thrashing.

MOTHER: Clive . . . please!

FATHER: He needs the skin taken off his back with a triple-thonged bamboo-backed leather strap . . . That's what *he* needs.

MOTHER (*taking* HUGO'S *arm protectively*): Clive, you remember what the doctors in London said.

FATHER: Doctors! (*He spits.*) What doctors need is a damn good flogging . . . you know what the Ottoman Turks used to do with loonies —

MOTHER: He is *not* a loony, Dada, he —

FATHER: They used to tie them to a tree and beat them senseless . . . they didn't have any nonsense.

MOTHER (*trying to get* HUGO *away from the car where he is still compulsively tinkering*): Hugo come and lie down, it's been a long journey.

HUGO: Don't you want to see the remould on the cylinders? . . . It's a super little job . . . Vivian's done it on his Packard Fastback — goes like a bomb . . .

FATHER: Oh!, let me just kick him . . .

Meanwhile, back on Darkstones Moor, the wind has increased, and huge black clouds are looming. DORA is walking up the road, hair and clothing in disarray. She looks vainly for help, to left and right. Desolation. Nothing in either direction.

Back in the comfort and warmth of Moorstones Manor, in a rather pleasant baronial living room, FATHER with a large scotch and soda is gazing reflectively at a series of Chinese prints depicting various acts of corporal punishment. MOTHER is doing some crochet work. She suddenly lays down her work and looks up.

MOTHER: But Dora was such a *nice* girl, dear.

FATHER: Well she can't have much upstairs, if she spends her time with a loony like Hugo.

MOTHER: I don't think we ought to just leave her there, Dada.

FATHER: Damn good for her if you ask me. You know what the Malays used to do to find if a man was really a warrior or not . . . they used to tear out his . . .

A doorbell rings.

Who's that?

MOTHER: It'll be Charles and Ruth, dear.

FATHER: Oh, that pair . . . come to ruin my weekend again, I suppose.

MOTHER: They've come all the way from London for your birthday, Clive . . . the least you can do is to be civil to them.

FATHER: They only come down to see whether I'm dead or not. Well, (*and here he stands with surprising sprightliness.*) . . . I'll be upstairs if they want me.

He disappears. MOTHER sighs wearily and prepares herself. MANNERS, the butler, enters.

MANNERS (*lugubriously*): Charles and Miss Ruth . . . M'lady . . .

Enter a young man with an expensive and tasteful tweed suit and a rather mature, sophisticated, London lady. This is RUTH, very self-possessed, very Sanderson. The young man is Lady Chiddingfold's smoothly elegant younger son, CHARLES.

MOTHER: Charles. (*She gives him a peck on the cheek.*)

CHARLES: Hello Mumsie . . .

RUTH: Hello Lady Chiddingfold . . .

MOTHER: Hello Ruth my dear (*She kisses her.*) I'm so glad you're here, we've had the most awful time with Hugo you know . . . he's left Dora alone on Darkstones Moor.

CHARLES: Yes we passed her in the car . . .

MOTHER: How was she?

CHARLES: Oh, very distraught . . . didn't look at all well . . .

RUTH: She only had a summer frock on, poor gel.

MOTHER: Oh dear . . . well come and get warm . . .

CHARLES: Where's Daddles?

She vaguely motions to the doorway.

MOTHER: He's upstairs . . . in his lair, dear.

CHARLES: Well, better go up and say hello . . .

CHARLES *with a flashy smile, makes for the door.*

MOTHER: Well . . . would you like a cup of tea Ruth dear?

RUTH (*with a knowing lift of the eyebrows*): Well perhaps something a little stronger, I feel, after that journey, Lady Chiddingfold . . .

MOTHER: Coffee?

RUTH (*a little thrown*): Er . . . No . . . I meant something a little stronger in the sense . . .

MOTHER (*helpfully*): Bovril with two spoonfuls . . . or Marmite . . .

RUTH: No . . . I was thinking of something more in the line of . . . whisky?

MOTHER: Bovril and whisky?

RUTH: No . . . just the whisky.

MOTHER: Ah! I'm so sorry Ruth my dear. (*She pulls a bellcord to summon Manners.*) Of course! I'm in such a damn muddle at the moment. (MANNERS *appears.*) Ah, Manners, a whisky, please.

MANNERS: With Bovril, M'Lady?

MOTHER: No, no, just a whisky, Manners.

MANNERS: Yes, m'lady.

He withdraws. Upstairs. The billiard room. SIR CLIVE *is playing a fairly bad game and grunting with the effort. The door opens and* CHARLES *enters.*

FATHER (*without looking up*): Hello Charles . . .

CHARLES: Hello father . . .

A pause. FATHER *slowly lines up another shot.*

FATHER (*with feeling*): Bloody Oscar Wilde!

CHARLES: What, father?

FATHER: Bloody Oscar Wilde . . . you know . . .

CHARLES (*clearly quite uncomprehending*): Ah yes . . . yes.

Another silence. They're obviously not very good at talking to each other.
FATHER takes a shot and slowly straightens up.

FATHER: How's the Foreign Office?

CHARLES: Oh fine . . . we've painted the Whitehall side, and we're making a start on the West Front next week.

FATHER: Still no chance of a job inside it?

CHARLES: No I'm afraid not, Father . . . far too dim . . .

FATHER (*glancing at him*): Yes I suppose so.

Downstairs RUTH has just been handed a large pint mug of whisky which she cradles awkwardly, trying politely not to draw attention to the huge glass, with a tiny smear of whisky across the bottom.

MOTHER (*noticing*): No, Manners, whisky in a *whisky* glass . . .

MANNERS: Yes . . . m'lady.

He takes the mug.

MOTHER: And no toast . . .

MOTHER hands him back a plate of buttered toast, which he has just put down on the table beside them. RUTH tries to rally the conversation to cover these eccentric faux-pas.

RUTH: The gardens are looking delightful, Lady Chiddingfold.

MOTHER: Oh yes . . . they're all over sixty, you know. Knowles is ninety-seven — took him nineteen hours to pull up a weed the other day. Clive wants to have them all neutered . . .

RUTH: No . . . I said the *gardens* . . .

MANNERS appears with a whisky in a saucer shaped champagne glass, with a cherry on a stick in it.

MOTHER: Ah . . . here's you whisky at last . . .

RUTH discreetly takes the cherry out, with a slight frown of distaste, and drops it behind her.

Shall we . . . shall we go and join the men . . . ?

RUTH: What a super idea.

MOTHER: What . . . ?

RUTH: I said . . . what a super idea.

MOTHER: Yes, I can't understand it . . . we've got both the oil heaters on.

She smiles and opens the door.
Upstairs: the billiard room. The door opens and LADY CHIDDINGFOLD *and* RUTH *enter.* RUTH *is still doing her London best to draw everyone into the conversation.*

RUTH: I was saying to Lady Chiddingfold how fine the grounds were looking. She certainly has the green fingers in this family . . .

FATHER (*pausing before another bad shot*): The only chap I know who had green fingers was "Tooler" Moran in the K.O.L.I. He was beating some chappie in Burma for breathing too regularly, and you know, the vibration from the stick was so intense that poor old Tooler's hands turned into a mass of . . .

MOTHER: Not now Clive . . .

FATHER: Wonderful chap, Tooler. Homicidal maniac of course — but he was the finest soldier I've ever seen. One of the few chaps I know who was squeezed to death by an anaconda . . . All his innards . . .

RUTH *suffers a pre-vomitory twinge in mid-drink. The windows rattle, as if in sympathy, but it's only the storm . . .*

MOTHER: Oh dear! Listen to that wind.

FATHER (*carefully miscueing his shot*): Yes . . . it's going to be a hell of a night tonight . . .

MOTHER *parts the curtains slightly, looks out then lets them fall back. She turns and shakes her head sadly.*

MOTHER: Oh dear!

Back on Darkstones Moor: the storm is howling, the clouds are riven with

sheets of lightning. In the middle of it all is DORA. *She is in a terrible state, eyes staring, hair awry. She keeps staggering on. She falls into a ditch by the side of the road, and pulls herself out. Black slime coats her legs and her summer frock. She drags herself up and along the road.*

Back at Moorstones Manor: the family, except HUGO *and* DORA, *are sitting round the dining room table, well laid with plenty of food and wine in evidence.* SIR CLIVE *is in the middle of a story.*

FATHER: . . . so this chap . . . who was obviously the sort of commander wallah — big fellow . . . boils all over his forehead . . . he ordered the whole platoon to get their bayonets. Then he gets them to pull back their own finger nails . . . one by one, and put quick-lime . . .

This is too much for RUTH. *She moans and falls forward into her cottage pie head first. She lies, inert, with her face deep in the pie.*

FATHER   (*a little irritated by the diversion*): What's the matter with her?
CHARLES: Oh, nothing Father, she's just a touch squeamish you know.
FATHER: "Squeamish!" Huh! . . . Wouldn't have done me any good if I'd have been "squeamish" . . . we didn't have time for any of that "squeamish" nonsense. When you're fighting next to a chap who has both his knees hanging off you can't afford to start getting "squeamish". The only time I ever felt squeamish . . .

The door opens. HUGO *appears in a crumpled dressing gown.*

HUGO   (*with his usual eager grin*): Hello all! You never told me I was missing supper.
MOTHER: Hugo . . . darling!
FATHER: Oh My God! Here comes the family loony.
HUGO: Hello Charles! (*He cheerfully goes over and sits down beside his* FATHER.) Father . . . you know you used to have one of those Barracuda eight cylinders, with an overhead camshaft.
MOTHER   (*quickly, half rising*): Don't bother your father now Hugo, go back to bed and have a nice rest . . .

HUGO: Well, I tried re-lining the cylinders of the Morgan last week — to supe it up a bit — and apparently all you need with an overhead camshaft like the one you have is . . .

FATHER: Oh go away!

MOTHER (*sensing the inevitable scene*): Hugo, to bed . . . please!

HUGO: . . . is to re-align the throttle control . . .

MOTHER (*standing up*): Hugo . . . please, you're not well.

HUGO: I'm perfectly all right Mumsie, don't worry about me.

MOTHER *goes across and rings the bell.*

FATHER: Of course you are not all right you idiot . . . Yattering on about overhead camshafts and —

HUGO: Ah, but you see what I mean . . . on a four cylinder car it's the easiest way of . . .

MANNERS *enters.*

MOTHER: Manners, take Master Hugo back to his room, please.

MANNERS: Yes m'lady.

FATHER: And give him a damn good throttling!

MOTHER (*sharply*): Dada!

HUGO (*as he is yanked up rather sharply from his chair and led out*): That's what I mean . . . it's all in the throttle . . . an extra half a yard of cable attached direct to the carburettor feed and aligned at an angle to the cylinder block increases the compression ratio, and if you re-adjust the connecting rods like Toby did on his Jupiter . . .

The door closes, but Hugo's voice can still be heard down the passage.

FATHER: What a disaster! . . . I'd rather have a box of fish than a son like that.

CHARLES (*brightly, after a pause*): Looking forward to your birthday tomorrow, pater?

FATHER: No.

CHARLES: Oh.

FATHER: He only comes down here to see if I'm dead or not. Well I'm only eighty-seven and I've no intention of popping off yet. Do you know there was a colonel in our regiment who was eighty-nine years old and he could still skin a live goat with his bare nails. I saw him once bite a wolf . . . it leapt at him one night when he was lying outside the mess and he bit it in the throat, swung it around . . . flung it twelve feet over the kazi and it killed a chowdah wallah just as he was shaving. Mind you, not as bad as the night Archie Pettigrew ate some sheep's testicles for a bet . . . God, that bloody sheep kicked him . . .

In HUGO'S bedroom: LADY CHIDDINGFOLD is laying HUGO in the bed and adjusting the pillows behind him. HUGO is rabbiting on cheerfully the while.

HUGO: The trouble is, Ma, that on the specifications there's a black lead to the distributor head and a red lead . . .

MOTHER: Yes, dear, just rest now.

HUGO (*suddenly serious*): Do you think I'll ever get over it Mother? (*He starts making car noises.*) Brrm! Brrm!

MOTHER: I hope so dear . . . just keep eating lots of fruit . . .

A shot rings out from downstairs. LADY CHIDDINGFOLD *starts up in horror.*

Oh no! That'll be your father being murdered!

Meanwhile . . . on Darkstones Moor: A wild night. The moon appears dramatically from behind scudding clouds. DORA, *her dress soaked, has managed to drag herself down, off the moor, into the woods below. She staggers blindly on, the jagged lightning her only guide.*
Back at Moorstones Manor: the dining room. SIR CLIVE *is slumped forward with* CHARLES *bending over him.* RUTH *remains face downwards in her cottage pie.* MOTHER *rushes in with* MANNERS *following.*

MOTHER (*distraught*): What's happened . . .

CHARLES: Dada's been murdered.

MOTHER: Oh dear . . . but how?

CHARLES: I don't know who did it, I'd just gone across to the wall at the end to see if there was a secret door in it and I heard a shot and by the time I turned round he was dead.

MOTHER: Maybe he shot himself.

CHARLES: Yes that's probably it.

MOTHER (*looking round the room distractedly*): I can't see a gun anywhere.

CHARLES: Perhaps he shot himself and then threw the gun out of the window . . . to try and lay suspicion on the gardeners or something.

MOTHER (*examining the body*): He's been shot in the back.

CHARLES: Oh . . . Mama who would have *wanted* to kill him?

MOTHER: Well we all would dear, you know that . . .

CHARLES: Yes . . . I suppose so.

MANNERS: (*who has been bending over* RUTH *trying to extricate her from the cottage pie*): M'Lady . . . ?

MOTHER: Yes Manners.

MANNERS: It's Miss Ruth . . . she is . . . dead as well, Ma'am.

MOTHER: Oh, not now Manners, please . . .

CHARLES *gives a "Gosh aren't things in a jolly awful mess" face, and looks to his* MOTHER *anxiously.*

MANNERS: Yes, M'Lady, I just thought you'd like to know.

MOTHER: Yes, Manners . . . I do appreciate it . . . it's just that with my husband being murdered, and having Hugo in bed and everything.

CHARLES: Can we read the will now, Mumsie?

MOTHER: No dear!

CHARLES *looks disappointed.*

Look, darling . . . first of all we must sort out in here. How many people are dead?

CHARLES: Well there's Daddy . . .

MOTHER: Yes.

CHARLES: And poor old Ruthy . . .

MOTHER: That's two . . . right.

CHARLES: And what about Hugo?

MOTHER: Hugo's not dead!

CHARLES: Well he is not very well . . . you know . . . his problem, Mumsie.

MOTHER: Yes, but I only want to know who is actually dead, dear.

CHARLES: Well, perhaps I'd better go and check on Hugo. He's awfully quiet.

CHARLES *makes for the door.*

MOTHER: All right . . . but don't give him a shock dear, please. Don't tell him what's happened.

CHARLES (*as he goes out*): No I'll be ever so careful.

CHARLES *disappears into the hall.*

MOTHER (*looking around the room with ever increasing anxiety and distraction*):
Manners?

MANNERS: Yes, M'Lady?

MOTHER: Go and check the gun case immediately.

MANNERS (*making for the door*): Yes'm.

MOTHER: Oh . . . and Manners . . .

MANNERS: Yes, M'Lady?

MOTHER: Tell Edith we will only be three for lunch tomorrow.

MANNERS: Yes, M'Lady.

MOTHER: And forever.

MANNERS: Yes'm.

He leaves.

MOTHER: Oh dear!

She hardly knows what to do. She decides to go and attend to her husband and just reaches his prostrate form when the telephone rings. MANNERS *re-enters soundlessly.*

MANNERS: The telephone, ma'am . . .

MOTHER: Yes. Thank you Manners. (*She lowers her husband, and, looking confused and distraught, goes over to the phone and picks it up.*) Hello?
. . . Oh hello, Madge . . . yes . . . yes . . . yes . . . yes . . . oh dear, what a shame! I'm so sorry . . . and he's got to have the whole lot out has he? . . .
Yes . . . well I'm sure he'll be better for it . . . they say that . . . yes . . . oh *yes* . . . Look, Madge . . . can I . . . no . . . no . . . you just keep him off fats and milks for a while will you . . . yes . . . I see . . . Madge can I . . .
oh, salads and things yes . . . yes . . . yes . . . Madge can I ring you back?
No! No! It's just that a couple of people have died and I . . . what? No, one shot, one drowned, I think . . . yes it *is* a shame . . . What? . . . Clive *was* one of them, yes . . . shot in the back . . . afraid so . . . oh yes it is . . .
he *was* eighty-seven . . . Look, Madge, I really must — what? No I'm sure it's better Frank had it out . . . yes at least he'll be able to sit down properly again . . . yes . . . yes . . . (*A gun shot rings out from an upstairs room.* LADY CHIDDINGFOLD *looks up in horror, and tries to get away from*

the phone, but Madge continues relentlessly.) . . . at the cottage hospital, yes, they *are* very nice . . . yes I'm sure . . . Look, Madge, I must dash, I've heard another . . . in a ward of his own, yes that's so much nicer . . . (*The dining room door opens slowly. CHARLES enters and stands just inside the door with a guilty-little-boy look. LADY CHIDDINGFOLD eyes him with a growing sense of alarm.*) Oh yes, quite . . . Look I must dash really now, Madge. I think someone else has been mur- . . . what? Yes of course I can give you a lift . . . right . . . right . . . yes yes at three o'clock outside Lewis's . . . (*She makes to put the phone down.*) . . . What? All right, just *in*side Lewis's . . . yes . . . all right . . . yes I know . . . by the umbrellas . . . Bye . . . (*She finally manages to put the phone down.*)

CHARLES: Mumsie . . . it's just as well I looked. Hugo *is* dead.

MOTHER: *Hugo's* dead!

CHARLES: Yes, I didn't see who did it again. I was talking to him one minute then suddenly I looked under the bed to see if there was a trap door to a secret passage underneath the house when there was this shot and I turned, and there was Hugo, Dada's eldest son, who stood to inherit everything, dead. Definitely dead.

MOTHER: Oh dear! . . . Oh dear! What *will* the neighbours think?

CHARLES: That's *three* dead now, Mumsie . . .

MANNERS: (*who has appeared in the doorway, silently, as usual*): Shall I call the police, M'Lady?

MOTHER: (*looking at CHARLES rather significantly*): It may not be necessary, Manners.

CHARLES: No I don't think there is much that the police could do. A waste of the ratepayers' money really.

MOTHER: Would you leave us for a moment, Manners?

MANNERS: Yes'm.

He leaves. The door clicks shut. A pause, then.

MOTHER: Charles . . . ?

CHARLES: Yes Mumsie pie?

MOTHER: Charles, I'd rather keep this in the family, if we can . . .

CHARLES: Quite agree, Mumsie, don't want to . . .

MOTHER: So be completely honest with me. Did you kill them . . . Charles?

CHARLES: No of *course* I didn't, Mumsie!

MOTHER: You killed Aunt Mabel.

CHARLES: Oh that was ages ago.

MOTHER: Well if you didn't, who *did*?

A sudden noise outside makes them turn. Through the shrieking of storm and wind they catch the chilling sound of someone . . . or something, being dragged across the gravel of the forecourt.

What was that?

She moves over to the window and draws the heavy curtain aside. As she does so there is an unearthly scream and a banging on the front door. She looks at CHARLES *in terror, and rushes out into the hall.* CHARLES *follows. The banging on the door becomes more urgent.*

MOTHER   (*eyes wide in fear*): Who on earth could it be? It's half-past twelve!

CHARLES   (*helpfully*): Jehovah's Witnesses?

MANNERS crosses the hall ahead of them takes a few steps to the door. Opens it wide on the final desperate bang and there . . . is DORA! *. . . soaked, her summer frock torn, covered in mud, blood, and looking terrible.*

MOTHER: Dora!

The next morning: Moorstones Manor. The storm has passed, leaving behind a clear sky. It's cold but fine and the gardens and house are bathed in sunshine. LADY CHIDDINGFOLD *is gardening, working away in sensible tweed skirt, scarf and stout gum boots, tying up flowers to stakes and occasionally tearing out weeds and dropping them into a garden basket beside her. Birds sing, and she hums to herself busily. It is a gentle, idyllic scene. Suddenly it's shattered by a gunshot from inside the house.* LADY CHIDDINGFOLD *stops in mid-weeding and, raising her eyes heavenwards straightens up and listens. No sound. She shouts —*

MOTHER: Charles!

No reply. She walks a couple of paces nearer the house, and shouts again.

Charles, dear! Have you been murdered?

CHARLES *in pyjamas, dressing gown and cravat, emerges from the front door holding a smoking shot-gun.*

CHARLES: No Mumsie! I was just cleaning one of Pater's old twelve bores and it went off.

MOTHER: Oh dear . . . it gave me such a shock! Thank God it didn't hit anyone.

CHARLES: Er . . . well it did hit *someone* Mumsie.

MOTHER: Who?

CHARLES: Hugo . . .

MOTHER: But he's dead already, dear.

CHARLES: Oh yes that was the lucky thing.

MOTHER: Well *do* be careful, dear. *(She goes back to the gardening.)* If I were you I should put them away.

CHARLES'S eyes light up.

CHARLES: Who? . . . Manners and Dora?

MOTHER: No, the guns, dear.

CHARLES saunters down to the flower bed.

CHARLES *(banteringly)*: Frightened of the police, Mumsie?

MOTHER: No, of course not, dear . . . I just don't want anyone else murdered, that's all.

CHARLES: Who . . . er . . .who were you ringing up this morning, Mother?

LADY CHIDDINGFOLD looks up sharply from her gardening then resumes digging rather deliberately.

MOTHER: If you must know, dear, I was phoning up Dr Farson.

CHARLES: Who's Dr Farson?

MOTHER: He's a very clever doctor from Inverness . . . and he happens to be an old friend of your father's . . . he's agreed to see Dora and . . . and perhaps help find out who killed your father and poor Hugo.

CHARLES *(with some irritation)*: Oh Mumsie, it doesn't matter who *did* it . . . the fact is that both of them *are* dead . . . Hugo definitely . . . and we ought to open the wills and see how much money and land we are all getting so I can go back to London on Monday.

MOTHER *(weeding)*: Oh I know how busy you are, Charles darling, it's just that I can't let all these murders go by without doing *something* and Doctor Farson is a very clever man and what's more he'll be discreet about it. Now go and put some things on dear.

CHARLES *(obstinately)*: Mumsie . . . he'll only say that they've been murdered and you know what that means.

MOTHER *(patiently)*: Well let's see dear . . . he may find it wasn't murder . . . they might have fallen on the bullets or something.

CHARLES *(grumpily)*: I know . . . they'll all start looking at me as if I murdered them, just like they did with Aunt Mabel.

MOTHER: Well you *did* murder Aunt Mabel, dear.

CHARLES: There you go, Mumsie . . . even you're holding it against me.

MOTHER: I'm *not* holding it against you, dear . . . now please just go and get ready. I'm coming in as soon as I've finished with this wretched trailing bindweed. *(She pulls a huge tuft up vehemently.)*

CHARLES   (*not moving*): You know Dada never allowed doctors in the house.

MOTHER: Well he was a stupidly stubborn man, dear, and look what happened. He nearly died when he took his appendix out with the grapefruit knife, but he wouldn't listen to anybody. We told him where it was, we showed him in the book, but he took out his liver, part of his colon and twelve feet of greater intestine before he even *found* the appendix. It took him four hours and *eighteen Daily Telegraphs* to stem the blood. Well I'm not having that sort of thing happen again, thank you.

She gives one last tug at a particularly stubborn weed, which reluctantly comes loose, revealing — briefly — a whitened human skull. LADY CHIDDINGFOLD covers it hastily and gets to her feet, carrying her basketful of weeds. She makes for the house.

CHARLES   (*walking along beside her*): I think we ought to bury them in the garden and get on and read the will.

MOTHER: You can't just do that sort of thing dear . . . we have to have coroners and and funerals.

CHARLES: Well why! Why do we have to have a funeral?

MOTHER: People *like* funerals dear.

CHARLES: We didn't have a funeral for Aunt Mabel.

MOTHER: Well we know why that was dear, now please.

She turns on a tap beside the wall and starts to wash mud off her boots.

CHARLES: Why? . . . why did we never have a funeral for Aunt Mabel?

MOTHER: Because we couldn't find her, dear.

CHARLES: We found most of her.

MOTHER: Charles please! I'm not telling you again.

CHARLES: I'm going to open the will.

He walks off towards the house determinedly.

MOTHER: You can't, Charles dear.

CHARLES: Why not?

MOTHER: Because it's not here for a start, it's at the solicitors.

CHARLES   (*wilfully*): All right, I'll give him a ring.

MOTHER: Charles, if you . . . (*He disappears indoors.*) Oh! You're worse than your father.

The dining room. Some time later: at the table FATHER and RUTH are both in the positions they died in the night before but are covered in sheets. At the other end of the immaculately laid table CHARLES and his MOTHER are having their lunch in silence, broken only by the occasional slurping of soup. MOTHER has a piece of paper and pen beside her.

MOTHER (*referring to piece of paper*): When I write to the *Telegraph*, do you think I should put "passed peacefully away" or just "passed away" . . . ?

CHARLES: "Shot away"?

MOTHER: Don't be silly dear . . . "suddenly" . . . perhaps that's better? . . . yes . . . (*She reads off the paper.*) "Chiddingfold, Sir Clive, suddenly at Moorstones Manor on October 19th aged eighty-seven". That's rather beautiful isn't it . . . nice and simple.

CHARLES: "Suddenly shot clean through the head, at Moorstones Manor . . ." . . . ?

MOTHER: Charles dear, it's four pounds a line now, you know.

CHARLES (*laying down his soup spoon with the air of one who has a revelation to impart*): I rang the solicitor this morning, Mumsie. Do you know Hugo left all his money to Dora?

MOTHER: How about "suddenly in the night"?

CHARLES: He's left her fourteen thousand pounds and seventeen cars, Mumsie.

MOTHER: Poor Dora.

CHARLES (*quickly*): Yes, perhaps I'd better pop up and see her. (*He gets up.*)

MOTHER: Now Charles *do* be careful, she's in shock.

CHARLES: I'm only just going to pop in and see if she's any worse, that's all.

He walks across to the door, but before he reaches it, he makes a quick sidestep to a long wooden chest, which he opens as nippily as possible, and extracts a twelve-bore rifle. He drops the lid, and is reaching for the door, when LADY CHIDDINGFOLD looks up.

MOTHER: Charles? . . . (*He turns.*) What's that?

CHARLES looks all round the room, feigning total amazement when his eyes finally light on the gun in his hand.

CHARLES: Oh this! . . . Just cleaning it, Mumsie . . . it's the last one . . . I thought I'd clean it while I was chatting to poor Dora.

MOTHER: Well don't point it at her darling.

CHARLES: Gosh no, I know not to do *that*.

He smiles disarmingly, rams home the bolt, and goes out.

MOTHER (*to herself*): "Very suddenly in the night" . . . "all at once in the night" . . . "quickly during dinner" . . .

The sound of a motor at full burst breaks her concentration. She looks at her watch.
A car draws up outside the house. It has obviously been driven hard, non-stop from Inverness and is stained and covered in mud. The bonnet steams like a racehorse after the Derby. The car is driven by DR FARSON, a lowland Scot, who has moved to Inverness and is undoubtedly played by Iain Cutherbertson, oh dear, what a long stage direction this is becoming.

Can we go up stairs to one of the empty bedrooms?

You are advised not to read any more of this stage direction but skip on to the next dialogue.
But for those who like stage directions, and there are such people, believe me, LADY CHIDDINGFOLD *approaches the* DOCTOR *who extricates himself from the steaming car. He's holding a small doctor's bag.*

MOTHER: Dr Farson! Welcome to Moorstones Manor.

MOTHER *shakes hands with the* DOCTOR *who gazes at her rather deeply.*

DR FARSON: Your husband told me so much about you . . .

LADY CHIDDINGFOLD *smiles politely, and shows him towards the house.*

MOTHER: Dr Farson, it really is most kind of you to come all the way from Inverness.
DR FARSON: Madam. If I had realised what a beautiful woman my hostess was to be, I'd have crossed the Seven Seas themselves to get here. I'd have fought wild beasts and flown through Time itself . . .

A shot rings out, bringing this passionate rhetoric to an abrupt halt. DR FARSON *reels back, blood spurting from his right shoulder.*

MOTHER: Charles!
CHARLES (*cheerfully, from an upper window, from which he is leaning with a smoking rifle*): Sorry.
MOTHER (*to* DR FARSON): That's Charles, I'm afraid . . . he has a thing about doctors . . .
DR FARSON (*he shouts up to the window, gamely, considering he has a dreadfully wounded shoulder*): Ah! Hello, Charles. Your father and I were in the Army together, you know.

Another shot blasts out and DR FARSON *reels back once more. Blood begins to pour out of his shoulder more profusely.* CHARLES' *head appears at the window again.*

CHARLES: Sorry! . . . Just cleaning it . . . fragment of bullet got stuck in the end of the barrel!
MOTHER: Oh dear . . . is your shoulder all right?
DR FARSON: Don't worry about me . . . (*He fixes her with his piercing, passionate gaze again, despite his two severe bullet wounds.*) This is nothing compared to the pain I feel in my heart. Can we go upstairs to one of the empty bedrooms?
MOTHER (*temporarily at a loss*): Ah . . . well . . . let's er . . . Er . . . Come in . . .
DR FARSON (*grabbing her hand*): I love you . . . I can't wait . . . (*He taps the bag.*) I've got everything.

LADY CHIDDINGFOLD *slides out of his embrace and walks firmly into the house ahead of him, trying not to wiggle anything.*

As they enter the hall of the Manor CHARLES *appears down the stairs, holding the smoking gun.*

MOTHER: Ah . . . this is my son, Charles . . . he is the one . . . who is *not* dead.

DR FARSON: . . . I was saying what a very beautiful, beautiful woman your mother is, what a very . . .

MOTHER (*quickly*): Charles, could you take Doctor Farson up to Dora's room please?

She takes the gun from him firmly. He leaves go of it with some reluctance.

DR FARSON (*his eyes lighting up*): Dora?

MOTHER: Yes, my daughter-in-law, she was . . . lost on the moor. She arrived here in an hysterical state last night.

CHARLES: I really don't think it's worth the doctor's time. She's slipping away fast, in fact she may be dead by now . . . I think she's got pneumonia or cholera.

MOTHER (*firmly*): Off you go.

DR FARSON *turns at the stairs and looks backwards at* LADY CHIDDINGFOLD *with deep consuming passion.*

DR FARSON: I will . . . I will be back . . .

MOTHER (*determined to be businesslike*): Yes when you've finished . . . there are some other people . . . to see.

They go off up the stairs. A few moments later, LADY CHIDDINGFOLD *hears them on the landing upstairs. She approaches as they emerge from* DORA'S *room.*

MOTHER: How was she?

DR FARSON: She is in a state of severe shock, Lady Chiddingfold, but I think she will recover. She had some traumatic experience last night she still finds difficult to describe . . . something terrible happened to her.

MOTHER: Is there anything you can do?

DR FARSON: Well, I rubbed some Vick on her chest.

MOTHER: Did that help?

DR FARSON (*slightly distantly*): Yes . . . Yes it did, thank you.

He smiles suggestively at LADY CHIDDINGFOLD.

MOTHER (*hurriedly*): Now if we just go in here . . .

They go into HUGO'S *room.*

MOTHER (*taking the sheet off* HUGO): This is my eldest son, Hugo.

DR FARSON (*examining him*): Ah! . . . he's been shot quite recently.

MOTHER: Well he was shot last night and then again this morning.

DR FARSON: Oh, I see.

MOTHER: By mistake.

CHARLES (*very irritably*): Now *he's* dead isn't he, Doctor? . . . I mean he's not going to recover, is he?

MOTHER: Charles, please!

DR FARSON (*replacing the sheet over* HUGO *and staring once again with deep passion at the deceased's Mother*): No . . . no . . . he is quite severely dead.

CHARLES: Well, I'll go and sit with Dora.

MOTHER (*desperately, with a quick and nervous glance at the* DOCTOR): Why don't you stay with us, dear?

CHARLES (*deliberately*): No, I think someone ought to be with her during her last hours . . .

He goes.

The dining-room, some time later. LADY CHIDDINGFOLD *is showing* DR FARSON *the corpses there. They have just put the sheet back over* RUTH.

MOTHER: And over here is my husband.

FARSON *is clearly very bored by the medical bit, and his only concern is with* LADY CHIDDINGFOLD.

DR FARSON (*not even looking at the body*): Oh dear.

MOTHER: Yes, I was wondering whether you could tell how or why it might have happened.

DR FARSON (*lifting the edge of the sheet cursorily and dropping it, then once more riveting* LADY CHIDDINGFOLD *with his eyes*): He's dead.

MOTHER (*expectantly*): . . . Yes . . .

DR FARSON: Shot . . .

MOTHER: Yes . . . but can you, for instance, say where from?

He advances rather suddenly towards her. She backs away. He stops, and his look of adoring passion hardens.

DR FARSON: I know what you're thinking . . .

MOTHER (*nonplussed*): . . . What? . . .

DR FARSON: You're thinking I've got a false lip.

MOTHER: No I wasn't.

DR FARSON: What's wrong with a false lip? People have false arms, false legs . . .

MOTHER: Absolutely nothing . . . I'm sure.

DR FARSON: All right, I *have* got a false lip! It's obvious, isn't it . . .

MOTHER: It *isn't* obvious, Doctor Farson.

DR FARSON (*bitterly*): Of course it's obvious. It juts out when the mouth's closed. It doesn't fit cleanly under the other one. It can't withstand hot soup! (*He collapses into a chair, head in hands.*) Oh . . . I was a fool. I thought

I'd take the cheap one . . . for an extra two hundred pounds I could have had a *new* lip . . . (*He shakes his head wretchedly.*)

MOTHER: Honestly, Doctor Farson . . . I really don't know which lip it is that's er . . . false.

DR FARSON: To think our love should end like this.

MOTHER: I think you're rather over-dramatising the situation, Doctor. I've never seen you before . . .

DR FARSON: Ah! . . . But I have seen you, Lady Chiddingfold. I have passed this house many times before . . . I have seen you at the window and in the garden . . . my heart was bewitched by you.

DR FARSON suddenly rises and takes her hands in his. Surprised by the suddenness of the movement, LADY CHIDDINGFOLD backs quickly away, dislodging her dead husband, who slumps forward. His head hits the table with a dull thud.

MOTHER: Oh, my husband!

DR FARSON (*urgently*): Forget your husband!

MOTHER: You're supposed to be examining him . . . (*She struggles. DR FARSON hangs on grimly.*)

DR FARSON: There's no point. I know he's dead. He died with a bullet lodged between the sternum and the crevascular nerve . . . and fired from this gun!

He produces a revolver from inside his coat, and brandishes it, wild-eyed.

MOTHER: Doctor Farson . . . *you!*

DR FARSON: How do you think I got here so quickly from Inverness? Because I've been watching this house for weeks . . . waiting . . . waiting to destroy all around you . . . so you could be mine . . . mine alone . . . just you and me, and then . . . and then — (*His face creases with heart-rending bitterness.*) — this bloody cheap lip lets me down! I love you! I have always loved you! Since that black day you married *him* — (*He points at the slumped corpse under the sheet.*) — instead of me!

He advances toward her, she backs away.

MOTHER: No, Dr. Farson! I can't *bear* being touched!

DR FARSON   (*stopping suddenly, and raising his revolver*): Lady Chiddingfold . . . if you reject me . . . *No one* shall have you!

He points the gun at her, finger on the trigger, and is about to squeeze when the dining room door flies open, MANNERS stands there, rifle raised. He looks far from obsequious.

MANNERS: All right . . . you! Drop that gun.

LADY CHIDDINGFOLD looks relieved.

MOTHER: Oh Manners! Thank goodness you've —

MANNERS: Stay where you are, M'Lady . . . or you'll get what I gave him. (*He nods at the dead body of SIR CLIVE.*)

MOTHER: Manners? . . .

MANNERS: Yes . . . "Manners", M'Lady . . . your humble, polite obsequious little lap-dog, Manners . . . (*He spits the words out with pent-up hatred.*) . . . Manners who opens doors and tells his master and his mistress when the telephone rings . . . well I decided it was time someone waited on me . . . someone listened to me for a change! That's why *I* killed him and that's why I killed Master Hugo . . . Because I'd had about as much as I could take!!

DR FARSON: Don't believe him. I killed them.

MANNERS: No . . . *I* killed them!

DR FARSON: I killed them!

MANNERS: I killed them . . .

DR FARSON: I killed them!

MANNERS: I killed them and I'll prove it to you.

He raises his gun, points it at LADY CHIDDINGFOLD and is about to blast her head off when there is a gunshot from upstairs. All stop and turn.

MOTHER: Oh my God! Charles is upstairs with Dora. He was going to look after her . . . Charles!

She rushes out into the hall. The others clutching their weapons, and temporarily forgetting their homicidal urges, follow. LADY CHIDDINGFOLD makes for the stairs shouting anxiously.

Charles! What have you — Dora! . . . ?

They all stop dead at the bottom of the stairs. DORA is standing on the stairs above them, holding a smoking twelve-bore.

DORA: It's all right, Lady Chiddingfold, I can look after myself. I looked after Hugo.

MOTHER: Oh . . . Dora . . . not you.

Madge . . . four people have
confessed already.

Te . . . le . . . phone,
mi lady.

DORA: Does it surprise you that your idiot son's fiancée wasn't that demure little girl you wanted her to be?

DR FARSON: She's lying!

MANNERS: I killed them . . .

DR FARSON (*rounding on* MANNERS): *I* killed them!

MANNERS: No you didn't . . . *I* did.

DORA: *I* did.

DR FARSON (*turning, desperately to* LADY CHIDDINGFOLD): Don't believe them, my little rosebud . . . it was me . . . honestly.

MANNERS: It was me.

DORA: It was not! You bastard . . . it was *me!*

A half-groan, half-shout is heard from upstairs.

CHARLES: It was . . . me!

CHARLES *appears on the upstairs landing. He is dragging himself to the balcony, blood pouring from a stomach wound.*

MANNERS (*rounding on* CHARLES *with contempt*): Of course it wasn't you . . . you're all talk!

CHARLES: I killed Aunt Mabel remember that!

MANNERS: *I* killed Aunt Mabel!

CHARLES (*so outraged he forgets his mortal wound for a moment*): Oh come off it! Everyone knows I killed Aunt Mabel!

MOTHER: Yes, he *did* kill Aunt Mabel.

DORA: All right, but you couldn't have killed your father . . . you were looking for a secret door to another part of the house.

CHARLES: Oh, that was just a silly story.

DR FARSON (*to* LADY CHIDDINGFOLD): They're all lying. I killed them because I wanted you all to myself.

CHARLES: I stood to gain much more than *you!* The entire estate — money — wealth — fortune . . .

MANNERS: But I had the *classic* motive! Brooding resentment, festering over a prolonged period, suddenly unleashed in a holocaust of violence!

DORA: What about *my* motive? Twelve years engaged to a man I hated, then turned out and made to crawl across the moor for forty miles.

DR FARSON: That's not a *real* motive . . . (*Proudly.*) Not like jealousy!

MANNERS: I had jealousy, mutual animosity, revenge, provocation and hatred over a period of over thirty-five years!

DORA: You couldn't hate a flea! . . . *servant!*

MANNERS: Don't say that!

DORA: You can answer the door, you can serve the dinner, but you couldn't kill a garden worm.

MANNERS: Oh no?

MANNERS *turns, fires and shoots* CHARLES, *who crashes through the bannister and falls with a cry onto the expensive hall carpet.*

DORA   (*after a not-unimpressed pause*): Well anyone can do that . . . Look.

She shoots the DOCTOR, *who falls, firing back as he does so.* MANNERS *fires, misses* DORA, *and shatters an expensive piece of Dresden china. The* DOCTOR, *who is not quite dead, wings* DORA. DORA *turns to fire back.* MANNERS *shoots the* DOCTOR *again and then* DORA. CHARLES *shoots* MANNERS. *So does* DORA. MANNERS *just manages to shoot* CHARLES, *as* CHARLES *shoots* DORA. DR FARSON *fires a last shot and rips a hole in one of the world's rarest paintings — Velasquez's "Man and a Psychiatrist".* CHARLES *is hit by a ricochet from* MANNERS' *shot at* DORA, *and dies.* DORA *slumps down four stairs and dies.* DR FARSON *shoots* MANNERS *and dies. The telephone rings.* MANNERS *drags himself towards* LADY CHIDDINGFOLD.

MANNERS   (*with dying breath*): L . . . ady . . Chidd . . . ingf . . . old . . . the . . . te . . le . . .e . . ph . . o . . n . . . . e. (*He dies with a final obsequious gurgle.*)

MOTHER   (*eyes wide, her face aghast with horror*): Oh thank you Manners. (*She takes the phone with a shaking hand.*) Hello? Oh . . . hello Madge . . . oh has he? Oh good . . . yes . . . Madge . . . could I . . . you what? . . . Do they? Oh well, that's very nice . . . no, well, I haven't really got a moment Madge . . . ? In *love* with him? Oh Madge . . . you can't be. Look four people have confessed already . . . Madge no . . . Madge . . . Madge don't . . .

There is the unmistakable sound of a shot at the other end of the phone.

Madge! . . . Madge?

LADY CHIDDINGFOLD *slowly replaces the receiver, and looks around at the scene of carnage, her beautiful hall filled with smoke and corpses. She shrugs her head wearily.*

Oh . . . dear!

THE TESTING
OF
ERIC OLTHWAITE

A Ripping Northern Yarn

THE TESTING OF ERIC OLTHWAITE

Denley Moor, Yorkshire, 1934.

The town is dominated by a colliery, whose big wheel is at rest, suggesting solitude and stagnation. A lone trombone, plays some rather moving melody. ERIC OLTHWAITE *walks along the "backs" of a line of terraced houses, beside the colliery. It's a grey day, and the rain falls steadily on the empty streets. The houses stretch back-to-back behind him, in long terraces, up the hill.*
As ERIC *walks through this dour northern townscape, he thinks aloud, in a thin high-pitched Yorkshire monotone.*

It were always raining in Denley Moor . . . I remember that . . . 'cept on days when it were fine, and there weren't many of them . . . not if you include drizzle as rain . . . and even if it weren't drizzling it were overcast, and there was a lot of moisture in the air . . . You'd come home damp . . . as if it had been raining . . . even though there hadn't actually been evidence of precipitation in the rain gauge outside the Town Hall . . .

He reaches the doorway of his anonymous stone-walled terraced house — number 58 Castle Street. He pushes the door open and disappears inside.

And the humidity level on the weather chart was a record nineteen point two . . .

Inside number 58 Castle Street, there is a small, plain, but well-kept room with a heavy iron kitchen range, a well-scrubbed table and two armchairs. MRS OLTHWAITE, *Eric's mum, is cooking away on the range. She occasionally stops to brush a wisp of hair from her tired eyes.* ERIC *hangs aimlessly around her. Rain beats on the windows.* ERIC *stares intensely at the frying pan for some while, then:*

ERIC: Black pudding's very black today, Mother . . .
MUM (*patiently*): Yes it is black today, dear.
ERIC: That's very black, that is . . .

MUM: Yes dear.

ERIC: Even the white bits are black . . .

MUM: Yes . . . dear . . . it is a very dark pudding today.

ERIC: Like the weather . . .

MUM (*looking up at him and rather sadly away*): Yes, dear.

ERIC moves to the window; he gazes out.

ERIC: Very overcast . . .

MUM: Mm.

ERIC, having looked at the rain for a full half-minute, moves slowly back and stares once more at the frying pan.

ERIC (*after a substantial pause*): Mum?

MUM: Yes, Eric?

ERIC: I don't think I've ever seen a pudding as black as that . . . 'ave you?

MUM (*forced to say something*): I dare say I have . . . son . . . I've seen some very black puddings in my time . . .

ERIC: But most of them . . . even if the white bits aren't black . . . they're kind of . . .

MUM: That's enough dear . . . go and get some coal, will you?

She hands him the coal hod. ERIC picks it up, and walks across to a rather smart sideboard with a glass cabinet on top, with one or two glasses, treasured pieces of china, and pottery in it.
He pulls open the doors to reveal that the sideboard cupboard is full of coal. He starts to fill the coal hod abstractedly.

ERIC: Mum . . . ?

MUM (*wearily*): Yes . . . son . . . ?

ERIC: Do you know Howard? . . . Howard Molson . . . ?

MUM: Yes dear . . .

ERIC (*finishing shovelling, shuts the doors and brings the hod over*): He's got a new shovel.

He sets the hod down by the fire and stands back to see the effect of this revelation on his MOTHER.

MUM: Oh . . .
ERIC: Aye, it's a lovely shovel . . . it's got a big brass handle.
MUM: Oh good . . .
ERIC: He's going to put it near his other one . . . you know, the one as . . .
MUM: Yes dear . . . er . . . look . . . give our Irene a call will you, tell 'er 'er tea's ready . . .
ERIC (*resignedly*): Righto . . .

He goes to the bottom of the stairs and shouts up to Irene, then back to the table where MUM *is starting to lay for tea.*

It were always like that at home. There were never time to discuss things. As soon as I raised an interesting topic . . . me mum would always find something else to do . . . or she'd be too busy . . . Sometimes she'd feign death just to avoid talking to me. It was the same with me dad . . .

The door flies open and MR OLTHWAITE, *black and grimy, heaves himself into the little room, wiping his hands on a towel. He carries an enamel tea-can which he drops down on the table.*

DAD (*in a thick Yorkshire accent*): Bonjour, Marie . . . (*He flops into his chair.*) Oooh . . . quelle journée au bas de la terre . . .

He'd pretend to be French when he came in, hoping I wouldn't talk to him.

ERIC: Dad, you know Howard Molson?

MUM *hands a portion of black pudding across to* DAD.

MUM: Not now dear . . . you can tell he's tired . . . let 'im 'ave his tea . . .
ERIC: He's got a new shovel, Dad . . .

DAD (*ignoring him, says loudly*): Oh, je suis tres fatigué demain, Vera.

MUM: Oh yes, dear . . . eh bien . . . le repas est prêt.

DAD (*nonplussed*): What?

MUM: Yer supper's ready . . .

IRENE OLTHWAITE, ERIC'S elder sister, comes downstairs. She wears violently over-rouged make-up and a vaguely flighty dress. She is obviously keen to liberate herself some time, with somebody.

And our Irene, me sister . . . she was just downright rude . . .

IRENE sits down at the table, and reaches for a hunk of bread.

ERIC (*eagerly*): Irene — guess who's got a new shovel, then?

IRENE: Oh, shut up . . . you boring little tit . . . !

DAD (*sharply*): Irene! Taisez-vous! . . .

MUM: That's enough, dear!

IRENE: Well, he's such a short-arsed little creep . . . he's driving me out of me tree . . .

MUM: Irene!

She hands her some food. They all munch in silence.

Meals were always the same . . . Every time I tried to start a conversation, our dad would feign a bilious attack and have to leave the room . . .

As ERIC *turns to his* DAD, DAD *clutches his stomach, leaps dramatically up from the table, and pausing only to take two enormous slices of fruit cake, rushes out to the back door . . .*

As soon as they'd finished supper, Mum and Irene would go for a walk round the cemetery, and leave me on my own . . .

MUM *and* IRENE *finish their tea with well practised speed and start to get up, leaving* ERIC *sitting there forlornly, with a half eaten mouthful of bread and black pudding.*

. . . until one morning . . .

Some days later: the sitting room/kitchen at Castle Street is empty, everything has been stripped clean. All that remains is the table. There's a note on it, held down by a piece of coal. It's early morning. Shafts of sunlight filter through the drawn curtains . . . ERIC *comes downstairs, talking as he does so.*

ERIC: You know Howard Molson's shovel I was telling you about, . . . Mum . . .? Well, he broke a bit off the top of the handle — I meant to tell y —

He breaks off and looks around, puzzled, as he enters the bare room. He draws the curtains back, . . . then he sees the note on the table . . . He reads it.

Me mum and dad had run away from home . . . they said they couldn't stand it any longer. But they didn't say what . . . maybe it was the damp weather, more prevalent this year than last, admittedly. Irene had gone as well, and they left no address . . .

He opens the back door. He looks out, and his face drops.

They'd even taken the outside toilet.

The wooden toilet hut has been removed — a toilet roll blows pathetically on its holder, and the chain flaps in the breeze. All the other fittings have gone. He shuts the back door sadly.
A little while later, the back door opens again and ERIC *comes out. Pulling his coat on, he walks through the back gate and along the backs of the terraced houses.*

The rest of that day . . . despite the likelihood of drizzle from an occluded cold front moving slowly east to cover all areas by lunchtime — I looked for them all over Denley Moor.

ERIC wanders the streets of Denley Moor, asking at the garage, the black-smith, tinsmith, looking into doorways, and under benches, and into backyards, and under tarpaulins for traces of concealed parents. Eventually he emerges onto the empty platform of Denley Moor station, he looks one way and then the other. It's deserted, the rain falls — steadily.

Why? Why had they run away? Was it something I'd said? Or was . . . it just the inevitability of living with an average rainfall of twenty-eight point four inches for the rest of their lives? There was only one person I could turn to . . .

ERIC makes up his mind, turns off the platform and out of station.

. . . Enid Bag, whose father kept racing vultures up in Scarsdale Road.

ERIC walks briskly up the road, and stops at the back gate of a house:

ERIC: Hello Mrs Bag.

MRS BAG, a formidable lady in her mid-sixties, powerful and businesslike with a face like a week-old haddock reacts to ERIC with distinct lack of enthusiasm.

MRS BAG: Oh, hello Eric.

She carries on hanging out her washing. ERIC removes his cap and enters the yard. MR BAG, wrinkled and weathered by sixty-eight hard years in this bleak little town, is attending to his birdcages. There is one vulture in each. He's obviously rather more fond of his racing vultures than any other form of life. His natural cheerfulness has just about survived thirty-nine years of marriage.

MR BAG (*popping his head around a cage*): Hello Eric.
ERIC: Hello Mr Bag. Is our Enid in?

MR BAG: Aye, she's upstairs in't bedroom.

ERIC: Oh thanks.

He makes for the back door.

MRS BAG: Hey — you're not going up to her bedroom, my lad!

ERIC: But I only want to talk to her.

MRS BAG: Well, she's got a young man up there.

ERIC: Oh. Who is it?

MRS BAG: I don't know. Somebody she met.

ERIC: She's supposed to be walking out with me.

MRS BAG: That's right Eric. And don't you forget it.

ERIC: Well, what's our Enid doing upstairs with a fellow?

MRS BAG (*aggressively*): She's just having a little fling, that's all.

ERIC: Oh.

An upstairs window slides open and ENID *leans out. She is prematurely careworn and wearing a rather disarranged slip.*

ENID: Who is it, Mum?

MRS BAG: Eric Olthwaite . . .

ENID: Oh.

ERIC: Can I talk to you, our Enid?

ENID (*unenthusiastically*): Yes . . .

ERIC: It's very important.

ENID: Well, what is it?

She speaks to ERIC *utterly without enthusiasm and is obviously not going to budge from the window.*

ERIC (*looking round and shouting his news back to* ENID, *rather reluctantly*): Guess what?

ENID (*flatly*): Howard Molson's got a new shovel.

ERIC (*disappointed*): Oh, who told you?

ENID: You did. Yesterday. Six times.

ERIC: Oh.

ENID: And four times on Tuesday.

ERIC: Oh well. I wasn't going to say that today, it were something else I wanted to tell you. Enid, it's me Mam and Dad and our Irene . . . they've run away from home.

ENID: I'm not surprised.

ERIC: What d'you mean?

ENID: Well they never did like you, did they?

ERIC (*dumbfounded*): Didn't they?

MRS BAG (*brushes past him as she goes inside with washing*): Hurry up, our Enid. You can't go talking all day.

ENID: Yes, our mam! Well, goodbye, Eric.

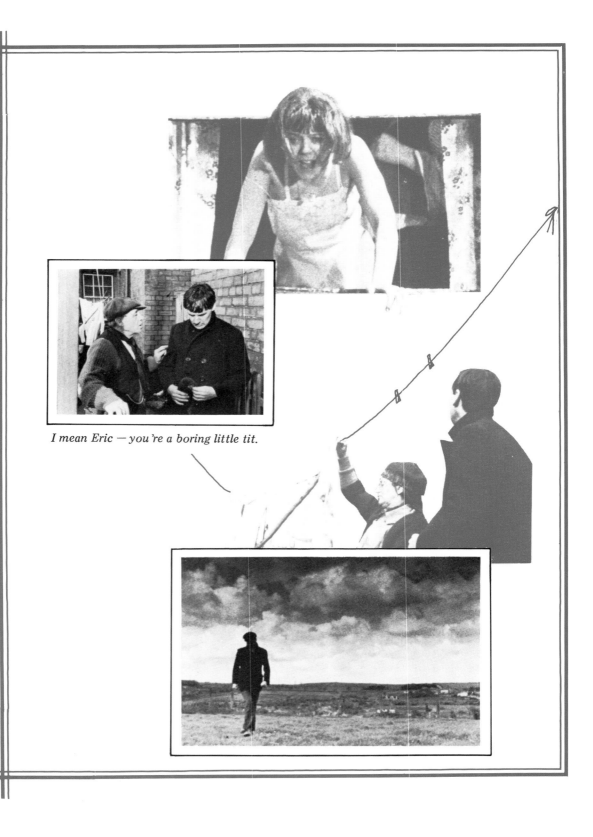

I mean Eric — you're a boring little tit.

As she disappears inside and closes the window, the dim shape of a man in braces and shirt-sleeves can be seen in the room behind her.

ERIC   (*shouts*): Hey — Enid!

The window is firmly closed.

Enid!

He turns dejectedly. This brings him alongside MR BAG *who is looking a little embarrassed by this scene and is applying himself to his birds with renewed dedication. He has a leather glove on one hand, to meet the Vulture Feeding Safety Regulations.*

MR BAG   (*indicating the more vicious of the two predators*): He's a naughty one, this Julian. Call him a racing vulture — he's nothing but trouble! You know, we had Reg and Doreen Molson here t'other day, and Rita had left window open, we'd just got sat around for Sunday joint . . . and in flaps Julian . . . he rips the lamb apart just as Rita's carving . . . took the whole thing off. Reg Molson — daft bugger that he is, tries to save his portion . . . and old Julian takes a couple of his fingers off . . . oh terrible mess! And Doreen, . . . well of cause, she looks like raw meat anyway . . . and . . .

ERIC: What did our Enid mean, Mr Bag? She said me Mam and Dad never did like me.

MR BAG   (*his face clouds as he realises he can't stall any longer*): Oh . . . well I suppose you had to find out some day . . . lad . . .

ERIC: Find out *what*, Mr Bag?

MR BAG   (*turns from his cage in some embarrassment*): Well . . . look Eric, it's like this . . . there are some people in life who are . . . you know — interesting people — good company, fun to be with . . . the kind of people who, when you meet them on the street, your heart lifts and you say to yourself: "Ah! There's old So and So! Isn't it grand to see him!" People who make you glad . . . people who make you feel that life's worth living . . . (*ERIC nods, cheered for a moment by this reassuring old man.*) Well, you're not one of them, Eric. (*ERIC's smile vanishes.*)

ERIC: What d'you mean, Mr Bag?

MR BAG: I mean, Eric — you're a boring little tit.

ERIC: That's just what our Irene said.

MR BAG: Aye — she's got her head where her mouth is, that girl.

ERIC   (*more crestfallen than ever*): Oh.

MR BAG picks up a dead chicken from an enamel basin beneath the cage, and slings it in to Beaky and Julian. Wiping his slightly bloodied hands, he walks up to ERIC and puts his arm round him. The yard is filled with the terrible screeches of Beaky and Julian ripping chickens apart. MR BAG leads ERIC gently towards the back gate.

MR BAG: Look, Eric, d'you mind if I give you some advice?

ERIC: (*numbly*): I don't suppose so.

MR BAG: Well, you've got to pull yourself together, lad . . . you've got to *do* something . . . you've got to make something of your life . . .

ERIC: You mean buy a new shovel, like Howard M . . .

MR BAG: No, forget about Howard Molson's shovel.

ERIC: It's *brand* new.

MR BAG: Eric . . . you can't make yourself more interesting by buying a new shovel . . . or even a hundred new shovels . . .

ERIC: A *hundred!* That'd be good!

MR BAG: No no . . . it's what you are yourself that counts, Eric. You remember what your Uncle Arthur said before he died?

ERIC: Eurggghh . .!

MR BAG: No no — before that. He said: the one thing you've got to learn is to pull *yourself* up in this world . . . and that's what you've got to do, Eric. Get out there and pull yourself up . . . you're the only one who can.

A particularly violent scream rends the air. MR BAG *looks back towards the cage apprehensively, and then pats* ERIC'S *shoulder.*

It's up to you, Eric.

He hurries back to the cages. There is a frightful scream. ERIC *bites his lip and moves off. That same afternoon* ERIC, *hands thrust deep in pockets, and cap pulled down, climbs onto the moors above Denley.*

It were difficult to accept that I were boring . . . especially with my interest in rainfall . . . but that day I climbed up on Skanley Tor . . . and as I looked out over the familiar grey world around me . . . I knew he were right . . . I had to *do* something with my life . . . something that would stretch my capabilities to the limit . . .something that would make me into a man! . .

ERIC looks up, jaw set firmly — an inspirational look in his eyes for the first time in his life. He's fired with a new spirit of determination.

. . . I applied for a job in the bank.

The Yorkshire Penny Bank: Denley Moor Branch: ERIC, in smart blue serge suit and best cap stands in front of a tiny BANK MANAGER who is only just visible behind the enormous desk. The MANAGER is small, weedy and talks in a high boring monotone, similar to ERIC'S. The conversation sounds like ERIC in stereo.

BANK MANAGER: I'm afraid you're too dull and uninteresting for us, Mr Olthwaite . . .

ERIC: Am I?

MANAGER: Yes. I'm afraid so.

ERIC: Oh.

MANAGER: You see, to get on in banking nowadays, you've got to be hard and ruthless.

ERIC: I didn't realise that.

MANAGER: It's a cut-throat business is banking, in which only the strong succeed.

ERIC: Oh dear.

MANAGER: To get where I am now, I've had to tear men apart with my bare hands.

ERIC: Did you really?

MANAGER: Men have come through that door, with their heads held high, thinking they are God Almighty, and they have left broken and utterly crushed by my hardness and ruthlessness.

ERIC: Oh, have they?

MANAGER: I have had men the size of W.G. Grace weeping openly in front of me. Men as tall as Ramsay MacDonald have thrown themselves out of windows and under railway trains and cast themselves into the quicksands because of my unyielding and implacable nature.

ERIC: Oh, I don't think I'd like to do that.

MANAGER: No, I can see you're not the kind.

ERIC: I'd better try and get a job somewhere else, then.

MANAGER: Yes. That would be a good idea. I should if I were you. I think . . .

He is cut short by a shot and a scream from outside. He looks up terrified as the door flies open and a GUNMAN bursts in. He is shabbily dressed, Northern working class. He wears a rough cloth cap pulled down over his head, and a scarf hides the lower part of his face. He is genuinely rather real and frightening. He brings with him an atmosphere of impending violence.

ROBBER: Put yer hands above yer heads . . . both of you . . . (*To the BANK MANAGER, whose head is still only just visible above top of desk.*) You . . . stand up!

BANK MANAGER (*pathetically*): I *am* standing up.

ROBBER: Throw the keys on the desk.

The BANK MANAGER does so.

You! Open up the safe!

ERIC hesitates. He looks at the little BANK MANAGER.

BANK MANAGER   (*to ERIC*): Hurry up!

ERIC picks up the keys and goes over to the safe and starts to open it.

BANK MANAGER   (*to the ROBBER*): You won't shoot us, will you?
        ROBBER: Shut your face.
BANK MANAGER: Yes sir. Thank you.
        ROBBER: Come on you — hurry!
          ERIC: I . . . I . . . can't do . . . it.

His hands are shaking as he tries to get the key in the lock.

        ROBBER   (*pushing ERIC aside*): Get out of the way.

The ROBBER kneels down at the safe, while keeping the others covered, he turns the key and opens the door. The safe contains cash boxes, deed boxes and two large bags of money. He stands back and motions to ERIC with his gun.

        ROBBER   (*to ERIC*): Pick up the bags!
          ERIC: Yes sir.
BANK MANAGER: If you want any more, there's another safe in the . . .

The ROBBER threatens the MANAGER with his gun.

ROBBER: Shut up!

BANK MANAGER (*quickly*): Yes sir!

ERIC gets the bags out, staggering slightly under their weight. The ROBBER jabs his gun in the direction of a small window high on the wall.

ROBBER: Out of the window, you!

ERIC: What *me?*

ROBBER (*fiercely*): Yes, MOVE!

ERIC: Oh yes.

ERIC staggers to the window and, dragging the money with him, starts to clamber out awkwardly. The ROBBER follows. Outside the bank the ROBBER drops onto the path beside ERIC. No sooner are they out than an alarm bell rings. The ROBBER looks round desperately. At that moment a limousine draws up on the opposite side of the road, where there is a small crowd gathered outside a shop which is about to be officially opened. There are bunting and flags flying. A red carpet runs from the door to the pavement. The proprietor stands proudly by the door. A small girl with a bouquet of flowers, and a smart little dress, stands waiting for the big moment of her life.

ROBBER: Get in the car!

ERIC: What car?

ROBBER (*hurrying him across the road*): That car!

They rush across the road and reach the limousine. The moment it stops they leap in. Once inside the limousine, the ROBBER points his gun at the back of the uniformed CHAUFFEUR's head.

ROBBER: Get going!

CHAUFFEUR (*immaculate, and quite unruffled*): Yes sir.

The limousine glides off again, having hardly stopped. The little cheering crowd watch it go, their cheers disintegrating. The proprietor is left holding out his hand rather limply, and the little girl with her bouquet of flowers is about to burst into tears.
Inside the limousine the ROBBER turns to ERIC and starts in surprise. ERIC is squashed up on the back seat between a MAYOR and MAYORESS in full regalia. ERIC looks hopelessly lost and embarrassed. A moment's pause.

MAYOR (*conscious of the gravity of his office*): You'll never get away with this, you know.

ROBBER: Shut up! (*He turns to the CHAUFFEUR again.*) Come on — let's get moving, fast!

CHAUFFEUR: Certainly sir. Fast as I can, sir? (*He is quite unflappable.*)

ROBBER: Yes . . . come on!

The limousine suddenly speeds up, and goes skidding round a corner. The little crowd reacts in amazement. Inside the MAYOR *and* MAYORESS *and* ERIC *are flung around. The speeding Mayoral limousine screeches past a parked police car. There is a slight pause and the police car pulls out after them, bell clanging. Inside the limousine, the* ROBBER *glances over his shoulder.*

ROBBER (*to the* CHAUFFEUR): Take a right quick!
CHAUFFEUR: Certainly sir.

The car swerves violently to the right, with a squeal of brakes.

ROBBER: Reverse and take a left!
CHAUFFEUR: Yes, of course, sir.

A well-polished shoe jams down on the footbrake. The car screeches to a halt amidst smoke and dust. The MAYOR *and* MAYORESS *are thrown forward, with* ERIC, *only more violently this time. The car roars back in reverse and turns left. Then leaps forward amidst dust, smoke, burning rubber, noise, and roars back the way it's come. On the way it passes the police car now going in the wrong direction. The police car skids to a halt then and there, and executes a wild three-point turn.*
Outside the shop the crowd are looking with some interest in the direction of the roar of engines up the street. Suddenly the limousine shoots past them and all the heads turn like a tennis match. A mixture of stunned surprise and curiosity on the faces. They all turn in unison as the police car roars past and again all the heads swing. Inside the limousine:

CHAUFFEUR: Where shall I be dropping you, sir?
ROBBER: Shut up! Just keep going.
CHAUFFEUR: Of course, sir.

The limousine roars out of the town into the open country. The MAYOR *is staring at* ERIC. ERIC *looks rather uncomfortable. He thinks about concealing the bags of stolen money, but can't, and just smiles back unconvincingly. The* MAYOR *is fat and well-fed and the moorland flashing by is reflected in the fine gloss finish of his heavily brylcreamed hair. He narrows his hard, piggy eyes and looks at* ERIC.

MAYOR: Don't I know you, lad? Aren't you Jean-Pierre Olthwaite's boy?
ERIC: Er . . . yes, that's right . . . you might have seen me outside the Town Hall. I come to look at the rain gauge every Sunday.
MAYOR: Oh aye.
ERIC: It's a lovely rain-gauge.
MAYOR (*suspiciously*): Is it?
ERIC: It's a pity with a rain-gauge like that that Denley Moor has such a

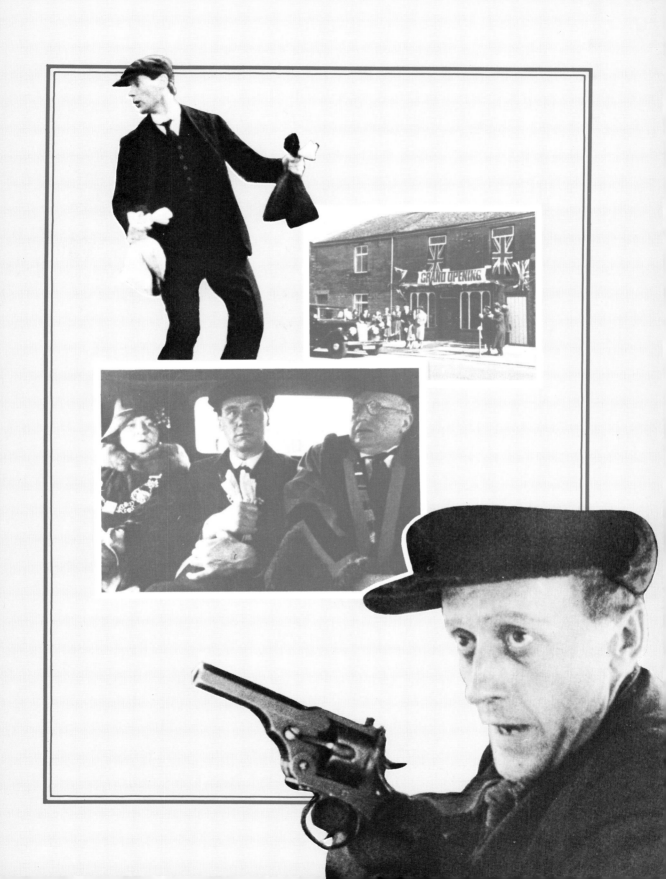

comparatively static mean annual rainfall rate . . .

MAYOR (*as a penny slowly drops*): Oh aye . . . you're the boring one, aren't you?
ERIC: Yes . . . that's right.

The ROBBER *realises that they are about to be overhauled. He turns to the* CHAUFFEUR, *and jabs his gun at him again.*

ROBBER: O.K. Turn left!

He does so.

ROBBER: Stop here!
CHAUFFEUR: Certainly sir.

The limousine screeches to a halt, on a deserted moorland track.

ROBBER (*turns to* ERIC): All right! Get out!
ERIC: What me?
ROBBER: Hurry!

ERIC *starts to get out, but the* CHAUFFEUR *has beaten him to it and is already holding the door open in the best tradition.* ERIC *and the* ROBBER *pile out.* ERIC *struggles with the money bags.*

CHAUFFEUR (*as the* ROBBER *gets out*): Shall I be waiting for you sir?

But the ROBBER, *spurred on by the sound of a police car getting nearer, has taken to his heels and is running up towards the rocks, forcing* ERIC *in front of him. The police car screeches to a halt beside the limousine. Two* POLICEMEN *give chase behind them, while a third* CONSTABLE *has the* MAYOR, MAYORESS *and* CHAUFFEUR *out of the car and is frisking them, despite the* MAYOR'S *protests. The* ROBBER *and* ERIC *climb higher and higher onto the summit of the crags.*

ERIC: Do *you* find me boring?
ROBBER (*breathlessly*): Just shut up!

He turns and fires a few shots at the pursuing POLICEMEN. ERIC *jumps out of his skin. The two* POLICEMEN *dive for cover. The* ROBBER *prods* ERIC *with the still smoking gun.*

ROBBER: Keep moving.
ERIC: Oh yes . . .

He sets off faster than ever. The POLICEMEN *start crawling towards the rocks more respectfully.* ERIC, *with fear in his soul, is struggling manfully with the sacks of loot.*

ERIC: I mean . . . you would *say* if you found me boring . . .

The ROBBER fires again. The POLICEMEN flatten themselves.

ROBBER: What?
ERIC: Would you say if you honestly found me boring?
ROBBER: Run quick!

They run at full pelt across the moor and find themselves beside a fast-moving rocky stream, leaping precariously from rock to slithery rock, the ROBBER spurring ERIC on, until suddenly they both skid to a halt, staring ahead in horror. They are standing on top of a sheer eighty foot drop, a waterfall beside them plunges, foaming and roaring into a gorge. There is no way out.

ERIC (*a little breathlessly*): I mean . . . people *do* find me boring.

The ROBBER takes a quick look over his shoulder, then down again at the torrent. He sees the POLICE gaining on them, makes up his mind and gives ERIC a push.

ROBBER: Go on — you first!
ERIC: Er . . .

His voice trails off into a prolonged wail as he plunges eighty feet. The ROBBER leaps after him. They seem to have disappeared into the torrent below, when suddenly, ERIC'S head pops out of the water. ERIC'S frightful voice is just audible above the roar of the raging waters.

ERIC: That's why I was going to join a bank, so I'd have something interesting to talk about . . .

The ROBBER pops up as well, freezing and spluttering.

Don't you think? Don't you think it would be interesting being in a bank?

The ROBBER grabs hold of a rock at the edge of the stream. He pulls himself onto the shore and then rescues ERIC, who is steadily sinking beneath the weight of the bags of money, to which he's tenaciously clung throughout. They fall exhausted onto the shore. The ROBBER drags a bedraggled but still smiling ERIC further ashore, away from the river and behind a tree.
The POLICE look down at the torrent, shake their heads, and give up the chase.
The ROBBER turns to ERIC.

ROBBER: Give me those. (*He motions to the bags of swag.*)
ERIC (*handing them over*): You didn't mind me asking about . . . about being boring . . .
ROBBER: What's your name, son?
ERIC: Eric. What's yours?
ROBBER (*hesitating*): Arthur . . .
ERIC: Hello, Arthur.
ROBBER: No. I'm afraid it's goodbye, Eric. (*He checks the magazine of his gun.*)
ERIC: What d'you mean, Arthur?
ROBBER: You don't think I can afford to let you go, do you?
ERIC: What are you going to do, Arthur?
ROBBER: I'm going to have to kill you . . . Eric.
ERIC: What . . . completely?
ARTHUR: Well, obviously, it wouldn't be killing you if it wasn't completely.
ERIC: Our Dad was always saying he'd *half* kill me. (*He laughs at his little memory, but the ROBBER just clicks his chamber shut.*)
ROBBER: Goodbye, Eric. (*He raises the gun.*)
ERIC: I wouldn't tell anyone anything. Honest, Arthur.
ROBBER: You think I can take that risk? There'll be a fat price on my head, lad, you'd be a fool not to take it.
ERIC: I'm not interested in money, Arthur.
ROBBER (*sharply, uncomfortably*): Stop calling me "Arthur".
ERIC: I don't want the money, honestly.
ROBBER: Don't give me that! Of course you want the money. That's all anybody's interested in! (*There is a slight pause. The ROBBER straightens his arm out and points the gun directly at ERIC's head.*) Now don't look at me while I do it.
ERIC: I'm sorry. (*He looks away.*)

The ROBBER struggles with himself to do the dastardly deed. He shuts his eyes, his finger tightens. He's about to squeeze the trigger . . .

ERIC: Arthur . . . ?
ROBBER: What is it?

He opens his eyes, obviously a bit glad of an excuse to prevaricate.

ERIC: D'you think if I had more money people would find me interesting?

ROBBER: Well of course they would, lad! You look at the nobs up in their big houses, wi' their big bellies and their big cigars — you don't think people go fawning round them because they *like* 'em do you? It's their money they like! Now keep your head still.

ERIC: Sorry.

The ROBBER takes aim again.

Arthur . . . ?

ROBBER: What?

ERIC: You're an interesting person . . . aren't you?

ROBBER: What d'you mean?

ERIC: Well . . . do you have a lot of money?

ROBBER: I do *now*.

ERIC: No, but before.

ROBBER: Don't talk daft, lad. The likes of me don't have money. We have grind and sweat and tears and filthy homes and hungry kids — we don't have money.

ERIC: But people don't find *you* boring, do they?

ROBBER: What d'you mean, lad?

ERIC: Well our Irene says I'm a boring little tit, so does Mr Bag . . . and me dad . . .

ROBBER: Well you don't want to listen to them . . . what do they know . . . ? Head up!

ERIC puts his head up, and the ROBBER, with a terrific effort of will, is about to blow it off, when —

ERIC: Me mum finds me boring, too.

ROBBER: She what?

ERIC: Me mum . . . she ran away from home just to avoid me.

ROBBER (*with heartfelt indignation, though still holding the gun at ERIC's brain*): Yer *mam?*

ERIC: Aye . . . she left with me dad and Irene . . .

ROBBER: Where's she gone?

ERIC: I don't know.

ROBBER (*with real feeling*): 'Ee, that's bloody terrible that is . . . no mam's got any right to do that.

He starts to . . . yes . . . choke back a tear . . .

ERIC: I suppose if I'd been more interesting she wouldn't have gone.

ROBBER (*really getting in quite a bad emotional state*): . . . That's . . . not the point . . . no mam should *ever* leave her 'ome and little ones like that . . .

ERIC: Well I *did* used to go on a bit . . .

ROBBER: A mam's place is with her family and her loved ones . . . (*Chokingly.*) I tell you, Eric, if my mam had stayed at home I wouldn't be doing this now . . .

ERIC (*a little embarrassed*): Really?

ROBBER: Aye . . . she were a grand mam . . . really . . . (*Voice cracking.*) . . . best you could have . . .

ERIC: Oh, mine wasn't the best . . .

ROBBER: Our mam . . . (*He chokes back the tears.*) . . . our mam used to make toad-in-the-hole like no-one else could. . . . Every Tuesday night me dad'd bring home these great big sausages from Hopkinson's . . . (*With a supreme effort of control he manages to keep holding the gun up.*) . . . And . . . and she'd make batter as thick as clotted cream, and we'd all sit around . . . and we used to . . . call it . . . Mam's Special . . .

A tear trickles down his cheek, ERIC *is genuinely moved, as he squints sideways at the barrel pointing straight at him, but now shaking dangerously with the* ROBBER'S *sobs.*

ERIC: Er . . . shall we sit down?

ROBBER: Yes . . . let's . . . sit down.

They sit.

ERIC (*a little embarrassed, and trying to cheer him up*): My mum, you know, used to make the blackest black puddings you ever saw.

ROBBER: What . . . (*Blowing his nose.*) . . . really black, were they?

ERIC: Oh yes. Some days even the white bits were black and I . . .

ROBBER (*looking up with genuine interest*): Even the *white* bits?

ERIC: Even the white bits were black!

ROBBER: I've never seen a pudding like that . . . though I did once see a pudding with . . .

Some time later. By now it is nightime, on the same lonely stretch of river bank. ERIC *and* ARTHUR *are still waiting where they were, rapt in conversation, oblivious to the wind and cold.*

ROBBER: . . . what sort of shovel was it?

ERIC: It was an oak-shaft, Spear and Jackson Number Three, with a reinforced brass handle . . .

ROBBER: Nickel scoop?

ERIC: No . . . the scoop's steel with a copper rim edging.

ROBBER: And Howard Molson got it *new*?

ERIC: Yes . . . it were only four pounds!

ROBBER: Only four pounds . . . that's a lot for a shovel. I just hope he keeps it safe.

ERIC: Well as far as I know he kept it next to his other one.

ROBBER: Oh yes . . . that's very sensible.

ERIC: But, Arthur, you know what happened . . . ?

ROBBER: Don't tell me . . .copper edging came loose on't scoop . . . ?

ERIC: No . . . no . . . a bit of the handle broke off.

ROBBER: What! Off a Spear and Jackson Number Three!

ERIC: Aye.

ROBBER: I don't believe it . . . whereabouts?

ERIC: On the inside handle grip . . . the brass hadn't been moulded into the embrasure properly and a crack had developed along the underside rim.

ROBBER: And how long had he had it?

ERIC: Couple of weeks.

ROBBER: Incredible . . . I've never heard of that before . . .

ERIC: Well . . . it does happen . . . even to the best shovels . . . (*A short laugh.*)

They pause in satisfied reflection.

ROBBER: You know, Eric, it's silly I know . . . but it's nice to be able to talk to someone about shovels.

ERIC: Oh . . . well . . . that's not me main interest.

ROBBER: No?

ERIC: Oh no . . . there's something I'm much more interested in than that . . .

ROBBER: What's that?

ERIC (*impressively*): Rainfall in this area.

ROBBER (*suddenly pointing at him*): *That's* where I've seen you before!

ERIC: What?

ROBBER: The rain gauge in the Town Hall gardens . . .

ERIC: Do you go there?

ROBBER: Every Sunday!

ERIC and the ROBBER, eyes shining with the discovery of a total identification of common enthusiasms talk on animatedly.

That night, as we talked excitedly about shovels and precipitation, Arthur and I decided we had so much in common, that we would form a gang, dedicated to pursuing our common interest. Arthur, with his long criminal record, was loth to divulge his name, so we called ourselves . . . the Eric Olthwaite Gang.

The next few weeks: The Eric Olthwaite gang in action.

A car wheel screeches round a corner.

A window is smashed by a brick.

A POLICEMAN *blows his whistle, frantically.*

ERIC *and* ARTHUR *turn into the glare of a police torch, two* POLICEMEN *running after* ERIC *and* ARTHUR.

A safe door swinging open and a gloved hand going in.

ERIC *and* ARTHUR *hi-jack a small grocery delivery van. The police give chase. Gunshots are exchanged.*

A series of newspaper headlines tells the story:

"OLTHWAITES IN ROTHERHAM BANK SIEGE TERROR,
Manager tells of Night of Boredom", "OLTHWAITE GANG MOVES
NORTH, Big Shovel Haul in Darlington", "OLTHWAITE
GANG STRIKE AGAIN, Poor to Get Free Rain Gauges",
"OLTHWAITE HITS CUDWORTH!, Weather Records Missing".

Enid Bag's bedroom in Scarsdale Road, Denley Moor: we see that ENID *is on her bed reading a paper, wide-eyed. Gone is her usual flat boredom. A* MAN *with his jacket half-off is fumbling with* ENID'S *bra, trying unsuccessfully, but urgently, to loosen it.*

ENID   (*reading from the newspaper*): The Eric Olthwaite Gang have struck again from their hideout on the North York Moors . . . Posing as members of the public, they entered Cudworth Public Library and while Eric Olthwaite, leader of the self-styled gang . . . oh get off! (*She wriggles irritably away from the attentions of the* MAN *and goes on reading, increasingly impressed.*) . . . daringly engaged the librarian in conversation, his colleague removed daily average rainfall records for the last twelve years . . . the Olthwaite Gang is now wanted by police in three counties!

ENID *gets up from the bed just as her companion has begun renewed assaults on the bra. She walks over to the window without a glance at him, and throws it open.*

ENID: Mum! Mum! . . .

Down in the yard MRS BAG *is taking down a line of washing. Mainly sheets, shirts, etc., which have been torn to shreds by an obviously claw-like force. There is no sign of Beaky and Julian except for feathers and patches*

of blood spattered around the yard. Ominously, there is no sign of MR BAG *either. The doors of their cages are open and hanging at a crazy angle, broken and bent.*

Mum . . . 'ave you read about Eric Olthwaite? He's wanted by police in three counties!

MRS BAG: Yes . . . I don't believe it . . .

ENID: Do you think he wants a moll?

MRS BAG: Who'd want a mole . . . dirty little things, dig up your garden and leave great holes in the park.

ENID: No, a *moll* . . . like, a gangster's moll.

MRS BAG: No, love, you get back upstairs and have a good time . . .

ENID: Oh, Mum . . . no . . . I'm bored with it . . .

MRS BAG *(goes back to hanging up the washing)*: You're only young once, Enid . . . if you don't have a fling now, you never will. I promised your father before the accident that I'd never stop you having it off with anyone . . . provided they respected you . . .

ENID comes out of the back door pulling her coat on and trying to restore some order to her hair. Her eyes at last have a spark of life in them.

ENID: I'm bored with it, Mum . . . I want to go and be with Eric, up there on the Moors, living dangerously, . . . living life to the full.

MRS BAG: Don't be daft! Get back upstairs!

ENID *(defiantly)*: I'm *off* mother! You may never see me again till tonight.

She walks out of the back gate.

MRS BAG *(bellows after her)*: Well don't come crying to me that we never let you have it off!

ENID runs off down the road.

The Manager's office at the Yorkshire Penny Bank, Denley Moor: the BANK MANAGER *is reading the paper out in his little whining, dreadfully monotonous voice, to the* MAYOR, *who is looking dolefully out of the window.*

BANK MANAGER: I see Eric Olthwaite's got himself a moll.

MAYOR: They're bloody pests . . . they are . . . what does he want one of them for?

BANK MANAGER: No . . . a gangster's moll . . . you know, to join his gang.

MAYOR: Oh aye.

BANK MANAGER: I wonder if he wants a bank manager. It's so boring here . . .

MAYOR *(grimly)*: You think bank managing's boring . . . you want to try being Mayor.

BANK MANAGER: Well they *did* ask me, but I were too small . . . I couldn't fulfil all the functions . . .

The MAYOR'S *eyes suddenly light up.*

MAYOR: Hey . . . just a minute! I've had an idea.
BANK MANAGER: What . . . for the Carnival . . . ?
MAYOR: Come on . . . get your coat on.
BANK MANAGER (*plaintively*): I've *got* me coat on.
MAYOR (*impressively*): We're going to see Eric Olthwaite.

Meanwhile, outside a bank in another town, ENID *is at the wheel of the Olthwaite Gang's getaway van. She taps her fingers on the wheel, suddenly, she looks up. A* POLICEMAN *is eyeing her suspiciously from across the road. The doors of the bank fly open and* ERIC *and the* ROBBER *dash out down the steps. The* POLICEMAN *starts to run, but* ENID *puts her foot down, the doors of the van slam, and it revs up and speeds away as the* POLICEMAN *arrives, just too late.*

Our gang became feared and notorious throughout the Leeds and Pudsey area.

The police give up the chase yet again.

. . . One of the most exciting things about being on the run was the chance it gave me to compare rainfall conditions in various parts of the country. For this reason alone, I didn't really want to go back to Denley Moor with its static mean average of 28.4 inches per year. But one day, everything changed.

A deserted moorland track: early morning. The getaway van bounces up the track towards a small cottage.

We returned to our hideout to find that we had a visitor . . .

ENID (*at the wheel*): Who is it?
ARTHUR (*raising his revolver*): Oh, no, it's the bloody police. I knew they'd find us . . .

ERIC: Stop, Enid, I'll give them a warning.

The car skids to a halt.

ARTHUR: No, leave it to me . . .

The van bounces to a halt. ERIC gingerly opens the door and shouts towards the black shape of a car bonnet just visible behind the wall of the cottage.

ERIC: Come out or else!

There is a pause. Then a voice from behind the wall.

VOICE: Eric . . . ?

A shape appears. ARTHUR shoots, realising too late that it's the MAYOR of Denley Moor. The MAYOR falls, poleaxed.

ERIC (*truly shocked*): Oh heck! We've shot the Mayor.

Outside number 58 Castle Street, Denley Moor, Eric's birthplace. A small crowd. Flags are up. This anonymous house now literally hums with life. A handful of pressmen and a couple of photographers rush into the house . . .

Now, back in Denley Moor I became famous in a way which I had never expected . . .

Inside number 58, the room is buzzing with life. Big pictures on the wall of ERIC *(life size).* IRENE *is busily answering fan mail. Piles of shovels and rain gauges about the place.* IRENE, DAD *and* MRS OLTHWAITE *are dressed up to the nines.* DAD *sports a carnation in his buttonhole. A period photographer takes flash pictures and* MRS OLTHWAITE *is by the stove talking to a gaggle of* PRESSMEN, *clamouring for information.*

FIRST PRESSMAN: Mrs Olthwaite, was it always shovels he talked about?

MUM *(giving forth quite happily and discursively)*: Oh yes . . . he were very keen on shovels . . . it was Howard Molson's new shovel that he admired most.

SECOND PRESSMAN: Did he talk about other things . . . ? We hear he was very keen on rainfall?

MUM: Oh yes, rainfall was always a big interest. *(Proudly.)* He could identify over forty different types of drizzle.

The pressmen scribble eagerly in their notebooks.

ANOTHER PRESSMAN *(urgently)*: Anything else. Mrs Olthwaite?

DAD *(scrubbed and spruce)*: Tell 'em about the black puddings, dear!

PRESSMEN *(eagerly)*: The black puddings? Yes! Tell us about the black puddings! . . .

MUM *(with mock reluctance: she's really having the time of her life)*: Oh well . . . he used to be very interested in the colour of black puddings.

More scribbling by the press.

FIRST PRESSMAN: How black they were?

MUM: Yes, that's right.

Scribble scribble. Much filling of notebooks.

DAD: Especially *very* black ones. He were interested in them!

MUM: Oh yes . . .I remember him once saying about a black pudding I were cooking that even the white bits were black!

This is greeted with appreciative pleasure by the press, who are scribbling feverishly, much laughter, and great interest.

A PHOTOGRAPHER: Over here! Mrs Olthwaite . . . in front of Eric's photo . . . great . . . Smile, please!

Flash of phosphorous flare as MUM *smiles at camera. Suddenly there is a shout from someone over by the door.*

VOICE: It's raining!

MUM: Raining?

DAD *(looking out of the window)*: Yes, it's raining love . . .

IRENE: What . . . light drizzle . . . ?

DAD: No . . . it's moderately heavy . . . slightly slanting . . . I'd say it's rain . . .

IRENE *writes all this in a book. She too has become a total enthusiast.*

I'll go and check the gauge. . .

He makes for the back door.

PRESS: Can we have a picture of you checking the gauge, Mr Olthwaite?

DAD: Yes, lads, come on.

The PRESSMEN *bundle enthusiastically out of the back door, interviewing as they go.*

FIRST PRESSMAN: Is it Eric's own gauge you'll be using Mr Olthwaite?

There is a sudden commotion.

VOICE FROM OUTSIDE: The car's here, Mr Olthwaite!

DAD *(turns at the doorway to the kitchen)*: Oh righto! I'll do the gauge later.

FIRST PRESSMAN: Could Mrs Olthwaite check the gauge as well? We'd love a picture of the two of you — ?

DAD: Sorry, lads! We'll have to go!

He ushers MUM *and* IRENE *towards the front door.*

SECOND PRESSMAN: How many shovels has Eric got now?

DAD: I'm sorry — you'll have to come to the Town Hall and ask him yourselves . . .

SECOND PRESSMAN: Is there one he likes particularly?

DAD: I'm sorry lads . . . must go . . .

They push their way through the throng. Outside a cheering crowd engulf nothing less than the Mayor's limousine itself. A CHAUFFEUR *is holding the door open. Inside the* MAYOR, *his arm in a sling, the top of his head bandaged, not looking well, but beaming as best he can, sits next to an even more proudly beaming figure. Amazingly, it is* ERIC, *in newly pressed suit. The* PRESSMEN *throng round the car asking inane questions.*

Just one more! Look over here, please. Eric! Give us a smile . . . Can you do a silly walk?

Flash bulbs go off. Then the mayoral car sweeps the OLTHWAITES *away.*

. . . The Mayor had made me an offer I couldn't refuse . . .

Inside Denley Moor Town Hall. A large crowd, flags and flowers. Above the stage a huge photo of ERIC. ERIC *and his family sit in a line on the stage, behind the* MAYOR, *who though badly wounded is in the middle of a stirring speech to a proud audience.*

MAYOR: . . . And, ladies and gentlemen, who has . . . given Denley Moor all this? Whose interests and whose personality have made this town famous throughout the length and breadth of the country — ladies and gentlemen — I give you someone who has made me the happiest man in the world — (*Momentary twinge of pain from the bullet wounds.*) — by graciously accepting my offer to be the next Mayor of Denley Moor . . . my old friend . . . Eric Olthwaite.

Terrific applause, the crowd rise to him. ERIC *shakes hands with the* MAYOR, *who in turn applauds him, then shuffles back to his seat.* ERIC *steps up to the microphone, and clears his throat modestly.*

ERIC (*in his numbingly boring monotone, which hasn't changed one bit*): What I remember most about Denley Moor was that it were always raining. (*Applause . . . all listen enraptured.*) 'cept on days when it were fine, and there weren't many of them . . . not if you include drizzle as rain . . . and even when it were drizzling . . .

Later that same speech:

. . . and I remember saying to her "black pudding's very black today, Mother" . . . (*Applause.*) . . . and she said, "Yes it's very black today, dear . . ." (*More applause.*) so I said . . . "Yes that's very black that" (*Audience laughter and applause.*)

At the back of the hall, two grown-ups are listening with a twelve-year-old son beside them, fidgeting.

MOTHER (*turning sharply to the little boy*): Behave yourself will you!
KID: It's so *boring* . . .
MOTHER (*with a smile of pride at the man on the stage*): No, it's not . . . it's interesting!

The Ballad of Eric Olthwaite

There was a lad from Denley Moor
From Castle Street he came,
He made this dark town proud again
Eric Olthwaite was his name.

Oh Eric, Eric Olthwaite
You're the one they're singing for
Eric, Eric Olthwaite,
The King of Denley Moor.

Oh he told the world of shovels
To be found in Denley Moor,
Of the rainfall that was static here
At twenty-eight point four.

Oh Eric, Eric Olthwaite,
You're the one they're singing for
Eric, Eric Olthwaite,
The King of Denley Moor.

Having checked the rainfall average
From the rain gauge he would run to
See Howard Molson put his shovel
Next to the other one.

Oh Eric, Eric Olthwaite
You're the one we're singing for
Eric . . . Eric Ol . . . thwaite,
The King of Denley Moor.

ESCAPE FROM STALAG LUFT 112B

ESCAPE FROM STALAG LUFT 112B

omewhere in Germany, 1917.

There is total darkness. All we can hear is the sound of men snoring. Suddenly there is a slight noise . . . a match is struck and lights up the blackened face of MAJOR PHIPPS. He looks around furtively, then lights a candle beside him.
There is by now enough light to reveal that MAJOR PHIPPS is in a P.O.W. hut, which contains a dozen or so beds. MAJOR PHIPPS is in a bed, but fully dressed in the traditional costume of a Bavarian peasant — except for his army vest. He checks his watch by the light of a candle and carefully slips out of bed . . . and crosses to a bed on the other side. There he bends down and softly shakes the sleeping man . . .

PHIPPS: Ginger! . . . Ginger!

The MAN wakes . . .

Ginger! . . . The escape's on!

"GINGER"
GINGERBERRY (*wearily*): What . . . ?
PHIPPS: It's on, Ginge . . . the big escape! Let's go . . .
GINGER: No . . . no. I don't want to go . . .
PHIPPS: Ginge . . . this is the big one . . . the big escape!
GINGER: No . . . no . . . I want to get some sleep.

He turns over, away from PHIPPS and settles himself comfortably back to sleep . . . PHIPPS pauses for a moment . . . shakes his head rather crossly and moves round to another bed . . . He crouches down beside a snoring soldier.

PHIPPS: Dusty!

He shakes him . . .

Dusty!

He wakes . . .

Dusty . . . time to go!

DUSTY (*uncomprehendingly*): Go . . . ?
PHIPPS: The escape! . . . it's *on* tonight . . .
DUSTY: Oh not tonight . . .
PHIPPS: It's dead right for it, plenty of cloud . . . two guards off sick . . . and the wire's down in number two compound.

There is a pause.

DUSTY: I haven't packed anything . . .
PHIPPS: Oh come on! Dusty . . . we've got to get through the wire before they change sentries . . .
DUSTY: Look . . . *you* go . . . Major . . . I've got this damn cold I can't shake off and I'm still rather bunged up . . . I really want to get rid of it . . . you know . . .
PHIPPS: Don't you want to get back to Blighty? See Norah and the kids?
DUSTY: Yes . . . well obviously . . . but I don't want to arrive back all sniffling and sneezing and have to go straight to bed.

PHIPPS *looks even more fed up, and stands up.*

DUSTY: Sorry!

PHIPPS *goes to another bed . . . and wakes another man.*

PHIPPS: Jenkinson! (*Impressively.*) It's the big one!

128

JENKINSON shakes his head with a trace of annoyance and turns over. PHIPPS, increasingly desperate, goes to the next bed . . .

Carter!

There is a bleary grunt . . .

Carter . . . We're going through the wire tonight!

CARTER: Oh piss off!

PHIPPS stands in the midst of the darkened hut glaring round at his dormant colleagues. A shaft of moonlight falls across his face. He draws himself to his full height and launches himself into a fine rhetorical tirade which is slightly hampered by the need for absolute silence.

PHIPPS (*whispering heroically*): What's the matter with you all? (*Slight groans of:* "Oh dear he's off again". *A lot of shifting.*) Where's all that British spunk? (*A slightly embarrassed silence.*) Well, whatever you lot do, *I'm* going tonight! (*A muffled and very half-hearted* "Good Luck!" *from under a nice warm blanket.* "Cheerio!" *from under another.*)

SOMEONE ELSE: Shut the door!

PHIPPS: This is your last chance . . . Is anyone going to come with me?

Silence. You could hear a pin drop. Just the sound of the sentry marching past outside reminding us of the need for silence. Suddenly a searchlight shines around the hut and PHIPPS has to flatten himself against a wall. The footsteps recede. PHIPPS lowers his voice even more for a final assault on their consciences.

Anyone? . . . Anyone at all? . . . Anyone want to come just a bit of the way? No? Right! That's it! I'll do the whole damn escape by myself! Right!

He starts to gather all the pieces of equipment which are hidden around the hut. He is obviously annoyed and tends to make rather more noise than he should. He pulls a rope ladder out of the stove and the wooden rungs clunk against the side with an echoing reverberation. He unscrews the flue of the stove and takes out a couple of carefully-hidden dismantled picks. The metal flue bangs loudly. Muttered "Sh!" and "Quiet" from the others. He reaches up to the roof and pulls down a couple of wooden planks to pull out a whole pile of heavy metal tools wrapped up in a sheet. The whole thing crashes down to the floor striking PHIPPS a glancing blow.

PHIPPS: Damn!

OTHERS: Oh! For heavens' sake! Honestly! Sh!

At this, PHIPPS' temper snaps. Loaded down ludicrously with all the gear for the escape, several haversacks, heavy tools, coils of rope, the rope ladder, picks, wire-cutters and a silly Bavarian hat with a feather in it, he turns on the others vehemently.

PHIPPS (*no longer bothering to whisper*): You miserable bunch of layabouts! You lazy, loafing lot of cowards! Don't you know there's a war on out there! . . .

At this moment a prison siren starts. There is the distant sound of German shouting followed by the sound of running feet and dogs barking. PHIPPS's voice rises as he delivers his impassioned appeal, and a searchlight beam starts to sweep the hut.

Don't you realise there are people out there fighting to keep this world safe and free for people like you! Well I'm going back to join them d'you hear? . . .

The sirens are increasing in volume, the German voices and running feet are getting nearer.

. . . I'm not staying here! Kicking my heels while there's Boche to fight and Hun to kill!

His voice has risen to a crescendo, oblivious to the German voices which are now almost outside the door. He moves towards the door with some difficulty.

I'm off! Going! Getting out! You won't see me again when there's a war to win. Goodbye!

He slams the door behind him. There is a sudden silence outside and a slight pause. Then we hear PHIPPS's voice from outside the hut.

PHIPPS: Oh . . . hello!

German shouts. Dogs bark. Sounds of PHIPPS being set upon. The others huddle back under their blankets. Snoring recommences. As PHIPPS is frog-marched away, a COMMENTATOR's voice takes up the story.

Major Errol Phipps of the Royal Northumberland Regiment, was a legend amongst British prisoners in the First World War . . . He had attempted over five hundred and sixty escapes . . . two hundred of them before he left England . . . On arrival in Germany he escaped regularly every day, and twice a day at the weekends . . . On June the fourth, nineteen seventeen, after escaping six times in one day, Phipps found himself being taken by the Germans to the most notorious prison-camp of all — STALAG-LUFT 112B.

Bavaria: June 4th 1917:

A small open-backed German truck bounces along a country road. In the back are two British officers: PHIPPS *and* NICHOLSON. NICHOLSON, *who is upper-crust and rather genial — is lounging against the partition between van and driver's cab,* PHIPPS *sits between two guards. Opposite* PHIPPS *is an N.C.O. —* VOGEL, *rather a fat, unpleasant little fellow, hot in a uniform that's a little too small for him.* PHIPPS *is looking all around him.*

NICHOLSON:	Where are you from?
PHIPPS:	Er . . . Reigate . . .
NICHOLSON:	Ah yes . . . know it well . . . I'm a Dorking man myself . . .
PHIPPS	(*looking around him, his eyes flicking from guard to guard*): . . . Ah . . . yes . . .
NICHOLSON:	Do you know the Eel and Partridge?
PHIPPS:	No . . . I don't, old chap . . . (*He turns to the* GUARD *next to him.*) . . . cigarette?
FIRST GUARD:	Ah . . . thank you . . .
NICHOLSON:	Nice pub . . . just outside Banstead . . . do you know the barman has this amazing . . .

As the GUARD *looks down to take the proffered cigarette . . .* PHIPPS *grabs him and pushes him to the floor and throws himself out of the truck with a great shout. The truck skids to a halt,* NICHOLSON'S *head thumps against the driver's cab . . .* PHIPPS *runs away with the* GUARDS *chasing him shouting.*

GUARDS:	Achtung! Achtung!

The scene fades and when we return, PHIPPS *is bruised and battered and handcuffed to one of the* GUARDS. NICHOLSON *is recommencing his story as if nothing had happened.*

NICHOLSON:	Anyway the barman at the Eel and Partridge has this marvellous old dog — Benjy . . . D'you know what he can do? . . .
PHIPPS	(*half-heartedly, through a bruised mouth*): No!

I'm a Dorking man myself.

He's not listening to NICHOLSON. *He's busily trying to lift a key on a string out of the pocket of the* GUARD, *who is dozing slightly.*

NICHOLSON: He's the *only* dog, and I kid you not, the only dog I've ever seen who can drink six pints of beer and sing "Give me the Moonlight". Honestly, I swear as God's my witness, Phipps, I've seen that dog, totally pissed, sing all four verses, and with his foot . . . mark you . . . with his foot . . .

PHIPPS has succeeded in undoing his handcuffs and once more leaps out.

GUARDS: Achtung! Achtung!

NICOLSON *raises his eyes heavenward, as the truck skids to a halt, causing him to bang his head sharply against the driver's cab once again. Again the scene fades and when we return* PHIPPS *is terribly battered, with a bleeding nose and both eyes closed up. He is trussed up entirely and manacled to both guards.*

Major Phipps escaped nine more times on that fatal journey but each time he was recaptured within fifteen yards of the van. It seemed that at last the Germans had broken the soul of the most hardened escaper of them all, for once inside the gates of Stalag Luft 112B no-one had ever escaped.

The truck bounces to a halt outside the main gate of a prison camp. PHIPPS *looks out of the window . . . his eyes narrow . . . as he reads:*
"STALAG LUFT 112B"
The gates open and the truck drives in past a group of British prisoners . . . being taught to whistle "Colonel Bogy" by a suspiciously Alec Guinessian character. He is COLONEL HARRY HARCOURT-BADGER-OWEN, *the Camp C/O.*

COLONEL: No no! (*He hums a few bars of 'Bogy'.*) Up on the note . . . (*He whistles.*) Once more, let's get it right.

The truck draws up outside a long hut . . . with a very neat herbaceous border reminiscent of any English suburban flower bed . . . It's being watered by a P.O.W. He looks up with momentary interest as the truck draws up, and NICHOLSON *and* PHIPPS *are bundled out . . .* VOGEL *orders the* GUARD *to untie* PHIPPS. *Then he brushes* PHIPPS *down, and puts his cap back on straight, and generally tries to improve on* PHIPPS's *heavily battered appearance.* PHIPPS *and* NICHOLSON *are then pushed rather roughly into the hut. Inside two or three* ENGLISH P.O.W.'s *are sitting around reading or smoking pipes . . . They look up . . .*

VOGEL (*reading off paper*): Major Nicholson and Major Phipps . . .

A rather officious little English officer, ATTENBOROUGH, *rushes up, looking appalled . . .* NICHOLSON *proffers his hand.*

NICHOLSON: How do you do . . . my name's . . .

ATTENBOROUGH goes straight past him and up to the Germans.

ATTENBOROUGH: What are you doing in here?
VOGEL: (*slightly nonplussed*): *Was?*
ATTENBOROUGH: How *dare* you come in here . . . this is British sovereign territory . . . you know that damn well . . .
VOGEL: Vee are delivering prisoners . . .
ATTENBOROUGH: You are not delivering "prisoners", you are delivering British officers, and when you deliver British officers you wait outside the door until a member of the Arrivals Committee, being in previous receipt of an allocation form signed by your Commandant, comes to receive them.
VOGEL: Listen . . . 'oos vinning the bloody war . . . ?
ATTENBOROUGH: Don't you dare use language like that in front of a British officer.
VOGEL: (*as if getting off his chest something that's been bothering him for ages*): Vell . . . it gets on my wick . . . all this . . . You're supposed to be prisoners . . . you come here because you got captured . . . because you're not very good at fighting. And all vee get is . . .

ATTENBOROUGH turns and points to another OFFICER who is working on a piece of erotic sculpture. He smokes a pipe and wears a polo neck army sweater.

ATTENBOROUGH: You see that man over there — that's Captain Walcott — he won three DSO's and made a single-handed night attack that destroyed four German positions. Over there's Sergeant-Major Errol — he was the first of the Warwickshire Fusiliers over the top at Mons. Archie Tucker — Lieutenant

Tucker to you — Commander of the first ship to break the North Atlantic blockade in 1915 . . .

VOGEL (*surlily*): They still got captured.

ATTENBOROUGH: And lucky for you they did! You might have had the French in here . . . or the Greeks . . . or the Poles . . . Imagine that . . . a prison camp full of Greeks . . . hanging their washing out of the window, combing their hair all the time . . . would you like that? Would you really like that? Cleaning up after them whenever they've finished cooking . . . would you rather have that, than a prison camp full of some of the finest soldiers of this or any other war?

VOGEL: Vell, it's just not fair.

ATTENBOROUGH: Just because you haven't got the guts to get captured.

VOGEL (*protesting*): I voss nearly captured vunce . . .

Jeering from the British prisoners . . .

I voss! I voss next to a man who voss captured . . .

Sarcastic shouts of: "Oh yes, I had a brother-in-law who was captured"; . . . "I had an auntie who was captured, honestly"

Suddenly Phipps saw his chance. While his friends were causing this diversion, he would test the so-called impregnability of Stalag Luft 112B.

PHIPPS *makes a lunge for the door, wrenches it open and dashes out, slamming it behind him. The Germans wheel round awkwardly.*

VOGEL (*a trace of desperation in his voice*): Now look what you've done! All right! Don't anybody move! (*To his* GUARDS.) Get them back on their beds!

The GERMANS *are trying to get the door open, and tying themselves in knots in the process.*

ATTENBOROUGH (*to* WALCOTT): Get his gun quick!

WALCOTT *and another grab the* GERMAN'S *rifle, after a bit of a scuffle, he hands it to* ATTENBOROUGH . . .

ATTENBOROUGH (*to* VOGEL): Right . . . we'll see who's boss here!

ATTENBOROUGH *strides up to a window smashes the glass and points the gun out at the retreating figure of* PHIPPS, *who's making straight for the wire.*

Hey, you! Major! Come back!

He fires . . . PHIPPS dodges the bullet.

Phipps! Come back! D'you hear. (*Fires.*) This is your last warning.

He fires again, and PHIPPS falls, clutching his arm, only inches from the wire. ATTENBOROUGH withdraws the rifle and shakes his head wearily as he tosses the rifle back to the German guard.

VOGEL: (*between gritted teeth*): Thank you . . . Herr Attenborough . . .

ATTENBOROUGH: You couldn't run a bloody jumble sale, could you, Vogel . . .

VOGEL'S eyes narrow murderously, but he controls himself, and beckons to the GUARD. They march out and slam the door. ATTENBOROUGH looks out of the window. PHIPPS, lying just short of the wire, is clutching his freshly-wounded shoulder. He looks up at the wire, then back to the hut with a puzzled and disturbed expression. Then his head drops as he loses consciousness. Some time later we discover PHIPPS sitting on his bed. His shoulder is heavily bandaged and his arm is in a sling. The others are sitting around, playing chess, smoking, reading, wanking. WALCOTT works on his sculpture, which is becoming increasingly explicit. ATTENBOROUGH is talking to WALCOTT. They keep looking over in PHIPPS' direction. PHIPPS notices and half smiles at them, but they look away. The door of the hut opens and COLONEL HARCOURT-BADGER-OWEN enters cheerily. ATTENBOROUGH stands up smartly and the other men make moves to stand up.

COLONEL: (*to ATTENBOROUGH*): Hello, Buffy!

ATTENBOROUGH: Hello, Biffo!

COLONEL: (*to another*): Hello, Squidgey! Hello Dumbo!

OTHERS: Hello Biffo!

COLONEL: Hello Bo-Bo!

BO-BO: Hello Biffo!

COLONEL: At ease, chaps.

BADGER-OWEN has a brief word in the ear of ATTENBOROUGH. ATTENBOROUGH

replies and BADGER-OWEN *flashes a quick rather troubled glance in* PHIPPS *direction, and then begins to walk up the hut, smiling at the men as he goes.*

Hello Tosh . . . Hello Smudger . . . Hello Spiker, how's the leg?
SPIKER: Nearly finished sir.

SPIKER, *with a plucky grin, goes back to sandpapering his newly completed left leg.*

COLONEL: Good, damn good . . .

The COLONEL *continues his progress down the hut. He stops at one bed, where a man sits with his head in his hands. Beside him on the bed is a recently opened letter . . .*

What's the matter Chips . . . ? Feeling low?
CHIPS (*an N.C.O.*): Yeah . . . it's nothing sir.

He looks up rather red-eyed. . .

COLONEL (*sympathetically*): I know . . . I know . . . (*Sitting on the bed beside him.*) I sometimes feel like that . . . cigarette?
CHIPS: Er . . . yes . . . I've got one somewhere sir . . . (*Rummages in his pockets.*)
COLONEL: Is there anything I can do . . . Chips . . . ?
CHIPS: No sir . . . it's just I heard that . . . I heard that the wife's married . . . married again sir.

He gets out the cigarettes, and tearfully offers one to the COLONEL.

COLONEL: Ah . . . Have you got any tipped?
CHIPS: Er . . . no . . . no . . . sir . . . just these . . . I've got a cigar . . . but I was saving that for . . .
COLONEL: Ah, that'll do . . . marvellous . . .
CHIPS (*on the verge of total breakdown*): It's just that . . . she was . . . she was

everything to me . . . sir . . . everything I ever wanted . . . We've had such good times together sir . . . Last leave was the best time we ever had . . . then this. (*He motions to the letter.*) I just don't know how she could do it!

COLONEL: Where's the cigar?

CHIPS (*choking back tears*): Oh . . . it's on top of the locker sir . . . behind the photo . . .

COLONEL: Ah yes . . . thank you.

The COLONEL roots about on top of the cupboard.

CHIPS: I feel so helpless sir . . . I want to be back there with her . . . but it's too late . . .

COLONEL: Can't see the cigar anywhere.

CHIPS: Oh, it must've dropped down behind, sir.

COLONEL: Ah, fine . . .

The COLONEL starts to move the cupboard as discreetly as possible. This is not at all easy as it is a big heavy thing.

CHIPS (*confidingly*): It's funny, sir . . . I've never told anyone but . . . well . . . there was a time, early on, when we didn't get on that well . . . she . . . she . . . had an operation . . . (*Pause.*) down there . . .

COLONEL (*from behind cupboard*): Can't see it!

CHIPS: . . . and . . . well . . . after that she didn't like . . . "doing it", sir . . .

COLONEL: What?

CHIPS (*raising his voice reluctantly*): She didn't like "doing it" . . . sir . . . for a bit . . .

COLONEL: Is *this* it?

He holds up a cigar in a single container in rather feminine gift wrapping with a red bow around it.

CHIPS (*apologetically*): Oh yes . . . sir . . . She sent it last Christmas . . . I was saving it for . . .

COLONEL: Thanks. (*He tears off the gift wrapping.*)

CHIPS: But just recently . . .

COLONEL: Got a light?

CHIPS starts to rummage in a drawer.

CHIPS: But just recently, you see, sir . . . It all got so good I . . . I was just living for the day when we'd be together again . . . and . . .

He produces the matches.

COLONEL (*taking the matches and lighting up*): Well . . . don't worry, Chips . . . Inter-hut Cricket Shield tomorrow.

CHIPS   (*choking back the sobs*): Yes, sir.

COLONEL: There's a trooper. May I keep the matches?

CHIPS   Oh . . . yes sir . . . (*He breaks down totally, all the pent-up grief and anguish of many weeks pours out in a flood of uncontrolled tears.*)

The COLONEL *moves away cheerfully, pausing to light the cigar. He looks towards* PHIPPS, *and wanders over to his bed. He grimaces at the cigar, and drops it discreetly in the fire.*

COLONEL: So you're Phipps, are you?

PHIPPS: Yes, Colonel.

COLONEL: I'm Harry Harcourt-Badger-Owen, but the senior ranks call me 'Biffo'. I'm the C.O. here. Got any cigarettes?

PHIPPS: No, I don't smoke, sir . . . prefer to keep fit. (*Confidentially.*) You never know when the moment might come, sir.

COLONEL: The moment?

PHIPPS: To escape, sir. To get back home . . . fight the Boche . . .

COLONEL: Ah yes, I know how you feel . . . the trouble is, this damn place is virtually impossible to get out of, as I believe you, er, learnt early on.

PHIPPS: Well I've had a few ideas. I've started a glider, made entirely out of toilet roll holders . . . and . . .

COLONEL: Yes . . . ah you see we have a sort of agreement here about escapes. We have a system whereby all escape plans have to be submitted to an Escape Committee. The Committee then recommends some of them to a full session of the Escape Board, and whichever plan has a two thirds majority is put to a secret ballot, and the plan with the most votes then becomes the official plan and goes to the Escape Plan Review Committee, and if they like it, they'll commission a feasibility study.

PHIPPS   (*eagerly*): When's the next meeting?
COLONEL: June the fifth.
PHIPPS: June the fifth!
COLONEL: Er yes . . . three-thirty, but for God's sake don't tell anyone.
PHIPPS: But that's four months away!
COLONEL: Yes . . . the trouble is what with Easter coming up and then there's the start of the cricket season and . . .
PHIPPS: But the war might be over by then!
COLONEL: Well let's hope not . . . obviously . . .
PHIPPS: Look I've already got the main part of the fuselage started, all I need is a couple of your men to help me with the wings . . .

PHIPPS'S eyes are agleam with enthusiasm and pride, as he opens up his locker-cupboard to reveal the partially completed skeleton of a glider fuselage filling the entire cupboard. He pulls it out. The COLONEL reacts with horror.

COLONEL: For God's sake put that away!

The COLONEL tries to shut the door on the glider.

PHIPPS: Hey! Watch out!

PHIPPS makes a grab for the door, but the COLONEL keeps pushing.

COLONEL: Shut it you damn fool!
PHIPPS: Careful!

The door slams and there is a sickening crunch of squashed glider. PHIPPS looks horrified, the COLONEL hot and angry.

COLONEL: Now listen, Phipps, I don't want to hear of any escape plans except through the correct channels, d'you hear?
PHIPPS: There's four thousand toilet rolls in there!
COLONEL: I'm sorry, Phipps, but this is our camp and we do things our way.
PHIPPS   (*picking up his broken glider pieces*): You bally idiots! What's the matter with you, don't you want to escape?
COLONEL: There's a proper way of doing it Phipps!
PHIPPS   (*contemptuously*): Like sitting around on your arses until the war's over?
COLONEL: Listen, Phipps, either you play it our way, or you don't play it at all.
PHIPPS: I wouldn't play it your way — not while there's a war to win! I'm going to escape. D'you hear me? I'm going to escape — even if I have to do it on my own!

There is a tense silence. Everyone in the hut has gone quiet. Their eyes are turned towards PHIPPS and the COLONEL.

COLONEL (*rising*): You will be on your own, Major Phipps. I can assure you of that.

The COLONEL *gets up. They look at each other in confrontation for a moment. Then the* COLONEL *turns and walks towards the door of the hut.*

COLONEL: Cheerio, Spiker! Pads out for Junior Leagues tomorrow!

SPIKER: Righto, Biffo! Remember I'm going in number three this year. (*He carries on sand-papering his leg.*)

COLONEL: Cheerio, Smudger . . . Cheerio, Buffy . . .

ATTENBOROUGH: Cheerio Biffo . . .

COLONEL: Cheerio, Squidgey . . . Cheerio Bongo . . .

BONGO: Cheerio Biffo!

TOSH: Who's Bongo, Biffo?

COLONEL: Another name for Squidgey, Tosh!

TOSH: Damn good, Biffo!

COLONEL: Cheerio Bo-Bo, Cheerio Dumbo . . .

GENERAL VOICES: Cheerio, Biffo.

The COLONEL *leaves.* PHIPPS *looks defiant. He holds a few pieces of his glider — a few toilet rolls stuck together. He stares around but the others look away immediately, and busy themselves at whatever they're doing.* CHIPS *is still sobbing hopelessly the meanwhile.*

Several days later: a cricket match is in progress in the compound. It is a makeshift game with improvised pads, skilfully improvised stumps and bats, made from old Red Cross food parcel crates etc. and pads made from pilfered motor-cycle parts. The German guards stand around watching impassively. PHIPPS *is not joining in — he is a solitary figure, stalking the empty part of the compound, surreptitiously making a map of the camp. He looks across at the cricket match with distaste as somebody hits a terrific six right over the wire fence of the camp. General cheering. A* FIELDER *goes up to a guard, and after a few words, leaps up the wire and climbs out of the camp.* PHIPPS' *distaste changes suddenly to wide-eyed admiration for the simplicity of this escape plan. The* FIELDER *drops down the other side, and scampers away at great speed. When well clear of the camp, he picks up the ball, throws it back and climbs back into the camp.* PHIPPS *admiration (somewhat mixed with jealousy) relapses back into contempt. He turns on his heels and leaves them to get on with their cosy cricket match.*

As the weeks went by, Major Phipps' contempt for the attitude of his fellow-officers, drew him into an ever-deepening isolation as he dedicated himself, night and day to the one goal of escape . . .

We see the P.O.W.'s in a line, turning over their flower bed. At the end of the line is PHIPPS, digging with somewhat greater urgency than his comrades. Two of the officers step back to admire their display and suddenly realise that PHIPPS is actually getting deeper and deeper into the flower bed — he is in fact almost up to his waist. They glance at each other, and then quietly bring this to the attention of the German guards. PHIPPS is hauled out and marched away, glancing bitterly at his fellow British officers as they stand there with their little pots of flowers.
The next we see of PHIPPS, he is systematically working through the camp latrines, stealing toilet rolls. As he stealthily opens the last latrine and pinches the toilet paper, there is an angry shout of indignation from within.

COLONEL BADGER-OWEN: Hey Phipps! Phipps! Bring it back . . . !

PHIPPS races off with his precious load.

Working entirely alone, and with a mind obsessed with his desire for freedom, he almost became a recluse, hardly ever speaking or communicating with his comrades, as his plans neared completion . . .

By this time we have seen him carrying all the toilet rolls furtively into a woodshed. On the door is the sign: EINGANG VERBOTEN
He locks himself in. Inside the woodshed is the huge frame of his almost

completed glider made from toilet rolls. He now puts the finishing touches to it and stands back.

Until after months of this solitary work, the great day arrived . . .

Inside the hut: PHIPPS *is asleep in bed. Suddenly we hear sounds of commotion in the distance.* PHIPPS *slightly opens his eyes. There are shouts of "Achtung! Achtung!" off. A siren wails in the background and there is a rending crash as the door of the hut is kicked open.* PHIPPS *blinks, and wakes finally as the sound of footsteps clatters towards him. He opens his eyes . . .* VOGEL *and two German guards stand over him with rifles pointed at his head . . .* VOGEL *glares down. He's clearly very angry . . .*

VOGEL: Vere are zey!?

PHIPPS: You're not supposed to come in here you know —

VOGEL: Shut up! Vere are zey!

FIRST GERMAN GUARD
(BIOLEK) (*aside to* VOGEL): He's right, you know, we're not really meant to come in here . . .

VOGEL: Shut up! You tell me vere zey are, or I blow your head off!

BIOLEK: We're definitely not allowed to do *that*, Herr Unteroffizier.

VOGEL: Please! Stop telling me my job. (*To* PHIPPS.) Vell . . . ?

PHIPPS: What are you talking about!

VOGEL: Zem . . . (*Indicates the hut.*) . . . Vere have zey gone?

PHIPPS looks up and round the hut for the first time since his rude awakening. Every bed in the place is empty . . . He is amazed.

VOGEL: Vas it a tunnel? A vire job . . . Huh?

PHIPPS (*hollowly*): You mean they've *escaped!*

VOGEL: Of course they've bloody well escaped!

BIOLEK (*to* VOGEL): Language!

VOGEL *just bites his lip at this and manages to suppress his extreme anger. He turns to the* GUARD.

VOGEL: Look! Who's side are you on?

BIOLEK: I'm on the side of justice, Mein Herr, and legality.

VOGEL: Oh Christ!

PHIPPS (*incredulously*): Without me? They've escaped without telling me?

VOGEL: I vouldn't look so pleased if I vere you, Major Phipps, vee'll find zem eventually — vether you help us or not . . . but if you vere to co-operate and tell me exactly vere they are heading for, I vill make things a little easier for you.

BIOLEK: They're pretty easy for him already. You want to say you will make things harder for him, if he doesn't co-operate.

VOGEL: Listen to me! All of you! (*He turns to* BIOLEK *and the two other German guards.*) Things will not be easy any longer. I promise you that . . . from

Tragedy struck — Peace broke out.

now on prisoners will be treated as prisoners . . . I'm fed up with all zese silly rules about vere I can go and vere I can't go and vot I can say and vot I can't say . . . all that name-rank-and-number shit! . . . Vee are the wictors and you are the wanquished . . . remember that!

PHIPPS: The swine . . .

VOGEL (*his voice rising to a pitch of barely controlled hysteria*): No . . . no there is no messing about . . . from now on I tell *you* vot to do . . . you don't tell *me* vot to do . . . because vee are vinning and you are losing . . . and I vill boss you around if I vont to, as much as I like . . . Now tell me vere zey are, and I vill go easy on you.

BIOLEK: No . . . you will make things *more* difficult . . . if he *doesn't*.

VOGEL: I know vhat I'm saying!

BIOLEK: It's just stronger . . . the other way round . . . that's all.

VOGEL: I don't need to make it stronger . . . I'm in charge. I can do vot I like . . . Come on . . . Vere are your nasty colleagues — hah?

PHIPPS makes a move to the window.

Watch him!

The second GUARD grabs him roughly and pulls him back. VOGEL slaps PHIPPS across the face.

BIOLEK (*in alarm*): Herr Vogel! What about the Red Cross?

VOGEL: To hell with the bloody Red Cross! (*He quietens down, tries to regain a shred of self-control and goes on with patient desperation.*) Listen . . . Listen . . . How can you have a war in which nobody does anything bad to each other? There's no point in a war in which everyone goes around saying, "Good evening", "How are you?", "Hello old chap," "Have some of my chocolate".

BIOLEK: Yes, but surely there are humanitarian considerations which are applicable even in wartime.

VOGEL: Oh I know! There is nothing I like better than to give people my chocolate, or say, "Good morning, how are you?" But the conditions of wartime create an unreality which calls for a different sort of moral code.

BIOLEK: Are you saying we should abrogate basic responsibilities for our fellow men because of some disagreement over the size of the Austrian Empire?

VOGEL: No — I'm saying there is a moral code which supersedes our individual moral codes in time of war.

The SECOND GUARD looks at his watch. VOGEL notices and snaps himself out of this philosophical aside.

BIOLEK: But what you're saying is . . .

VOGEL: No! I don't vont any more argument! From now on this prison camp is going to be run as if there vere a war on! (*He points dramatically to PHIPPS.*) Take him to the cooler!·

BIOLEK: What's the "cooler"?

VOGEL: Oh my God, just get him out of here!

BIOLEK *(to the second GUARD)*: "Cooler"?

The second GUARD shrugs and shakes his head.

VOGEL: Move!

PHIPPS pulls himself erect.

PHIPPS: Do what you like, you'll never keep me in here now!

VOGEL *(thrusting his face right up against PHIPPS)*: Major Phipps, in this prison camp there are over forty-five highly trained, fully-armed German guards, if you think vee can't look after one cowardly British officer . . .

PHIPPS: Don't you *dare* call me cowardly!

BIOLEK *(to VOGEL)*: We haven't got a "cooler".

SECOND GUARD: At least . . . we don't *think* so.

BIOLEK: We're still not quite sure what a "cooler" is . . .

VOGEL: Shut up!

PHIPPS: Just because the others left without me, doesn't mean I'm a coward. I've escaped more times than all of *them* put together!

VOGEL: Vell this is one time you're *not* going to escape! By the time I've finished vith this place, *nobody* . . . will ever . . . escape . . . again!

In the next few days, VOGEL carries out his threats, with a whole host of extra security precautions: German soldiers sweating putting up new barbed wire, big arc lights being heaved into position; extra machine guns being installed; two soldiers hammering a new sign outside the camp:
"MINEFIELD" — "ACHTUNG MINEN"
Back in the compound, we hear the voices of German soldiers and sounds of feet running at the double and the heavy clattering of equipment.

BIOLEK: Left right left right left right . . .

From round the corner of the hut comes MAJOR PHIPPS at the double

*surrounded by a squad of heavily armed guards all doubling with him.
They are obviously exhausted. They bring him to attention in the middle
of the yard.* VOGEL *is standing there with the* KOMMANDANT *standing behind
him on a little dais with a rope round it. The* KOMMANDANT *looks rather
unhappy.*

BIOLEK: Prisoners! Prisoners! Shun!

PHIPPS comes to attention.

VOGEL: Prisoners will answer their names. (*Consults clip board.*) Phipps!
PHIPPS: Here.
VOGEL (*with a terrific flourish turns and salutes the* KOMMANDANT): Alle hier, mein
Kommandant!

The KOMMANDANT *salutes wearily. The soldiers are just recovering and
getting their breath back when* VOGEL *shrieks at them again.*

VOGEL: And now! Cricket! At the double! Ein, zwei! Ein zwei!

*The guards look long suffering and wearily turn about and double off with
PHIPPS. We see PHIPPS engaged in various activities — vaulting, cleaning
his teeth, going to the lavatory etc. There are never less than six heavily
armed guards sweating beside him; everything's done at the double.*

**Vogel's pressure was tremendous. Every move Phipps made was watched
and controlled by guards, working sometimes eighteen or twenty hours a
day. There seemed, at last, no way out . . .**

Finally we find PHIPPS *asleep in bed. Around him are at least fifteen guards, their rifles pointed in his direction. One has a machine gun trained at his head. They are still in full uniform and obviously so exhausted they seem to be dropping off, as well as* PHIPPS. *Suddenly there is a footfall and the door opens. They all stiffen, as* VOGEL *enters, he looks round imperiously. He adjusts* BIOLEK'S *rifle to point more directly at* PHIPPS *head, and adjusts the posture of another guard. He nods with some satisfaction and then leaves. The guards look at each other. There is obviously much disgruntlement and they cast glowering looks after* VOGEL. *There is a pause during which the Germans exchange glances. Then* BIOLEK *leans forward.*

BIOLEK: Pssssst!

PHIPPS *doesn't move.*

Pssst!

PHIPPS *opens one eye and looks up in some surprise.*

 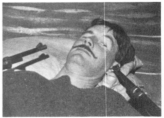

PHIPPS: What do you want?
BIOLEK: We wondered if . . . (*He stops and looks at the others.*)

The others nod encouragingly.

PHIPPS: What?
BIOLEK: We wondered if . . . you were . . . thinking of escaping at all . . .

PHIPPS *narrows his eyes and looks from one guard to the other.*

PHIPPS: You don't think I'd tell *you* do you?
BIOLEK: No, of course not . . . of course not . . . it's just that . . . (*He pauses again and looks at the others.*)
PHIPPS (*getting irritated*): What?
BIOLEK: Well . . . (*A bit embarrassed now.*) . . . if you are . . . we wondered if we could perhaps come with you . . .

PHIPPS *stares at them incredulously.*

PHIPPS: You!

BIOLEK: We want to get out of here. We can't stand it any longer . . .

PHIPPS (*a sudden look of suspicion crosses his face*): What is this?

BIOLEK: You don't know what it's like.

SECOND GUARD: Vee're not happy here.

General murmurs of agreement from the other haggard-looking guards.

PHIPPS: Vogel making it too tough for you eh?

BIOLEK (*indignantly*): No . . . it's not that, it's just that we used to have rules . . . we knew where we were . . .

SECOND GUARD: Vee all knew them off by heart.

BIOLEK: We had to — and Major Attenborough used to make sure we kept to them!

SECOND GUARD (*appreciatively*): He voss very strict.

General agreement.

He'd never have allowed us all in here like this!

BIOLEK: This is sovereign British territory! It is disturbing for us — we are highly trained, you cannot suddenly just make us do things that are not in the book.

SECOND GUARD: Herr Vogel has cancelled all leave, he has put up all these lights and vires. It's impossible to get out!

BIOLEK: But you know the camp better than anyone . . . please, you can help us escape . . .

Pause. They all look at him.

PHIPPS (*incredulously*): You really want *me* to help *you* escape!

BIOLEK: Oh it's not only us. The Kommandant wants to escape as well!

SECOND GUARD: Only vee've never done it before and you are doing it so often . . . please help us!

PHIPPS: Never! I will never co-operate with Germans!

BIOLEK (*hopefully, indicating the guard next to him*): Fritz here is Austrian.

PHIPPS: I will never besmirch the name of my country and my regiment by collaborating with the enemy!

SECOND GUARD: Oh *please!*

PHIPPS: When I escape, I will go in my own way and my own time. Now get off my bed.

They all look bitterly disappointed. PHIPPS *very obviously makes to go to sleep, a trace of a smile flicks across his face, then broadens into a satisfied grin.*

Phipps went back to sleep that night happier than for many weeks. The camp was falling apart before his very eyes. All he needed to do now was to choose his moment and effect the most spectacular escape in the history of the war . . .

With the muzzle of BIOLEK'S *rifle inches away from his nose . . . he drops
into a happy sleep. The scene fades. When we return, it is daylight, the next
morning.* PHIPPS *is sleeping very soundly indeed . . . snoring in fact. The
muzzle of* BIOLEK'S *rifle still by his nose. Suddenly he jerks himself awake.
A puzzled expression sweeps over his face and he looks along the barrel
of the rifle to find no one at the end of it. The hut is empty. Not a single
guard is left. The rifles have been tied into position on the backs of chairs.
But there is not one German to be seen. At an open window the curtain
blows in the breeze.*

PHIPPS   (*under his breath*): My God!

Suddenly there is a manic hammering on the door.

PHIPPS: It's open!

But VOGEL *in his manic anger can't open it himself. A splintering crash
and* VOGEL *bursts in, holding the door. He throws it away, and angrily
stalks up to* PHIPPS'S *bed. His clothing is in disarray. He has obviously just
scrambled out of bed and hastily thrown on the nearest bits of uniform
he could find.*

VOGEL: Vere are zey!?
PHIPPS: Who?
VOGEL: Qvit fooling I am in no mood for ze fooling. I warn you. I vont to know
          vot you have done viz my guards!
PHIPPS: I haven't done anything with them.
VOGEL: Vere are my forty-five highly-trained armed guards?
PHIPPS: How should I know?

VOGEL, *in his rage grabs him by the collar and half drags him up from the
bed.*

VOGEL: Listen!
PHIPPS: Now this really *is* against regulations. . . .
VOGEL: Sod ze regulations, I vont to know vere are my highly trained guards . . .
PHIPPS: Well they said something about escaping.
VOGEL   (*as if struck by thunderbolt*): Zey vot?

He looks around wildly.

PHIPPS: They seemed a bit fed-up with things here so . . . (VOGEL *sees the open
          window.*)
VOGEL   (*still unable to comprehend*): Escaping!

VOGEL *dashes to the window and looks out. Then he whirls round with an
expression of total disbelief.*

You are right! Zey are escaping!

PHIPPS: That's what I said.

VOGEL: Zey are escaping — do you understand! (*He starts to yell*). Stop! Halt!

VOGEL goes quite berserk. He rushes to the other end of the hut. Realises there is no door there. Rushes back to middle. Then rushes to the door. He races into the compound. He looks around wildly. Over to one side there is a cluster of German guards going through a hole in the wire. Some are already through and streaming away into the dawn. Suddenly a siren goes off. VOGEL spins round and looks up. He sees a couple of guards dropping down from a watchtower.

VOGEL: Stop! Steilbeck! Schwarzenburg! Woitkevitch! Stop!

He starts to run towards the tower. But then hesitates as he looks back at the wire again. He doesn't know which way to go. He starts towards the wire again, when an alarm bell starts to ring in another direction. He wheels round to see another cluster of twenty guards gathered round the main gate.

Mein Gott! Hunlich scheisslecker! Leave those alone!

The gates are flung open by the escaping Germans. VOGEL abandons the guards going through the wire — who are all through by now anyway — and races for the main entrance. But too late! The guards are streaming through to freedom.

You can't do this! I have not given permission! I have not said anything about leave! Stop!

He gets to the open gates. He raises his rifle.

I vorn you for the last time! Stop!

He takes aim . . . Then suddenly as he is about to fire he hesitates . . .

VOGEL suddenly has an idea. He turns and races back to PHIPPS who is at the door of the glider hut, looking round anxiously lest any of his escape

151

routes have been discovered. VOGEL *thrusts the gun into his hands and starts to push him with some force towards the compound gates.*

Stop them.

PHIPPS: What?

VOGEL: They are escaping . . . stop them at once!

PHIPPS: I am a serving British officer, Herr Vogel. I cannot obey your commands.

VOGEL *makes one last attempt to control his impatience. He is still pushing* PHIPPS *towards the gates.*

VOGEL: All right I am not ordering you . . . I am just asking you nicely . . . as a friend . . . *please* . . . shoot a few Germans . . .

PHIPPS: No — do your own dirty work, Vogel.

They have reached the gates.

VOGEL: Look! Vot's the point of the war, if you don't shoot Germans? (*Shakes his head in disbelief.*)

PHIPPS: It would be collaboration.

VOGEL (*slaps forehead*): Gott und Himmel! Bloody rules! I'm sick to death of zem. Give me zat!

VOGEL *grabs the gun and fires wildly after the guards. Then he suddenly stops and looks up. The blood drains from his face.*

VOGEL: Oh no . . . oh no . . . I hit the Kommandant . . . (*He swallows.*) Oh my God . . . I hit the Kommandant.

All is quiet beyond the wire now. In the far distance we can just see a small group of soldiers kneeling beside the dead KOMMANDANT. *They look up towards* VOGEL *as they drag him away.*

VOGEL: Oh no . . . (*He shakes his head in disbelief and when he speaks, he speaks quietly, pathetically, his head hanging like a broken doll.*) Where have I gone vrong? I didn't want to run a prison camp . . . it was just a job . . . I tried to do it well, but everyone shouts at me . . . they all know better than me . . . all my life people know better than me . . . and now look . . . I've killed the bloody Kommandant . . .

PHIPPS: What are you going to do, Vogel?

VOGEL (*turning on* PHIPPS): What d'you think I'm going to do? Zere's only vun thing I *can* do! I got to escape!

VOGEL *turns on his heel and races for the furthest end of the compound. He scales the wire with furious energy and leaps off into the distance.*

PHIPPS stands in the emptiness of the deserted prison camp. The gates swing idly in the wind.

For Major Phipps, this was the moment he had waited for for so long.

PHIPPS suddenly makes up his mind. He walks firmly to the gates. He shuts them and slides the bolts back.

Now at last he was free . . .

He starts to walk back towards the huts, a smile of happiness breaking across his face.

. . . free to complete the largest glider ever assembled inside a prisoner of war camp . . .

There is a visionary gleam in his eyes.

. . . free also to complete all those other plans already fermenting in his brain . . .

We see PHIPPS digging with a certain exaltation.

Undisturbed now by the constant attention of the guards he worked furiously on a network of tunnels so elaborate that they later became part of the Munich underground system. . .

We see PHIPPS adjusting a huge improvised catapult made out of floorboards, etc. especially designed to save the BBC money. This could be used for countless other productions ('It's a Knockout', 'The Generation Game', 'Glittering Prizes' etc. etc.) It's stage directions like this that save the British taxpayer money. Help to fight Britain's economic crisis with "Savo" stage directions. Sorry about that.

He built a catapult so powerful that it could fling him two hundred and

twenty-one miles across occupied Europe and into neutral territory . . . he was about to construct a hot-air balloon using only the little bits you pull off Elastoplast before sticking it on, when tragedy struck . . .

Scenes of rejoicing crowds on Armistice Day 1918.

Peace broke out.

Back in the empty compound, PHIPPS *stands alone holding a crumpled German newspaper in his hands. The headline is clear* "THE WAR IS OVER".

And so it was that, ironically, Major Errol Phipps became the only man never to escape from Stalag Luft 112B . . .

He flings the newspaper down forlornly and stands alone in the deserted compound . . .

He returned home to England, a broken man . . . and died three months later . . .

We see PHIPPS'S *gravestone. It bears the inscription:*

He was buried in Totnes Churchyard . . . but his body was found two years later over by the fence . . .

A little group of villagers stand by the fence examining a hole and a pile of earth, with wondering admiration.

Major Phipps had attempted his last and perhaps his greatest escape.

A crescendo of stirring Elgarish music.

A Ripping Story of Fear, Tragedy and Terror

THE CURSE OF THE CLAW

A *wild and stormy night. The wind howls and whistles. A crack of thunder, followed by a massive fork of lightning, illuminates an old and eerie house. Beside the house, the branches of leafless trees weave contorted shapes against the wild night sky. This is Maidenhead, 1926. At a downstairs window, a figure holds a curtain back and peers out into the darkness. It is* SIR KEVIN ORR, *a man in his late fifties, but with an aged and troubled face, which seems to have known no pleasure. His eyes dart around in fear, as he strains his tormented eyes into the darkness. The curtains fall back and the dim light of an old library reveals that his face is deeply lined. He turns slowly from the window and crosses, with a slight limp, to an armchair beside the flickering log fire . . . on the mantelpiece are half a dozen birthday cards, and in an elaborate little frame, the portrait of a fine-looking woman in her late thirties. This he picks up. He looks at it; sadly and with deep unhappiness upon his face. The wind howls, he stares at the portrait and shakes his head, echoing some unimaginable sorrow. A sudden sharp sound causes him to start and turn. But it's only the* BUTLER, GROSVENOR, *an elderly, shuffling, but venerable figure, bringing a glass and a decanter of claret, on a tray. He sets the tray down beside* SIR KEVIN *and pours a glass of claret.*

SIR KEVIN: Thank you Grosvenor . . . It's a cold night tonight . . .

GROSVENOR: Yes sir.

SIR KEVIN: God . . . it's on nights like this I wish Lady Agatha were here still . . . I miss her you know, Grosvenor.

GROSVENOR: Oh yes sir . . . we all miss her.

SIR KEVIN: Yes . . . (*Staring into the fire.*) . . . I suppose we do . . .

GROSVENOR: She had such a fabulous body, sir.

SIR KEVIN: (*a little thrown from his reverie*): . . . Er . . . yes . . . yes . . . She was a lovely woman . . .

GROSVENOR: Oh yes, she was a real dish . . .

SIR KEVIN: (*quickly*): Yes . . . she was a kind creature too . . . not a trace of guile or malice ever crossed her pretty face.

GROSVENOR: Oh yes . . . and in the evenings sometimes when she used to wear that black transparent sheath skirt . . . and the . . .

SIR KEVIN: (*hurriedly*): Yes . . . you can go now Grosvenor.

GROSVENOR: Yes sir, thank you sir . . . will you be requiring the naughty books tonight sir?

SIR KEVIN: (*crossly now*): *No* Grosvenor . . . thank *you*.

GROSVENOR: Thank you, sir . . . Goodnight sir . . .

SIR KEVIN: Goodnight.

He goes back to staring in the fire . . . GROSVENOR *makes for the door. At the door he turns.*

GROSVENOR: Sir?

SIR KEVIN: (*on the verge of another reverie*): Yes, Grosvenor?

GROSVENOR: If *you* won't be requiring the books sir . . . may I?

SIR KEVIN: (*briskly, dismissively*): Yes . . . yes, of course . . .

GROSVENOR Thank you sir.

GROSVENOR *leaves, happy. His footsteps recede . . . wind howls outside . . . curtains flap . . . suddenly a window blows open with such a crash that* SIR KEVIN *starts violently. He looks up, terrified, then relaxes a little when he realises it's only the wind. He goes over and closes the window and leans against it, in relief. He's in a highly nervous state.*
Suddenly a heavy, thudding bang from a distant front door, sets his, and the reader's pulses racing. His eyes widen fearfully, he listens. A moment of silence. Then, dull remorseless thuds from the door.

SIR KEVIN: Oh my God!

Almost entranced . . . he staggers out of the room and into the hall as the banging continues, heightening in volume and frequency till the house seems to be full of unearthly sound. SIR KEVIN *screams toward the huge oak front door, whence the noise, as of some unearthly creature demanding entry, comes.*

SIR KEVIN: Leave me alone! For God's sake . . . leave me alone! Oh! . . . please . . . You've tormented me enough!

He rushes to the door, and pulls back the bolts, scrabbling with terror; wind, howls, more banging, lightning cracks.

SIR KEVIN: Leave me alone!!!

He screams as he finally wrenches the door open. Outside in the pouring rain is a man in a mac. Moustachioed, well-spoken, youngish and wet through. He is CAPTAIN MERSON.

MERSON (*apologetically*): I'm terribly sorry to get you up at this time of night . . . but I'm afraid I'm lost.

SIR KEVIN (*much relieved*): Oh . . . Oh . . . Oh . . . that's all right . . . come in.

MERSON: Thanks ever so. D'you mind if I bring the rest of the expedition in?

SIR KEVIN: Oh no . . . please do . . .

MERSON: Er . . . some of them aren't awfully decent . . .

SIR KEVIN: What do you mean . . . ?

MERSON: Well . . . their . . . tribal outfit is pretty basic . . . if there were any ladies in the house . . .

SIR KEVIN (*sharply*): No! There are *no* ladies in the house.

MERSON turns and speaks rapidly into the stormy darkness.

MERSON: Eedi . . . an-o-loto, nimunti — ayag dal oh lava, occailo . . . no-wah, no mundalunga masa.

He turns to SIR KEVIN.

I've asked them to wipe their feet . . .

Six cold wet Asian bearers enter, wearing rather brief underpants and thin macs. They are drenched and unhappy, like holidaymakers caught in the rain. They're all very cold, and stand in a pathetic huddle, slapping their sides and blowing on their hands. SIR KEVIN shuts the door behind them. MERSON proffers his hand.

MERSON: My name's Merson, by the way, Captain Merson. This is awfully good of you . . .

They shake hands.

SIR KEVIN *(glancing at the huddled figures)*: Not at all . . . What . . . er . . . what's your expedition looking for?

MERSON: Well we're looking to see if there's a channel . . . a river passage linking the Ganges and the Brahamaputra rivers through Bhutan.

SIR KEVIN: But this is Maidenhead.

MERSON: Oh yes, well it's only our first day. We were supposed to change at Woking, and the damn stupid ticket collector put us on the Swindon platform . . . and of course most of my chaps are hill tribesman and really didn't know what had happened until we got to Didcot . . . so then of course we all piled out, across the bridge and caught the next train back . . . well that turned out to be the Oxford-Maidenhead stopping —

SIR KEVIN: Yes . . . well, you'd better bring them into the library . . . there's a fire there.

He motions them towards the library. They troop in wide-eyed and rather alarmed. SIR KEVIN goes to the bottom of the stairs, and shouts up.

Grosvenor!

GROSVENOR *(from a distant upstairs room)*: What is it, Sir? Crumpet?

SIR KEVIN *(a touch wearily)*: No . . . Grosvenor . . . it's not . . . Could you bring some towels and hot drinks to the library . . . ?

GROSVENOR *(appearing, mysteriously dishevelled, at the top of the stairs)*: . . . And the ropes, sir?

SIR KEVIN: No! Just the towels and drinks, Grosvenor!

GROSVENOR *(rather subdued)*: Yes, sir . . .

Meanwhile the Asian bearers are cowering at the door to the library. They look around at each other in fear . . . they seem reluctant to go in . . . MERSON *orders them in briskly.*

MERSON: Come in! Ada . . . odowa!

Reluctantly they enter, looking around fearfully.

MERSON: We only left Paddington at 4.30 and we've already lost three men.
SIR KEVIN: Oh . . . I'm . . . I'm sorry to hear that.
MERSON: Yes . . . they went on to Bristol . . . the trouble is they're head-hunters — that's what really worries me.

The natives look rather apprehensive . . . as if they feel something slightly amiss. SIR KEVIN *shows* MERSON *over to a chair by the fire. Suddenly one of the tribesmen falls to the ground with a strange cry. He is a little older and more distinguished than the rest. He wears an ornamental collar and has various other mystic appurtenances.*

SIR KEVIN: What's the matter with him?

The HEADMAN *is pointing at a sideboard, and mouthing prayers as if in an hypnotic trance.*

MERSON: Ah . . . I'm not quite . . . er sure. . .

The HEADMAN *begins to roll his body around rather sensuously, emitting low cries,* SIR KEVIN *watches in amazement,* MERSON *more in consternation.*

MERSON: They do tend to go in for these sort of fertility . . . er . . . dances, some of which to the Western eye are a little . . . er . . . frank. They are a very frank tribe, actually.

The others begin to join in. They moan softly and flick their bellies up and down suggestively.

SIR KEVIN: What are they doing now?
MERSON: Well I think this is the one about the three ladies and the gentleman.

He shouts at the natives.

Oom-wa! Om-wa! Ti-raree! You see where they come from — the Naga Hills in North-Western Burma, it's almost inaccessible, and their standards of behaviour there are . . .

On hearing this, SIR KEVIN *turns to* MERSON, *eyes suddenly wide, his frame animated with suppressed excitement.*

SIR KEVIN: *Where* did you say?
MERSON: I said where they come from is almost inaccessible and the standards of behaviour —
SIR KEVIN: Where did they come from?
MERSON: North West Burma.
SIR KEVIN: (*urgently*): The Naga Hills! Did you say the Naga Hills . . . ?
MERSON: Yes . . . about four hundred miles from Mandalay going north . . .
SIR KEVIN: (*his eyes widening*): Yes, I know . . .
MERSON: You know?

SIR KEVIN *grabs* MERSON'S *arm,* MERSON *looks rather bewildered.*

SIR KEVIN: Captain Merson . . . I think these people came here tonight for a purpose . . .
MERSON: Oh no . . . it's just that damn stupid ticket collector at Paddington.
SIR KEVIN: I think they've come to help me . . .
MERSON: Help you . . . I don't see how I . . .
SIR KEVIN: Yes! (*He goes to the fire, and turns, slightly wild-eyed.*) I want to tell you a story, Captain Merson. It is a story of fear . . . tragedy and terror . . . it is the story of a curse . . . a curse that is upon this house!

There is a sudden crack of lightning. The window blows open.
There is a final terrifying crash of thunder above the house, as we go into
SIR KEVIN'S *memories of his childhood. In his mind he sees a picture of*
peace and quiet and idyllic rural atmosphere. Birds singing, bees buzzing
etc. It is a beautiful sunny day in an idyllic English country garden. SIR
KEVIN *sees himself as a boy of ten or eleven sitting in his sailor suit looking*
very bored. His FATHER *is drinking tea rather formally. He is dressed in*
black and looks forbidding, as does his MOTHER, *who is occupied knitting*
a long woollen garment, with arms and legs like a huge baby-gro.
SIR KEVIN'S VOICE *describes the scene.*

**I was born in Cheltenham in 1881. My parents lived a comfortable but
austere existence in which they had little time for me.**

KEVIN *looks forlornly across the lawn.*

**They exerted an iron discipline upon their children. They had my sister
imprisoned for putting too much butter on her scone . . .**

At a small barred window at one end of the house, the face of a desperately
ill, tragic looking, thirteen-year-old girl stares out, through bars. Her hair
is matted, her wide-red eyes imploring from a sunken emaciated deathly
pale face. KEVIN *looks quickly away, and turns and walks away from the*
house, across the garden. He passes an obsessively neat flower-bed, beside
an obsessively neat lawn.

And my younger brother David was killed for walking on the flower beds.

In the middle of the flower bed is a little white cross, with the single
word "David" inscribed on it.

**And I hardly dared to think what they would have done to me if they
ever discovered I had a sweetheart, Agatha, who lived next door.**

*KEVIN looks to the other side of the lawn. A GIRL, about his own
age is looking towards him, over the fence.. She looks fresh and young,
simple and innocent. As she sees she has attracted KEVIN's attention, her
lips part into a sweet and innocent smile. She waves. KEVIN turns quickly
back to his parents, horrified in case they might have noticed.*

**But this passion . . . like all my passions . . . had to remain a dark and
guilty secret . . . I dared tell no one — not even Agatha herself . . .**

*KEVIN looks up again furtively. AGATHA has turned away and is trailing
off with her head hung, sadly. KEVIN gazes longingly after her, his heart
torn in two.*

**The only person I could talk to outside this drab and suffocating world
was my Uncle Jack.**

*The scene he is describing now shifts to Uncle Jack's Victorian house. It is
the same one as SIR KEVIN now lives in, but in those days it was severely
structurally unsound. There are uprights supporting parts of the roof and
huge wooden braces keep up several of the walls. The exterior is literally
crumbling. Windows boarded up, here and there. UNCLE JACK himself —
a disgusting, scrawny, pock-marked, pustule-ridden man with a ready smile,
is stripped to the waist and loading rubble, which has obviously fallen off
the house, into a wheelbarrow.*

**Uncle Jack was my childhood hero . . . He was so strong and so brave . . .
Ever since I'd been able to understand about hernias, I'd envied the care-
free way he'd lift up bits of falling masonry. . .**

In his mind's eye, he sees UNCLE JACK *straining at some spar, when suddenly another bit of the house starts to creak and crack.* UNCLE JACK *reacts and leaps into action running along the front of the house to grab a timber support before it falls.*

If some section of his house looked like falling down, Uncle Jack could run like the wind, without a truss or surgical appliance of any kind.

He now sees UNCLE JACK *cleaning out a waste-pipe and drain at the side of the house. With his bare hands he is depositing the filthy contents — black slime, lumps, dead rats etc. — into a wheelbarrow. He coughs cheerfully and bronchially the while.*

He was also totally unconcerned about contagious diseases . . . Tetanus, beri-beri, yellow-jack, yaws, typhus, pyorrhoea, dingue and blackleg were all old friends to Uncle Jack . . .

UNCLE JACK *turns and looks towards the road outside his house, whence he hears sound of horse and trap. It's* YOUNG KEVIN, *his* MOTHER *and* FATHER. *Their horse and trap draw up outside the entrance to Uncle Jack's driveway.*

The monthly visits to this strange old house were the only breath of life in the sterile world my parents inhabited.

Kevin's FATHER *peers towards the house with unconcealed distaste.* KEVIN *can't wait to jump down. His* FATHER *brings out his watch.* KEVIN *nods, jumps down, waves cursorily, and runs up the drive as the pony and trap drives off.*

KEVIN: Uncle Jack!
UNCLE JACK: Hello, Kev!

He has a hacking cough spasm.

KEVIN runs up to Uncle Jack and flings his arms around him. As he hugs him he obviously feels something under UNCLE JACK'S disease-ridden armpits. He pats UNCLE JACK under the arms.

KEVIN: What are these, Uncle Jack?

UNCLE JACK: (*beaming*): Buboes. Touch of bubonic plague I picked up last weekend.

KEVIN: Gosh . . . weren't you scared?

UNCLE JACK: What! A bit of old bubonic plague — (*He laughs.*) I should say not. So long as you get a rabid dog to lick the poison out you're all right . . . Want to see the rats?

KEVIN: Rather . . .

UNCLE JACK (*takes KEVIN by the hand and leads him towards the house: suddenly he stops, puts his tongue out and points*): See that! . . . Spots on the tongue.

KEVIN (*fascinated*): Yes . . .

UNCLE JACK (*impressively*): Yellow jaundice. First symptoms . . .

KEVIN: Terrific, Uncle Jack.

KEVIN gazes admiringly at him. As they go in to the front room, UNCLE JACK points to his neck, just below the hairline.

UNCLE JACK: And that's mange.

They both go into the house and the door slams with a crash. Bits of wood, masonry and glass crash to the ground in front of it. As usual, the porch (which looks precarious anyway) crashes to the ground as well.
Later that day, as darkness falls, KEVIN and UNCLE JACK are sitting before a fire, in one of the rooms of the house. The mantelpiece has come away from the wall and is held up by a crutch.

Sometimes I'd stay till the evening, and Uncle Jack would sit me down in front of a roaring fire and tell me stories of his travels round the world . . . of the women and the diseases that he'd had. How he'd given mouth-to-mouth resuscitation to cholera victims in Valparaiso, how he'd gone to Kazakhstan to catch a rare kind of plague, and how, when he lived in London, he'd contracted pellagra, lock-jaw and scurvy as a protest against the postal charges . . . But the years passed. I was sent away to school and saw less and less of Uncle Jack, until one day I heard he'd been taken seriously ill. It was the third year of the Boer War, and it was his birthday. I'd bought him a brand new bed-pan, and couldn't wait to give it to him . . .

It's nearly ten years later, KEVIN, *now a young man of twenty, is approaching Uncle Jack's house in the pony trap, with his* MOTHER *and* FATHER. *A doctor's carriage is at the door already,* MOTHER *and* FATHER, *tight-lipped, their noses twitching slightly at the smell, rein the trap to a halt.* KEVIN *senses something is wrong and races on to the house.* GROSVENOR, *the butler, is at the door, looking very sad.*

KEVIN: What's the matter Grosvenor?
GROSVENOR: He keeps asking for you, sir. The Doctor's just left now . . .

KEVIN goes upstairs. As he gets closer to the door of UNCLE JACK'S *bedroom, the sound of buzzing flies grows louder. He opens the door. The stench is terrible and* KEVIN *involuntarily gets his handkerchief out. On the bed lies* UNCLE JACK, *covered with very shabby bedclothes. Beside him on the table, beneath a film of dust, are a water-bowl and pitcher, and next to them a couple of birthday cards.*

KEVIN: Happy birthday, Uncle Jack!

He holds up the present. UNCLE JACK *is racked by a prolonged and dreadful coughing fit.*

KEVIN: Are you all right?
UNCLE JACK: I'm not long for this world, nephew.
KEVIN: (*tenderly*): Is it . . . the bubonic plague, Uncle Jack?
UNCLE JACK (*dismissively*): No! . . . no . . . that's no problem — just an itch or two . . . no . . . this is worse, nephew . . . it's . . . it's my birthday . . .
KEVIN (*a little puzzled*): Yes, I know I've brought you a pres- . . .
UNCLE JACK: A day I've dreaded for years.

KEVIN becomes aware of an uncomfortable eeriness in the atmosphere, as UNCLE JACK *continues.*

I haven't much time, Kev . . . go to the dressing-table . . .

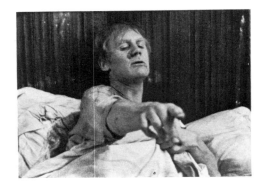

KEVIN crosses over to the dressing table — a dilapidated contraption.

Open the left-hand drawer.

KEVIN does so.

Put your hand in.

KEVIN does.

What can you feel?
KEVIN: A sort of furry thing.
UNCLE JACK: No — not the rats. Feel again.

KEVIN searches . . . suddenly stops dead. He has touched something.

KEVIN: A box?
UNCLE JACK: That's it!

KEVIN pulls out a solid dust-covered, but quite elaborately carved wooden box. It looks oriental.

Don't open it whatever you do . . . bring it here . . . quickly . . .

KEVIN crosses over to UNCLE JACK with the mysterious box. UNCLE JACK takes the box. He bites his lip and looks first at it and then at KEVIN. He takes a deep breath.

UNCLE JACK: Now stand back, nephew . . . on no account must you ever touch the thing that is in this box . . . Do you understand?
KEVIN *(not understanding)*: Yes.
UNCLE JACK: You promise?
KEVIN: Yes, Uncle Jack, of course.

UNCLE JACK seems satisfied. Then, slowly and cautiously and with obvious

fear in his heart, begins to open the box. The atmosphere of chilling horror seems to build as UNCLE JACK'S *trembling hands work at the clasp lock, raising the lid slowly, fearfully, until at last it falls open and there, revealed, is the hideously gnarled foot of some vast bird.*

KEVIN: What is it, Uncle Jack?
UNCLE JACK (*obviously in some emotional turmoil*): It is the Claw!
KEVIN: It looks pretty ordinary to me, Uncle Jack.

He puts his hand out to pick it up. UNCLE JACK *snatches the box away in alarm.*

UNCLE JACK: Don't touch it! Oh no, Kevin! There's nothing ordinary about this Claw . . . When I was given this, I was in Burma, Kevin. I was a young fit man . . . I only had malaria. I was cut off by the monsoon in a hill village . . . and what with the rain and the damp, the malaria turned to gangrene, and I was about to bite my leg off and spit it out — oh! . . . how I wish now that I had — when into my hut crawled a local tribesman, wearing the decorated headress and briefs of the Holy Ones. He thrust this . . . this . . . Claw into my hand.
KEVIN: Gosh!
UNCLE JACK: Like a fool I took it from him.
KEVIN: Well, why not? You didn't die.
UNCLE JACK: Because there is a curse upon it. This is the Claw of the Burmese vulture, which is sacred to the Naga tribesmen, for they draw from it their amazing sexual powers.
KEVIN (*shocked*): Uncle Jack!
UNCLE JACK: Ah! . . . It's true, Kevin. I never tried it, but my manservant, Grosvenor did . . .
KEVIN: Oh, I *see*. Is that why he always —
UNCLE JACK: When the missionaries arrived in Burma they destroyed every holy vulture, so they could no longer tempt the tribesmen to sin and lust. This Claw is all that remains. (*Wide-eyed,* KEVIN *listens.*) . . . The owner must return this Claw to the Holy Men of the Naga Hills before his sixtieth birthday or misfortune and death will be upon him and all who touch it! And I'm sixty today, boy.

UNCLE JACK sinks wearily back on the pillow, a rat scuttles from behind it.

KEVIN: I'll take it back, Uncle . . .
UNCLE JACK: Burma's ten thousand miles away, Kev.
KEVIN: I've got a new bicycle.

He reaches out to take the Claw.

UNCLE JACK: No! Don't touch it!
KEVIN: Please! Uncle Jack! Let me *try* to take it back, please.

UNCLE JACK thinks for some moments. KEVIN waits anxiously by the bedside.

UNCLE JACK: It won't be easy, Kev . . . the Claw is cunning . . . its power is strong . . .
KEVIN: Give it to me, Uncle.

UNCLE JACK stares hard at KEVIN for some time and then eventually closes the box and hands it gravely over to KEVIN.

UNCLE JACK: All right, lad . . . but keep it tight shut . . . never *hold* the Claw itself . . . whatever you do.

KEVIN takes the box eagerly but with a new respect for its strange contents.

KEVIN: I'll save you, Uncle . . . don't worry. (*He turns to go.*)
UNCLE JACK (*pulls himself up in the bed and manages a smile*): Kevin . . . if I'm still alive when you get back . . . I'll show you my cyst.
KEVIN: Gosh thanks, Uncle Jack!

KEVIN hurries off, his heart full of elation at being able to do something. UNCLE JACK stares after the young lad admiringly. As the door of the bedroom closes, part of the ceiling collapses showering UNCLE JACK'S bed with a fine layer of plaster and rubble.

Now all I had to do was to convince my parents . . .

Sir Kevin's story now shifts to the sitting-room of his parents' house. The three of them are sitting there. FATHER is sitting very straight-backed, perusing the newspaper somewhat minutely. MOTHER is knitting. KEVIN sits looking around him uncomfortably, his hands gripping the box tightly. A grandfather clock ticks in the silence. KEVIN looks around the neat little room with its stiflingly severe atmosphere and antiseptic silence. The walls have lots of little texts in frames hanging up. KEVIN casts his eye towards just three of them:—
"Being clothed we shall not be found naked" — *II Corinthians. 5. v.3*
"And they knew that they were naked and sewed fig leaves together and made themselves aprons" — *Genesis 3 v.7.*
"Thy nakedness shall be uncovered, yea thy shame shall be seen" — *Isiah 47 v.3.*

KEVIN: What are you making Mummy?
MOTHER: Something that will cover the entire human body, dear.

A slight pause. Silence reasserts itself.

KEVIN: Father . . . ?
FATHER: Yes, boy?
KEVIN: Where's Burma?
FATHER: It's in the Midlands, boy . . . in Warwickshire.
KEVIN: Burma?
FATHER *(correcting him)*: Birmingham.
KEVIN: No, Burma, Father.
FATHER *(definitively)*: There's no such place as Burma, boy.
KEVIN: It's a country with jungles in and mountains . . .
MOTHER: Your father has spoken, dear.

Silence descends once more. Seeing his parents engrossed in what they are doing, KEVIN cautiously starts to open the box. But the moment he has it open even a fraction of an inch there is a cry from his MOTHER.

MOTHER: Ow!

KEVIN snaps the box shut again.

FATHER: What are you doing, Mother?
MOTHER: The needle went straight into my finger . . . oh dear . . . I've never done that before . . . how careless . . .

KEVIN stares at the box in his hands.

FATHER: The sooner the entire human body is clothed, the better.

MOTHER: Yes, dear . . . ooh! (*She shakes her injured thumb.*)

FATHER: I think I shall detail that very incident in our next newsletter, then those who scoff and belittle our ideas may smirk on the other side of their cheeks . . . Good Lord!

His eyes are suddenly rivetted on the paper. KEVIN *looks up, snapping shut the lid of the box once again.*

MOTHER: What, dear?

FATHER (*tapping the paper*): There's a typhoon warning.

MOTHER: In the *Maidenhead Advertiser?* Are you quite sure, dear?

KEVIN'S *eyes widen. He glances down at the box in his hand.*

FATHER: It's in very large type . . . on the Sports page.

MOTHER (*comfortably*): Probably a misprint, dear.

FATHER: Yes . . . the work of evil men . . .

Silence falls on the oppressive little room again. After a moment KEVIN *looks up.*

KEVIN: Isn't it near India, Father?

FATHER: What?

KEVIN: Burma.

FATHER: Who on *earth* told you that?

KEVIN: I saw it in the Atlas . . .

FATHER: You're not to look at the Atlas, my boy it's an evil book . . .

KEVIN: It's not . . . it's ever so useful . . . it's . . .

FATHER (*with disgust*): It's filled with lewd and lascivious ladies, who know no better than to disport themselves for the carnal delight of . . .

MOTHER (*quickly*): That's not the Atlas, dear . . .

FATHER: Oh.

MOTHER: Why are you so interested in Burma?, Kevin?

KEVIN: I have to go there, Mother, as soon as possible.

MOTHER: Of course you can't go to Burma, dear.

KEVIN: I could join the Navy . . .

FATHER: I'll not have you debase yourself amongst those perverts . . .

KEVIN: I could go as an apprentice cook, they're always wanting . . .

FATHER (*snapping back firmly*): You'll stay here boy . . . where we love you.

KEVIN: But you don't understand . . .

FATHER: That's it. I've spoken.

KEVIN *in desperation wrenches open the box and shows them the Claw.*

KEVIN: Look!

FATHER: Put that away at once, sir.

KEVIN: I have to return it to the tribesmen of the Naga Hills.
FATHER: Put away that object of sin and shame.
KEVIN: It's a claw, Father . . .
FATHER: A *claw*? A *clamp* you mean! A sexual device to tickle the jaded sense of old men.

His FATHER makes to grab it, but KEVIN backs away in horror.

KEVIN: No! There's a curse on anyone who touches it!
FATHER: Give it to me at once, sir!

KEVIN backs away.

KEVIN: No, father!

His father advances.

FATHER: I will not have the trappings of whoremongery and free-lovism under this roof!
KEVIN: No, Father! Don't touch it!

His FATHER raises a protective hand to cover his MOTHER'S face.

FATHER: Turn away, woman! Lest it arouse you to unseemly lubricity! This is the devil's work.
KEVIN: No!

His FATHER wrests the Claw from KEVIN'S terrified grasp and holds it up.

FATHER: And to the devil it shall return! *(There is an unpleasantly sharp crack.)* Oh!
MOTHER: What's the matter, dear?
FATHER: I've just broken my leg.
MOTHER: How could you, dear?
FATHER: I was standing here and it just broke. *(Another crack.)* . . . Oohh! Aargh! There's the other one! I've broken two!

KEVIN looks up wide-eyed and speechless with fear. The wind suddenly blows the windows open. A crack of lightning. FATHER drops the Claw and collapses on the ground, clutching both his broken legs. MOTHER springs to his side. An unnaturally violent wind is howling outside.
KEVIN bends to pick up the Claw. As he does so, a sound above his head makes him turn. He looks up to see a timber beginning to crack, a bit of pre-collapse debris falls on him. He has the presence of mind not to touch the Claw himself. Instead he grabs a bit of his mother's knitting and drops the Claw into the box with it. Outside the typhoon is reaching its climax, tearing mercilessly at the little house. KEVIN climbs to the window, the strong gusts blowing his hair and clothes.

The Claw had already begun its evil work . . . I knew there was no time to lose. I had to get to Burma somehow . . .

KEVIN, fighting against the mighty wind and ignoring the screams of his parents, jumps from the window out into the storm-tossed night.

I was lucky. I got a job as Captain upon the Greasy Bastard, a tramp steamer which carried rubber goods and things for the weekend between London and Rangoon.

KEVIN, in Captain's uniform is standing on the bridge of the Greasy Bastard, a low, chunky vessel, not much larger than an ocean-going tug.

It seemed an unbelievable stroke of luck, but I knew that some time . . . somewhere — the Claw would start to work its evil influence. . .

KEVIN walks across to the door of the wheelhouse and enters. Inside is a HELMSMAN and next to him a CHIEF PETTY OFFICER, who is giving orders into the speaking tube to the engine room. This is CHIEF PETTY OFFICER RUSSEL.

RUSSEL: Fourteen starboard . . . Mr Jenkins . . . Three degrees sou' sou' east . . .

RUSSEL starts checking and cross checking the course and being generally efficient. KEVIN'S eyes seem drawn to the petty officer, but he looks away quickly and shyly as the glance is returned.

But even I was totally unprepared for the way in which the Curse was to manifest itself . . . We were four days out of London, when I began — to my horror — to notice what an extraordinarily beautiful Chief Petty Officer Mr Russel was.

MR RUSSEL turns and looks inquiringly at KEVIN, having caught his eye. MR RUSSEL is, indeed, extremely attractive. His fine features, almost delicately beautiful: soft-skinned and un-lined . . . his body too, hints at a slender femininity. . beneath his officer's tunic a moderately well-endowed chest is betrayed by a slight-straining of the buttons. KEVIN *blushes and looks away, bemused and troubled.*

A few hours later, in the evening, as the Greasy Bastard heaves its way through a heavy swell off the Portuguese coast, KEVIN *is lying on his bunk in his cabin. He looks troubled and is staring at the Claw in its box on a shelf beside him. He shakes his head and tries unsuccessfully to concentrate on a nautical book.*

Could the Claw be taking its revenge in this cruel way . . . ? My shameful passion for the Chief Petty Officer grew and grew, and I was helpless in its grip . . .

KEVIN *flings the book down and buries his face in his pillow. Suddenly there is a knock at the door.* KEVIN *jerks up, eyes wide. He tries to pull himself together.*

KEVIN: Come.

The door opens and in comes MR RUSSEL *himself.*

Ah . . . Mr Russel . . . (*He swallows.*)

They both swallow.

RUSSEL: Permission to speak with you, Captain?
KEVIN (*slightly breathless*): Yes?
RUSSEL: Well it's just that I . . . I've noticed you *looking* at me, Captain.
KEVIN (*quickly, highly embarrassed*): Well I look at all the men, Mr Russel . . . (*Attempts a laugh.*) I'm just a born starer, I suppose . . .
RUSSEL: Not the way you've been looking at me, Captain.
KEVIN: Please don't be offended, Mr Russel . . .
RUSSEL: I'm not offended, Captain . . . (*Meaningfully.*) That's what's worrying me . . .

KEVIN *is speechless. He tries to reply, but cannot. He swallows dryly.*

KEVIN: "Worrying" you?

RUSSEL: I don't know how to say this . . . Captain . . .

KEVIN (*breathlessly*): What?

RUSSEL (*dropping his eyes for a moment*): Ever since you first took over the ship, Captain . . . I've . . . I've felt attracted to you.

KEVIN: Oh God!

KEVIN turns away, fists clenched and stares blindly out of his porthole into the night.

RUSSEL: Does that repel you?

KEVIN (*dragging it out of himself*): I wish it did, Mr Russel . . . I only wish it did.

RUSSEL comes up behind KEVIN.

RUSSEL: May I touch you, Captain?

KEVIN freezes and shrinks away.

KEVIN: No! No! It's bad enough with a girl . . . but you're . . . you're a *man!*

RUSSEL leans his fists against the wall and closes his eyes. His breast heaves.

RUSSEL: I know! I know!

KEVIN (*focussing on RUSSEL'S chesty region*): You *are* a man, aren't you?

RUSSEL: Of course I'm a man.

KEVIN: I'm sorry, Mr Russel, I didn't mean . . .

RUSSEL: Don't be sorry. It's me that's sorry. You don't know what it's like . . . trapped in this man's body . . .

KEVIN: But what about . . . (KEVIN *nods at* RUSSEL'S *heaving bosom.*) . . . those.

RUSSEL: These. (*He looks down at them.*) Oh . . . I've been putting on weight there ever since I was sixteen . . . it's a recognised medical condition.

KEVIN: Have you seen a doctor?

RUSSEL: Doctors . . . surgeons . . . there's nothing they can do, they just say I'll grow out of it . . .

KEVIN (*swallows tentatively, and approaches* RUSSEL): Well . . . Mr Russel . . . since you *are* a man . . . maybe it would be . . . all right . . . for me to . . . rub something on them . . . for a bit . . .

It seemed as if the evil influence of the Claw was tearing away the last shreds of my manhood and dignity . . .

RUSSEL: Would you . . . Captain?
KEVIN: Oh yes . . . Chief Petty Officer.

They fall, locked in an illicit embrace, onto KEVIN'S bunk, in the very shadow of the Claw itself. The scene discreetly changes and we see the small boat from a distance, tossing in the waves . . . one porthole is lighted . . .

And yet, at that moment, something changed. As if the power of the Claw seemed to be suddenly weakening.

Back in KEVIN'S cabin. He and CHIEF PETTY OFFICER RUSSEL are sitting up naked in KEVIN'S bunk. RUSSEL'S long dark hair spilling across the pillow . . .

That night, we discovered that Russel had been wrong — he *was* a woman after all . . . it was a mistake anyone could have made, in the sort of society in which we had been brought up.

Some time later in the voyage, KEVIN is sitting on the stern of the Greasy Bastard surrounded by his pretty crew. Their jackets hang loosely open in the sunshine. They laugh gaily and happily.

We discovered that most of the rest of the crew were women as well . . . The voyage became suddenly idyllic . . . Free from the repressive society we'd left behind us, we began to talk frankly about ourselves and our bodies and our needs . . . I was happy for the first time in my life until one day, with the coast of Burma almost in sight . . . I realised I had once again underestimated the power of the Claw.

KEVIN is in his cabin. He looks tanned and fit. He's humming happily away to himself as he does his packing. The Claw is in its box beside his bed. There is a knock at the door.

KEVIN: Come!

The door opens and a deputation from the crew enters, headed by CHIEF
PETTY OFFICER RUSSEL, *looking quite ravishing. All the rest are women, apart
from a bearded* STOKER, *who is quite definitely a man. There is a slight
pause. They look a little uncomfortable.*

KEVIN: Ah! We'll be in Burma by tomorrow, eh men? All packed?

They look at each other.

RUSSEL: We're not going to Burma, Captain.
KEVIN: I beg your pardon?
RUSSEL: We're not going to Burma, Captain.
KEVIN: What do you mean? We're practically there.
RUSSEL: It's too good here, Captain. On board the Greasy Bastard we've all found
a freedom and happiness we can never find anywhere else. Let's not just
throw it all away . . .
CHIEF ENGINEER (*a flaxen-haired beauty*): Why can't we sail on like this forever?
KEVIN: Because I have to get to Burma.

The crew stand their ground, looking defiant.

KEVIN: Look . . . I know we've been happy together . . . I've learnt a lot about . . .
well . . . all sorts of things I didn't know before . . .
STOKER: Like stoking the boiler, sir?
KEVIN: Well that . . . and . . . er . . . *other* things . . . (*He eyes* RUSSEL *knowingly.*)
STOKER: I *meant* it metaphorically, sir.
KEVIN (*highly embarrassed*): Ah . . . yes . . .

KEVIN *decides it's time he came clean, he picks up the box containing the*
Claw and shows it to them.

KEVIN: Look! I have a trust to return this to its rightful owners . . . I cannot
betray that trust.

RUSSEL: You wouldn't let that come between us and our happiness!
KEVIN: A man's life depends on it.
RUSSEL: Our happiness depends on it too, Captain!

RUSSEL makes a sudden grab for the box, snatches it out of KEVIN's hands and races out of the cabin.

KEVIN: Mr Russel!

He gives chase, elbowing his way through the other men. RUSSEL, pursued by an increasingly frantic KEVIN, who is pursued in turn by the rest of the crew, races down the steps from the bridge, and runs the length of the Greasy Bastard until she reaches the stern, there she stops, and begins to open the box.

KEVIN: No! You don't know what you're doing, Russel!
RUSSEL: I do, Captain . . . I'm saving you . . . I'm saving all of us!
KEVIN: Russel! No!

RUSSEL clasps the Claw, holds it aloft, but before she can hurl it over the side, there is a tremendous explosion and a sheet of flame and debris fly hundreds of feet into the sky.

As the noise of the explosion dies down we move on in the story, and find young KEVIN, many weeks later, torn, battered, and slightly charred, walking forlornly up the driveway of UNCLE JACK's crumbling house.

I was the only survivor . . . A dreadful sense of foreboding gripped me as I returned to the house I had loved so much . . .

The chimney of Uncle Jack's house collapses, quite slowly, in a shower of brick dust. KEVIN walks slowly up the drive. He goes in the front door, the porch collapses as usual, only more so.

. . . During my absence Uncle Jack had grown weaker and weaker. He had caught a rare Spanish skin disease, which cheered him up momentarily, and a bout of myxomatosis, but apart from that it had all been downhill.

KEVIN walks through the house and up the stairs and into Uncle Jack's room. Uncle Jack is lying in bed at his last gasp. Flies buzz around him.

KEVIN: Uncle Jack . . .
UNCLE JACK: (*wearily*): Kevin . . . did you return the Claw?
KEVIN: (*lowering his eyes*): No . . . Uncle Jack . . . I'm sorry . . .
UNCLE JACK: Where is it boy?
KEVIN: It's in the Indian Ocean . . .

UNCLE JACK   (*as if caught by some sudden, unbearable pain*): Agh! . . . Oh . . . no . . .
                  no . . .
       KEVIN: I couldn't help it. I was nearly there, but . . .
UNCLE JACK: Of course you couldn't . . . I told you boy, the Claw's too strong . . . too
                  cunning.
       KEVIN: I'm sorry Uncle Jack . . .
UNCLE JACK: Listen, boy . . . I'm done for now, but I want you to promise me something.
       KEVIN: Yes?
UNCLE JACK: That Claw must be stopped . . . if it's allowed to go loose in the world for
                  too long it'll do untold damage.
       KEVIN: Yes Uncle Jack.
UNCLE JACK: One day . . . it will return to this house . . . you must be here, always, ready
                  for it, when it comes.
       KEVIN: How can it Uncle Jack?
UNCLE JACK: It will . . . it will . . . (*In considerable pain.*) Now boy, come here and have
                  a look at my . . . Aargh . . . Aargh . . . Aaaaarggghhh!

*UNCLE JACK dies spectacularly with prolonged gurgling, and rattling. KEVIN
looks on with deep sadness and utter helplessness.*

And so, Uncle Jack passed away . . .

*Three days later: the day of the funeral. A tolling bell. On the driveway
of Uncle Jack's house. MOTHER, FATHER and KEVIN are standing, all dressed
in black. FATHER is wearing his knitted black body coverer tied in a knot
over his top hat, giving him a truly ludicrous aspect. The doors open and
the coffin is brought out. The last remnant of the porch collapses. The
coffin is carried at rather a run by four men, all with faces screwed up and
handkerchiefs over their faces. Loud buzzing of flies as the coffin is hurried
past the family. There is an ominous creak, and one side of the coffin falls
off. One of Uncle Jack's arms flops out.*

Within a year, a series of strange misfortunes befell my family. My father
suffocated when a flock of starlings became entangled in his body coverer
. . . and my mother was carried off by a golden eagle at the Highland
Games in Braemar in 1921, and was never seen again. As for me — I was
named Uncle Jack's only heir; he left me his house and enough money
to enable me to marry my childhood sweetheart.

We now jump back into the present: back to the library of old Sir Kevin's house, where SIR KEVIN *is telling the story of the Claw to* MERSON. *The natives rumble weirdly in the background. There is an atmosphere of escalating terror.*

SIR KEVIN (*to* MERSON): We should have been idylically happy . . . but since then I have not slept through a single night. My hair has turned white and I have grown old before my time . . . waiting . . . waiting for the Claw to find its way back and wreak its terrible revenge . . .

MERSON is listening intently. He looks across at his native bearers. They are still in a trancelike state, moaning softly. The leader is still staring at the sideboard. They are all down to their briefs and occasionally they flick their hips or push out their stomachs provocatively.

MERSON (*eyes widening*): You . . . think the Claw *is* going to return . . . here . . .
SIR KEVIN: It *has* returned . . .

SIR KEVIN, *with a strange, almost manic stare in his eyes, moves from the mantlepiece, across to the sideboard, his voice thickening with emotion.*

Today is my sixtieth birthday . . . In the morning I came down to breakfast as usual, and I found Lady Agatha, my lovely wife . . . dead. And beside her, on the trapeze, was *this.*

He pulls open the door of the sideboard with a flourish and there, revealed, is the Claw!

MERSON: The Claw!
SIR KEVIN: Yes . . . the Claw!

At the sight of it the tribesmen moan even more ecstatically, rotating their bodies sensuously. They fall to the floor naughtily and prostrate themselves, all except the HEADMAN who looks hypnotically towards the sideboard.

. . . It has returned, just as Uncle Jack said it would. (*He indicates the tribesmen.*) . . . and they . . . they knew it was here, but they were almost too late. (*He addresses the HEADMAN.*) Now take it! Take it! Please take it back! and lift the curse that is upon this house for ever!

MERSON, SIR KEVIN and the others stare fearfully on as very slowly the HEADMAN walks to the sideboard, stretching out his hand. The tension reaches a climax as finally the HOLY MAN grasps the Claw and holds it up for all to see. At that moment there is a terrifying scream from outside the door. They all turn. The door flies open and GROSVENOR enters with a look of horror on his face.

SIR KEVIN: What *is* the matter Grosvenor?

GROSVENOR (*a handkerchief clasped to his face*): There's a man in my bed!

SIR KEVIN: I thought you liked that sort of thing.

GROSVENOR: He's a *smelly* old man sir, and he claims to have myxomatosis, and he's got an enormous lump in his armpit . . . —

SIR KEVIN's eyes widen at this news,

Only then did I realise that the Claw had one final, hideous, trick to play on me . . .

Even as SIR KEVIN *listens to* GROSVENOR's *descriptions of the smelly old man's most intimate details,* SIR KEVIN *himself is undergoing a physical change, suddenly he has shed ten years.*

SIR KEVIN (*now aged fifty*): It must be . . . Uncle Jack!

GROSVENOR (*he too has shed ten years*): . . . Oh . . . yes sir . . .

The door bell rings, SIR KEVIN *looks up. On that instant he has shed a further ten years.*

SIR KEVIN (*now aged forty*): I'll go Grosvenor . . .

GROSVENOR (*now aged forty*): Very well sir.

At that moment the door opens and LADY AGATHA *(deceased only that morning) pops her head round brightly . . . She looks fresh young and beautiful . . . about twenty-seven/twenty-eight years old . . .*

LADY AGATHA: Don't worry dear, I'll get it.

She goes out into the hall, leaving an even younger SIR KEVIN *gazing after her . . .*

SIR KEVIN (*now aged thirty*): . . . Lady Agatha . . !

He pursues her into the hall. At the door to the library, he shouts after her again, a look of disbelief giving way to extraordinary happiness . . .

SIR KEVIN (*now aged twenty*): Agatha! . . .

LADY AGATHA *turns . . . she is as beautiful as she ever was, but as* SIR KEVIN *looks at her, he helplessly finds himself shedding the years yet again. He's now the young boy old* SIR KEVIN *described earlier.*

KEVIN (*now aged ten*): Agatha . . . ?

AGATHA has become his young childhood love. Her eyes widen. She starts to come towards him. But even as she does . . . the front door swings open to reveal, resurrected, the forbidding, cast-iron features of Kevin's fierce FATHER and implacable MOTHER. They stare down at the couple, eyes blazing.

FATHER: Kevin! You'll come home this instant!
KEVIN: Oh please Daddy, we're having such a super time at Uncle Jack's.
MOTHER: Your father has spoken dear.

At this Kevin's father grabs him and pulls him out into the dark and stormy night where their carriage awaits. He admonishes him violently the while.

FATHER: I will not have you showing off your body in this place of depravity! You'll stay at home away from the lascivious glances of harlots and old men . . . (His voice trails away into the night.) . . . Where the concupiscence of the lechers and the ungodly cannot taint you . . . where . . .

The house too, has changed, and even as the sound of the retreating carriage dies on the wind, the old house crumbles and falls into a thousand pieces. All that remains intact among the rubble of these hopes and dreams and failures is . . . the Claw.

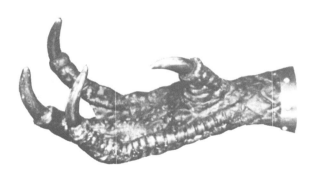

THE END

WHINFREY'S
LAST CASE

A Ripping Tale of Events
That Slightly Changed the Course of History

WHINFREY'S LAST CASE

An elegant London square. Time: the Present

A VERY FAMOUS PERSONALITY contemplates the hustle and bustle of London, then turns impressively and talks to a camera which follows his every move.

VERY FAMOUS PERSONALITY: Good evening . . . I want to ask you, if I may tonight, to join me in an experiment. An experiment to turn back time, to suspend belief in the here and now of a busy city, and to join me in the past. . . . Come with me now. (*He starts to move leading the camera with him*) . . . to a London before two wars, when this house (*He indicates a smart London residence just as a delivery van draws up against the kerb outside the house, completely blocking the* VERY FAMOUS AND CHARISMATIC PERSONALITY *from view. The* VERY FAMOUS PERSONALITY *continues to drone on obliviously, as the van's handbrake is applied and the engine rattles noisily to a halt.*

. . . was the London home of one of the most powerful men of this century. Through this elegant doorway . . .

An anoraked and stop-watched BBC PRODUCTION ASSISTANT *rushes out from behind camera and across the road to ask the van to move. She runs right across the path of an oncoming Vauxhall Viva de luxe, which skids to a halt with a screech of brakes.*

VERY FAMOUS PERSONALITY: . . . came and went the greatest names of pre-war days.

The P.A. approaches the driver, a MEAT PORTER, indicates the camera and asks him to move on.

. . . Kaisers, Tsars and Cabinet Ministers stood at these very windows . . .

The MEAT PORTER looks at camera, gets down from cab, and gives a cheerful nod and a wink as he goes to the back of the van.

. . . and on that balcony you see above me stood the King of England himself.

The DRIVER of the Vauxhall has now joined the helpless P.A. The DRIVER (a traveller in underwear from the Midlands) argues with the P.A. and points out how he nearly hit her.

The MEAT PORTER appears carrying a side of pig over his shoulder.

The owner of this quietly elegant residence was the legendary Gerald Whinfrey, the man who saved governments and ended wars . . . in an era when individual bravery and courage were still valued highly . . .

A terrible skid and rending crash is heard off. The Viva de luxe jerks forward. The TRAVELLER IN UNDERWEAR looks round in horror. His car has obviously been rammed. The MEAT PORTER is now quite blatantly waving at camera.

This is where our journey back in time must begin.

There is a sound of a police siren off. Slamming of doors, the MEAT PORTER gets into his cab and then out again. He performs a little dance for the camera, winking and mugging a lot. Halfway through a neat pas-de-deux an OFFICER OF THE LAW approaches, but before he can raise a truncheon the MEAT PORTER ceases his performance and nips smartly back into the cab.

. . . Take one last lingering look at this building and imagine yourselves back in the year 1913, the year of wars and rumours of wars, the year that saw the extraordinary tale (*The lorry drives off. The VERY FAMOUS AND CHARISMATIC PERSONALITY turns, at the crescendo of his oratory, to camera.*) of Whinfrey's Last Case . . . (*He comes forward and speaks to the director.*)

How was that? That felt good.

DIRECTOR'S VOICE   (*off*): One more time love . . . not quite right . . .

The VERY FAMOUS AND CHARISMATIC PERSONALITY *tears his beard off and bites the* DIRECTOR *in the head. But we don't notice, as we're busy going back sixty-seven years.*

The War Office in Whitehall, 1913.

In a war room with maps, charts of Britain, with markers all over them etc. are GENERAL CHAPMAN, *C-in-C of the Army and* LORD RAGLAN, *Chief of the Imperial General Staff. The door opens and* ADMIRAL OF THE FLEET JEFFERSON *enters.*

RAGLAN: Ah, Jefferson, glad you could get here . . . something pretty big's come up . . . sit down.

JEFFERSON   (*sitting*): What's the problem Archie?

RAGLAN: Well . . . we think the Germans may be trying to start the war a year early . . .

JEFFERSON: God! (*He looks aghast.*)

CHAPMAN   (*equally shocked*): I thought they were the one nation we could trust.

RAGLAN: We all did, Harry.

CHAPMAN: Dammit all, it's not as if we're *short* of people to have a war against.

RAGLAN: Well, suppose this damn rumour's true! . . . are we ready to start a war now?

CHAPMAN: Well, I don't know about your boys Jefferson, but we need at *least* another six months — we're still short of heavy cannons, two-point-five mortars, trestle tables.

RAGLAN: Trestle tables?

CHAPMAN: For the catering! We've only got six. You can't expect to train a man to the peak of military achievement and then ask him to eat off his lap. I mean if you spill things on some of those uniforms . . .

RAGLAN: What about the Navy, Jefferson?

JEFFERSON: We're short on spoons, mainly.

RAGLAN: No, I meant weaponry.

JEFFERSON: Ah well, we have fifteen Dreadnoughts at sea and twelve under construction.

RAGLAN: And the Germans?

JEFFERSON: Oh they've got everything: spoons, forks, knives, complete condiment sets . . .

RAGLAN: Ships Jefferson! Destroyers, Dreadnoughts?

JEFFERSON: Ah . . . er . . . well, the last they told us . . . it was twelve at sea and nine under construction . . .

RAGLAN: When was that?

JEFFERSON: Well I spoke to old Tirpitz at a sherry party about a month ago.

RAGLAN: Since then?

JEFFERSON: I haven't heard anything.

RAGLAN: Well this is what worries me. Intelligence think that the Germans are up to something very underhand.

CHAPMAN: Bloody Intelligence, they never did like the Germans.

RAGLAN: I'm afraid, gentlemen, they're pretty certain that the Germans have somehow opened hostilities without letting us know.

Looks of astonishment all round.

JEFFERSON: How the hell could they . . . ?

RAGLAN: I don't know how, or where or when, but we must find out, and put a stop to it before . . . (*a sharp crump as of a distantly exploding shell*) . . . what was that?

CHAPMAN: Sorry, it was my stomach.

RAGLAN: . . . Before the whole bloody country starts to panic . . . (*He stands up very straight, and gazes heroically out towards the Houses of Parliament.*) We can save this war and it can still be a Great War, but if we should fail . . . (*He looks round significantly.*) I need hardly say gentlemen, it could jeopardize our chances of ever having a war with the Germans again . . .

This really hits home. There is a long pause whilst the full awfulness of the suggestion sinks in.

JEFFERSON: What do you propose, Archie?

RAGLAN: Gentlemen, I think we have only one option: to ask Gerald Whinfrey to intervene . . .

JEFFERSON and RAGLAN: Whinfrey! Of course.

A London Club. The next day.

RAGLAN and CHAPMAN and JEFFERSON are sitting before a blazing fire. All heads are turned to WHINFREY at the mantelpiece as he swirls his brandy round the glass, stands up and takes a final drink, setting the glass down with a sharp crack on the polished marble surface. He turns to face the others.

WHINFREY: The answer is no, gentlemen. I'm afraid I can't help you this time.
RAGLAN: Whyever not, Whinfrey?
WHINFREY: Gentlemen, in the last four months I've brought the Balkan wars to an end; I've averted a revolution in Russia — for the second year running; I've sold twenty-three submarines to the French; annexed two new colonies and organized an armed uprising in Brazil. I've been saving this country every year since 1898 and I need a holiday.

All are stunned.

RAGLAN: *A holiday? . . . for how long?*
WHINFREY: A year . . . two years . . .
CHAPMAN: But . . . the war . . .
WHINFREY *(checking his half-hunter watch)*: The war gentlemen is your affair. Now if you'll excuse me I have to see George, he's lending me some fishing tackle.
RAGLAN: George?
WHINFREY: The *Fifth . . . you know . . . ?* (*He flashes a smile at the discomfited Chief of Staff and bows briefly.*) Good day, gentlemen, and good luck with your . . . war . . .

As he turns and walks out a PORTLY MAN in an armchair in the dark recesses of the club lowers his paper and calls after him.

PORTLY MAN: Don't forget you're giving my wife brain surgery next Friday, Whinfrey.
WHINFREY: Have to be after the holiday, I'm afraid.

WHINFREY sweeps out.

PORTLY MAN: Hey . . . look! I don't want her batty over Christmas!

A train rattles through a sunlit Cornish countryside. Inside a comfortable first class compartment, WHINFREY *is the sole occupant, he stares out of the window, alone with his thoughts.*

Truth to be told, I was fed up with being a hero. Having to save the country once or twice a week meant I could get nothing done at all. Well now, at last, I was going to sit back and enjoy a life of my own. I'd taken a short let on a cottage on the Cornish coast, as far away as I could get from the power politicking, and the Machiavellian intrigues of the men in Whitehall; somewhere where I could at last enjoy the real values of English life, whilst they still existed.

A small country station. The train comes to a halt with much hissing of steam, sunlight filters through the smoke. All is rather beautiful and idyllic.

WHINFREY *opens a carriage door and takes out a couple of bags and fishing tackle. He breathes in a generous gulp of fresh Cornish air and beams around happily. He can't immediately see any railway staff, however. Then he hears a footfall. He turns sharply as a* PORTER *steps out of the shadows. It is a rather distinguished man uncomfortably dressed in a brand new porter's outfit.*

WHINFREY: Ah! Porter, this is Torpoint, isn't it?
PORTER (*he looks oddly uncomfortable, and speaks English very correctly*): Er . . . no . . . no, not really.

WHINFREY: But the guard's just put me off here . . .
PORTER: Er . . . no. He must have been lying. Next stop.

WHINFREY turns in annoyance as, with a whistle, the train hisses and starts to move. WHINFREY dashes after it banging his knee on the long handles of a baggage trolley. He reaches the end of the platform and stops, breathlessly watching, as the train chugs away into the distance. He turns to remonstrate with the PORTER but finds the station platform empty. He picks up his bags and starts to walk back towards the exit. As he walks something catches his eye. He stops, walks across to the overgrown railings and, bending down, pulls some weeds away to reveal a clear, and quite recently painted railway sign which reads 'Torpoint'. He looks round. The PORTER has gone. WHINFREY looks up and down the platform. There is no sign of anyone. He struggles to the booking office . . . and peers in.

WHINFREY: Hello?

Silence.

. . . Hello!

The booking office is deserted but there is evidence of a freshly made cup of tea.

Hello?

But there is nothing save a gentle wheeze from a hissing kettle. With irritated resignation WHINFREY picks up his bags and walks out of the station.

There is nothing on the station approach, just a couple of porters' barrows and some milk churns. He looks around.

No sign of life. Then suddenly he sees movement ahead of him. In the distance the elegant figure of the PORTER scuttles off round a corner.

WHINFREY: Hey!

Angry and puzzled he looks around him and sees a pub about a hundred yards away. A couple of lights are on downstairs and it looks reassuring. A sign,

'The Queen's Head' creaks gently above the door. WHINFREY *brightens and, lugging his two heavy cases, approaches it. He pushes open the door.*

Inside the pub a fire flickers in the grate. It's all quite neat, and looks ready for people, but there is no-one there.
WHINFREY *looks around. Silence. Suddenly the voice of a little old lady is heard.*

OLD LADY   (*unseen*): Yes sir?

WHINFREY *looks around, he can't see anyone. He looks around behind him; still nothing.*

OLD LADY   (*unseen*): Can I help you sir?

He swings round to the bar, walks across to it and jumps suddenly . . . he's looking down . . . there is obviously someone very small down there.

WHINFREY: Oh . . . er . . . yes . . . hello! A pint of bitter please . . . (*With relish.*) Best Cornish Bitter!

A sound of shuffling, then a little old hand comes up and pulls the pump. Nothing more of this personage can be seen.

OLD LADY: You from Penzance?
WHINFREY: No . . . no . . . London.
OLD LADY: Where's that?
WHINFREY: What?
OLD LADY: Where's that?
WHINFREY: Well . . . er . . . it's sort of east, I suppose . . .
OLD LADY: Bodmin way?
WHINFREY: No further than that . . .
OLD LADY: Oh. Russia.
WHINFREY: No, not as far as . . . Russia.
OLD LADY: Latvia?
WHINFREY: No, not as far as Latvia . . .

OLD LADY:	Estonia?
WHINFREY	(*rather sharply*): Yes, how much is that, please?
OLD LADY	(*her hand lays the pint on the bar*): Two pence, please.
WHINFREY:	Oh thank you. (*He reaches for the money.*) Cheers! (*He drinks deeply and licks his lips with satisfaction.*) Er . . . excuse me, but is this Torpoint?
OLD LADY:	Yes . . . that's right.
WHINFREY	(*frowning to himself, briefly*): Ah . . . well I'm going to be renting a little spot called . . . er . . . (*he pulls a crumpled bit of paper out of his pocket and reads*) . . . Smuggler's Cottage.
OLD LADY	(*aghast*): Oh . . . terrible place.
WHINFREY:	What . . . ?
OLD LADY:	Terrible place to get to . . .
WHINFREY:	Oh?
OLD LADY:	Very dangerous. There's only the village taxi . . . that dares go along that road . . .
WHINFREY:	Ah, well that doesn't worry me. When can I get a taxi?
OLD LADY:	Oh . . . about five minutes.
WHINFREY:	Ah . . . that's perfect . . .

Five minutes later. A lonely moorland road.

There is a banging and clanking and a couple of sharp back-firings. Then a 1911 model T taxi chugs round the corner, weaving dangerously close to a 250-foot cliff top.

In the car WHINFREY *is sitting in the passenger seat whilst all we can see of the driver is a pair of old lady's hands turning the wheel. It is the* OLD LADY *from the pub. She chatters on quite cheerfully despite the fact that she can see nothing of the road.*

OLD LADY: It was at Smuggler's Cottage that a young retired vicar went mad . . . chopped his wife into six hundred and eighty-two pieces.

The car lurches slightly. WHINFREY *looks out apprehensively.*

OLD LADY: Bits of her were found in people's shoes for years afterwards . . .

Suddenly the car revs frantically. WHINFREY *looks even more disconcerted and grips the side.*

OLD LADY: Be a love and press that pedal down while I change gear . . .

As WHINFREY *grapples with the pedal, the* OLD LADY *goes on cheerily.*

Twenty years after that another retired vicar bought it. He used to organize knitting circles — 'Balaclavas for the Boer War' he called it. But not one of the old ladies ever came back from one of those knitting circles. Years later they were found embedded in the . . .

The car lurches wildly. A tyre skids in the earth terrifyingly close to the edge of the cliff.

WHINFREY (*anxiously*): I think you'd better stop . . .
OLD LADY: Don't like the gory details, eh . . . ?

With more violent revving the car frees itself and jerks forward haphazardly. The OLD LADY *continues to gossip on quite unperturbed.*

Well, a year ago a retired bishop took the cottage over. He had a huge cheese grater . . .

WHINFREY (*finally, decisively*): This is fine honestly, drop me here!
OLD LADY: All right, sir . . .

The car comes to a halt. WHINFREY *clambers out. They're at the very edge of a windswept vertiginous cliff. He reaches for his cases, then brings out his wallet for some money.*

OLD LADY: Don't worry, dear, pay me tomorrow when I bring the milk . . .
WHINFREY: Do you do *everything* round here?
OLD LADY: Oh yes . . . there's no-one else'll do this sort of work. All the young men have gone.
WHINFREY: Into the army, I suppose . . .
OLD LADY: Yes . . . I expect so.

WHINFREY *shakes his head.*

WHINFREY: What a waste!
OLD LADY: Mind how you go now . . .

The car revs up again.

WHINFREY: And you!
OLD LADY: Oh . . . I'm all right. I know this road backwards.

She starts to go into a grinding three-point turn. WHINFREY *sets his face to the wind, and looks ahead.*

He sees a lonely little stone cottage on the edge of a headland, he smiles and is about to set off towards the goal of his journey. Suddenly he hears the roar of an over-revved engine and a series of raucous crashes and bangs. WHINFREY *spins round to see the* OLD LADY *has reversed the car over the edge of the cliff.* WHINFREY *races to the top of the cliff and looks over . . .*

WHINFREY   (*calling*): Hello? Hello?

From far below the OLD LADY'S *cheery voice floats up from the wreckage.*

OLD LADY: Don't worry dear! I'm used to it!

The sound of an engine being put into gear from far below. WHINFREY *shakes his head then turns towards the lonely cottage. Far below a huge wave crashes in a mighty column of spray against the rocks.*

Further along the cliffs WHINFREY *struggles up a steep path. He stops at a broken down overgrown old sign. It reads 'Smuggler's Cottage' and has an arrow pointing ahead, and there is the cottage a hundred yards away.*

He shivers against the cold, picks up his bags and hurries towards it. As he approaches the door of the cottage, he drops his bags, looks for his key, and is about to put it into the lock when suddenly it's opened . . . A very distinguished but sternly remote professional lady in her early forties stands there with a lamp.

LADY: Mr Whinfrey?
WHINFREY: That's right . . . yes.
LADY: Welcome to Smuggler's Cottage.
WHINFREY: Oh thank you.

He enters and finds himself in a neat, but rather poky hallway, with whitewashed walls, stairs and a passage leading to a kitchen.

WHINFREY: This is very kind.

LADY: I am your housekeeper, Mrs Otway.

WHINFREY: Well this is most kind of you to bother.

MRS OTWAY: And this is my assistant, Mrs Partington . . .

A rather short young woman in a white apron appears and curtsies. WHINFREY *reacts with some surprise.*

. . . This is Mr Carne, the head steward . . .

A tall, distinguished, most unservile man appears from the passageway. He looks distinctly uncomfortable and is not un-reminiscent of the 'Porter' at the station. He bows rather stiffly.

CARNE: Evening sir . . .

MRS OTWAY: McKendrick the butler . . .

Another more elderly man appears and bows.

Mr Rothman and Mr Vickers, assistant butlers . . .

Two rather young fit men appear, again looking ill at ease and bowing rather unnaturally.

. . . McKerras the boot boy . . .

Another young man comes out of the shadows. WHINFREY *reacts in amazement.* MRS OTWAY *carries on busily.*

Mr Ferris . . .

WHINFREY: Mr . . . Ferris . . . I didn't catch what *you* do here . . .

FERRIS   (*a middle-aged man, looks distinctly unhappy*): . . . Er osteopath, sir . . .

WHINFREY: Osteopath?

MRS OTWAY   (*quickly*): Ostler!

FERRIS: Ostler . . . sorry ostler . . . yes . . .

MRS OTWAY (*by way of explanation*): . . . Ostler . . . stableman, you know. He attends to the horses.

FERRIS (*unconvincingly*): That's it.

WHINFREY: Well, I certainly didn't . . .

But MRS OTWAY *hasn't finished.*

MRS OTWAY: Mr Girton, master of the bedchamber . . .

GIRTON *appears down the stairs* . . .

MRS OTWAY: Mr Campbell and Mr Rowley, bedmakers . . . (*They appear.*) . . . and Mr Vinney, under assistant bedboy. (*He joins the throng.*) Monsieur Bientôt the cook . . .

A huge burly, un-French bullet-headed swaddy appears from the kitchen passageway in chef's whites with hat, behind him are two assistants also in whites.

. . . and the kitchen boys, Mr Rolfe, and Mr Tipkin . . .

The tiny hall is now packed with servants.

WHINFREY: Look, I don't know what to say, but . . .

MRS OTWAY: Say nothing, Mr Whinfrey. It's just traditional Cornish hospitality. I'll introduce you to all the gardeners tomorrow . . .

CARNE: We want you to feel absolutely at home here at Smuggler's Cottage. It's your holiday, enjoy it as you will, but don't go in the small bedroom at the end of the passage whatever you do . . .

MRS OTWAY: *Or* the basement . . .

CARNE (*silencing* MRS OTWAY *with a look*): Ssh!

WHINFREY: The basement?

CARNE: She meant the basins, Mr Whinfrey . . . don't get in the basins. They won't stand it.

MRS OTWAY: Mr Carne, show Mr Whinfrey to the bottom of the stairs.

CARNE: Yes of course. This way, sir.

They reach the bottom of the stairs in a couple of paces, but MRS OTWAY *carries on before* WHINFREY *can say anything.*

MRS OTWAY: Mrs Partington will show you to the top of the stairs . . .

WHINFREY *looks up at the poky winding stairs. There are about eight steps in all.*

Mr Girton will meet you at the top and take you round the corner, then Mr Vickers will take you to the door of your bedroom, and Mr Girton will take you inside.

MRS OTWAY *leaves with a severe but comprehensive smile.*

I trust you will be comfortable . . .

WHINFREY *climbs the narrow stairs and is making for his bedroom when a sombre, dark-suited manservant steps out from the shadows, with a polite formal smile:* WHINFREY *jumps.*

GIRTON: My name is Girton sir, I'm in charge of the upstairs section.

He indicates the bedroom door.

WHINFREY *enters the bedroom, with* MR GIRTON *leading. It's a traditional small cottage bedroom, with white-washed walls and very simple furniture. As they enter the room,* MR CAMPBELL *and* MR ROWLEY *stand to attention on either side of the mantelpiece . . .*

GIRTON: Passing through the door — (*He elaborately indicates what the door is.*) here, sir, you will find on your right — the bed. You will notice that it is laid with two pillows, but a further two pillows, or one bolster are available on request.
WHINFREY: Yes — thank you!
GIRTON: Should you require the pillows to be turned at any point, Mr Rowley will oblige until a proper pillow boy arrives tomorrow . . .
WHINFREY: Thank you!

GIRTON *goes across to the window and demonstrates elaborately.*

GIRTON: The curtains can be drawn, left . . . and right and left . . . and back to —
WHINFREY (*losing patience*): Mr Girton — that's *all*, thank you!
GIRTON: Yes of course, sir.

He ushers his two assistants out briskly.

WHINFREY *breathes a sigh of relief then starts again rather suddenly when he hears the door open. It's* MR GIRTON *again.*

GIRTON: Will you require a call, sir?
WHINFREY: NO! No thank you!
GIRTON: Well, I'll call you anyway sir, but don't in any way feel bounden by it.

GIRTON finally leaves.

*WHINFREY shakes his head, and slumps on the bed. There is a twang and a
yell from beneath the bed and WHINFREY leaps up.*

Who the hell's that?

*He crouches down and looks under the bed. A thin pasty-faced spotty youth
is clinging on to the underneath.*

VINNEY: Vinney, sir! I'm in charge of the under-mattress area.
WHINFREY: Look, go away *please!*
VINNEY   (*scrambling out*): Yes, sir . . .

*WHINFREY pushes the boy out, and leans against the door, shaking his head
wearily. Then he crosses to the bed, takes one last look under it and lies down.*

So began my first night at Smuggler's Cottage. I couldn't say it was the
holiday I expected, but I'm sure they were all good people trying to do their
best for me, and anything was preferable to the company of the warmongers
of Whitehall. As I sat and listened to the silence of the night, there was
something unutterably satisfying about not having to be anyone's hero . . .

The next morning. WHINFREY's *cottage bedroom. Sun fills the room.* WHINFREY
*opens his eyes, registers where he is. On holiday at last. He smiles for a
moment, then a frown of concentration replaces the smile. He listens.*

*In the distance, amidst the birdsong and the crashing of the sea on the cliffs
below, he hears another sound. It's the sound of men being drilled, as if on
an army parade ground. He pulls himself out of bed. Still listening. The noise
is still there. He goes across to the window and pulls back the curtain. His
eyes widen. He pushes the curtains right back and tries to pull up the window.*

It won't move easily. As he gives it a tug a voice close behind him causes him to start. It's GIRTON, *amiably charming as ever.*

GIRTON: They're the new gardeners, sir . . .

WHINFREY: But there must be seventy or eighty of them . . .

GIRTON: Lot to do in the garden this time of year, sir: planting, weeding, cutting off the dead heads, breakfast?

WHINFREY *(looks down at the gardeners, then back to* GIRTON*)*: What's going on here, Mr Girton?

GIRTON: Going on, sir?

WHINFREY: All these people . . .

GIRTON: They're all villagers, sir . . . We're just a normal happy Cornish fishing community.

WHINFREY: I never saw any fishermen.

GIRTON: Oh . . . they're always to be found, sir . . . In the pub usually . . . *(He laughs in a slightly forced way.)*

WHINFREY: There was no one in the pub at all yesterday.

GIRTON: Ah no . . . they weren't here yesterday . . . they were out all day . . . on the mackerel boats, sir . . . They'll be there today, though definitely. *(He turns to go.)* I'll put your kippers on, sir.

WHINFREY *turns to start dressing. He goes to the chair where his clothes were and stops in consternation. They're gone. His consternation is replaced by irritation. He marches, with brisk determination out onto the landing . . .*
He bends low along the little passage but is stopped in his tracks at the top of the stairs by the sound of MRS OTWAY *and* GIRTON *having a sharp exchange at the bottom of the stairs.*

MRS OTWAY: He mustn't leave here! D'you understand! It's as simple as that.

GIRTON *(who is holding* WHINFREY's *clothes)*: I've removed his things.

MRS OTWAY: D'you honestly think that'll stop him?

GIRTON: He'll look very silly.

MRS OTWAY: Look, you're supposed to be an assistant butler, just make sure he doesn't leave the house . . . drug his kippers or something.

GIRTON: I don't think you *can* drug kippers . . .

MRS OTWAY *(impatiently)*: Well just use your intelligence.

WHINFREY *darts back into his bedroom and pretends to be arranging his cravat in front of the mirror, when he hears* GIRTON's *footsteps in the passage. There is a knock on the door and a rather tentative voice.*

GIRTON: Mr Whinfrey, sir . . .

WHINFREY: Come in.

GIRTON *enters and comes up to* WHINFREY.

GIRTON: Er . . . I've just come to say, sir . . . that I forgot something earlier on.

WHINFREY *(a little cautiously)*: Oh yes . . . ? What was that?

GIRTON brings his knee up rather smartly into WHINFREY's groin. WHINFREY collapses on the floor.

GIRTON: I do apologize, sir. But it's an old Cornish custom.

He leaves, as WHINFREY makes to get up after him. There is a click, and the door locks. WHINFREY looks towards the door with grim determination.

Whatever was going on, it certainly wasn't my idea of the ideal holiday. I decided it was probably best to forgo the kippers.

He pulls himself up and paces the room. He tries the window. It's stuck fast. He tries the door. It's solid and well-locked. Then quite suddenly his legendary cool deserts him. He races round the room in a burst of hysterical panic, trying every exit unsuccessfully. He finally pulls himself together.

However, a brief inspection of the room was more than enough to convince me there was absolutely no way I could escape. The door was oak and triple locked, the window well guarded, and there was no other entrance or exit.

He sits on the bed in despair and throws a paperweight hard at the wall in frustration. It hits the wall and falls.

But I had forgotten one thing . . . This was smuggling country.

After a series of multiple clicks, a door panel in the wall mysteriously swings open. With an expression of amazement, WHINFREY rises to his feet and walks cautiously towards the hole. As he does so there is suddenly a click underneath him and he jumps to one side as a section of floor swings open to reveal a second set of stairs going down.

. . . No smuggler's cottage would be complete without at least one secret passage and this seemed to be no exception . . .

He backs against a bedside table which turns over to reveal yet another set of stairs leading into a second wall: Spinning round, he almost goes down the trap door, and saves himself by grabbing a bell-pull whereupon a sky-light unexpectedly opens up in the roof and a rope-ladder dangles down. He leans back on the bed in bewilderment. It slides back into the wall, revealing a cave beneath.

In fact I discovered no less than twenty-three different secret passageways leading out of my room alone.

He finds another in the cupboard under the washbasin, two more in the floor and one in another wall.

The only problem was which one to take and where did they all lead?

WHINFREY is dithering looking at first one and then the other, trying to decide which one to take when suddenly he hears voices outside the door. He freezes. Outside are MRS OTWAY and GIRTON.

MRS OTWAY: We *have* to kill him, Mr Girton.
GIRTON: But it's against all the laws of hospitality.
MRS OTWAY: He knows far too much already . . . Out of the way.

More bolts are slid back, WHINFREY looks round panic-stricken. He makes his decision and disappears into a secret hole. There follows a series of bangs and crashes. He reappears clutching an armful of brooms and cleaning things.

More voices outside.

GIRTON: I can't do it.
MRS OTWAY: Oh give that to me and you can wipe up.

WHINFREY hears the last bolt on the door being slid back. He hesitates no longer and disappears down the trapdoor in the floor and closes it just as the door bursts open and MRS OTWAY rushes in with a large meat cleaver in her hands. GIRTON follows with a kipper on a plate.

WHINFREY leaps into the darkness of the secret passage.

MRS OTWAY   (*hisses to* GIRTON): Forget the kipper! Get the gun!

She charges after WHINFREY *with a look of grim determination.* GIRTON *goes off to exchange his kipper for something more deadly.*

WHINFREY *dimly gropes his way along the walls of a subterranean tunnel. He stops, lights a match and is looking around when the match burns his finger. He lets out an involuntary cry and drops the match. He hears a distant, echoing voice.*

MRS OTWAY: That way. Quick . . .

I staggered on blindly, and after what seemed like hours I saw light ahead and found myself free of the dank, brandy smelling tunnels.

WHINFREY *emerges onto a rocky beach.*

I decided to make straight for the village and seek help there.

He starts to clamber up the cliff. MRS OTWAY *and* GIRTON *appear.* GIRTON *fires. A bullet sings off the rocks.* WHINFREY *dodges further shots and scrambles to the top of the cliff . . . He looks down at* MRS OTWAY *and* GIRTON *and runs on towards the village.*

He sees the reassuring, creaking sign above 'The Queen's Head' and hurries towards it. As he approaches he slows down and hesitates for a moment.

From inside the pub comes the umistakable sound of lusty German voices singing a Bavarian marching song.

WHINFREY *reacts in some puzzlement then reaches the door and pushes it open.*

Immediately the singing stops.

WHINFREY *sees that this time the small single bar, with a cheerful fire in the grate, is reassuringly full of fishermen, in navy sweaters and high-sided boots. There is much cigarette smoke. All heads are turned to* WHINFREY, *who stands, faintly ridiculous in pyjamas, dressing gown, and cravat.*

WHINFREY   (*reassured at the sight of these trusty fisher-folk*): Evening!

There is some clearing of throats and a few rather uncomfortable guttural greetings which just about sound like 'Good Evening'.

WHINFREY *approaches the bar. No one there. He looks around again. This time one of the fishermen smiles stiffly back. Silence.*

WHINFREY: How do you do? My name's Whinfrey — Gerald Whinfrey.

WHINFREY *holds out his hand to first fisherman who looks panic-stricken. A colleague, who looks a little senior, rescues him.*

COLLEAGUE   (*in a very smooth faintly German voice*): Er . . . that's Tony.
WHINFREY: Hello, Tony.

The man nods uncomfortably. WHINFREY, *who's still not caught on, turns expansively to the other fishermen. The smooth German sees no way out apart from introducing them all.*

SMOOTH GERMAN   (*increasingly unhappily*): . . . And this is . . . Eddie . . . and er . . . Tony . . . another Tony . . . and er . . . Wolf . . . Wilf, sorry, Wilf . . . and er . . . Eddie . . . and another Eddie and next to Eddie is . . .
YOUNG GERMAN   (*proudly, but with heavy accent*): Eddie!
SMOOTH GERMAN   (*very unhappily*): Yes . . . another Eddie.
WHINFREY: My God, it's nice to be among sane people again. (*Rather odd reactions from the uncomprehending Germans.*) I know this may sound ridiculous, but I've just come from Smuggler's Cottage — where some of the staff are trying to kill me —

A voice at the door interrupts him. WHINFREY *freezes.*

CARNE: Not so fast, Mr Whinfrey, they won't understand you.

WHINFREY *turns to come face to face with* CARNE — *the 'Porter', the 'Head Steward', now dressed as a vicar.*

CARNE: I congratulate you on your persistence Mr Whinfrey. You survive the taxi ride and now you survive a night at Smuggler's Cottage. But then *the* Gerald Whinfrey would . . .

Impressed mutters from the German 'Fishermen' — 'Whinfrey . . . that is . . . Gerald Whinfrey!'

WHINFREY: Carne?
CARNE (*clicking his heels and bowing*): Alfred Von Kahn, Mr Whinfrey, German Intelligence. (*Punctiliously he introduces.*) Fraülein Gerta Ottweg, my assistant (MRS OTWAY, *with cleaver, enters from the back door.*) . . . and Herr Gurtheim, head of our British Division. (GIRTON *with gun follows.*)

WHINFREY *looks around, slowly taking it in* . . .

WHINFREY: British Division?
CARNE: . . . A final beer perhaps for Mr Gerald Whinfrey?
WHINFREY: So long as the beer's not German as well . . .
CARNE (*with a smile*): No the beer is authentic. (*To the* OLD LADY.) Lotte, ein echt Cornisches Bier für mein Freund, bitte.
OLD LADY'S VOICE (*from behind the bar*): Jawohl! Mein Kommandant.

WHINFREY *turns sharply.*

A pause. The sound of shuffling, then a hand appears and takes a pint glass down. Pause. More shuffling. A hand comes up again on the beer pull.

WHINFREY: What's the game, Carne?
CARNE: Oh, it's not a game, Mr Whinfrey. We're trying to start a war. A war by other means, if you like. A war in which everyone gets a little territory and no-one gets hurt.
WHINFREY: Except the poor bastards who used to live here.
GIRTON: They're very happy . . .
WHINFREY: Well, where the hell are they?
MRS OTWAY: In Germany . . .
WHINFREY: You . . . 'captured' them, I suppose.
CARNE: No we offered them a two-year inclusive holiday in the Bavarian Alps. They all accepted very happily. Apart from the vicar, who chose Dortmund instead — he had a sister there.
WHINFREY: And you take their place over here?
CARNE: Absolutely. We have a highly trained force waiting to move into England. Six

hundred vicars, a thousand shepherds . . .

GIRTON: Two divisions of cockneys . . .

MRS OTWAY: Forty-four judges . . . a dozen eccentrics . . . eight hundred and fifty private nannies.

WHINFREY: And you expect to keep this a secret?

CARNE: We have succeeded until now, Mr Whinfrey.

MRS OTWAY: Until you came along.

She moves towards him. His eyes notice her gleaming cleaver.

CARNE: No. Let him have his drink first.

The OLD LADY slaps a beer noisily and contemptuously onto the bar.

WHINFREY looks round helplessly, then slowly picks up his beer and drinks. As he does so the tension increases.

WHINFREY sees GIRTON, CARNE. He registers MRS OTWAY still holding the meat cleaver.

He tries to drink slowly to save his life.

Out of the corner of his eye he sees the fishermen closing in.

The SMOOTH GERMAN comes close to WHINFREY.

He builds up a totally paranoid vision and quite suddenly WHINFREY snaps. He hurls his beer in the face of the nearest German, then races for the window. Hysterical panic sets in as he scrabbles with the lock. It won't move. He races back past the impressed but bewildered Germans and rattles the back door. That's locked. He stops and, aware that he's made a bit of a fool of himself, smooths his hair down, rearranges his cravat and gives up.

WHINFREY: All right, Carne . . . You win. What do you want?

CARNE: I just wanted to say . . . goodbye and thank you.

WHINFREY looks very bewildered. GIRTON comes up and grabs his hand.

GIRTON (*shaking hands*): Me too, Mr Whinfrey. I'm sorry about the little business of the knee in the groin earlier on. Wait till I get back to Germany . . . and tell my children I've met Gerald Whinfrey . . . It's a great moment. Good-bye, and good luck.

MRS OTWAY (*still holding the cleaver in one hand, shakes him by the other; she is looking at him in a totally new, adoring light*): Believe me, Mr Whinfrey, I would not have surrendered to anyone else but you. You are a brilliant man, you fooled us all.

Casting one last admiring glance at WHINFREY she also leaves.

SMOOTH GERMAN (*deeply impressed*): Goodbye Mr Whinfrey . . . a pleasure to meet you.

He shakes his hand. WHINFREY *is utterly confused.*

From outside we hear the sound of a lorry arriving — military shouts. The fishermen leave, casting impressed and awed glances at WHINFREY. *They have their hands up.*

CARNE: Yes, you're quite a man, Whinfrey. We thought this operation was foolproof. But we reckoned without you. I salute you. It has been an honour to be caught out by you.

There is a clatter of army boots outside and a BRITISH CAPTAIN *and three other soldiers break in.*

CAPTAIN: All right! Get hold of them . . . come on you lot . . . out in the front.

Hand searching goes on. Revolvers are thrown on the floor. The fishermen are lined up against the wall.

WHINFREY: What the *hell's* going on . . . ?

CARNE *is hauled out by the scruff of his neck. As he passes* WHINFREY *he smiles . . . in admiration.*

CARNE: Superb job!

Then the familiar figure of RAGLAN *enters, beaming, with* CHAPMAN. *Before* WHINFREY *can say anything he grasps his hand.*

RAGLAN: Well done Gerald! You've saved the country again. And to think we believed all that stuff about a holiday. Damn glad I followed my instinct and had you tailed.

CHAPMAN: These chaps won't see much of the war now.

WHINFREY: But there won't be a war now I've caught them for you . . .

RAGLAN: Oh, there *will*, Gerald. And it'll be a *proper* one, thanks to you.

CHAPMAN: Not one of those mean little jobs run by Intelligence.

RAGLAN (*beaming confidentially*): We got definite dates from the Kaiser earlier today — 10 o'clock August 4th 1914, in France.

CHAPMAN: And if this one's successful, they want to do a follow up!

WHINFREY suddenly catches sight of a rifle slowly being raised by the tiny OLD LADY behind the bar and aimed at RAGLAN, though RAGLAN, with his back to it and pre-occupied with his triumph, doesn't notice.

RAGLAN: You're a genius, Whinfrey. I don't know how you do it. Have a drink.

WHINFREY (*looking at the raised gun*): Er . . . No . . . No, you two have a beer on me . . . I'm . . . I must get back to the holiday.

He turns and backs out of the pub rather quickly.

RAGLAN (*as he disappears*): Marvellous chap.

Outside the pub British troops are piling the Germans into the back of a lorry.

As WHINFREY walks away we hear a shot from the pub. WHINFREY stops briefly. He adjusts his cravat — another shot. He gives a sort of enigmatic smile, and walks away . . . away across the lonely cliff tops, as the sea crashes remorselessly below.

GOLDEN GORDON

A Ripping Soccer Tale

GOLDEN GORDON

Barnstoneworth, Yorkshire, 1935.

Barnstoneworth is a stout little Yorkshire wool town. A bit faded at the edges; and its prospects for the future don't look bright.

A football match is in progress, but by the sound of it, not going very well. Looking down on the dark streets of Barnstoneworth all that can be heard this Saturday afternoon is the occasional sound of a ball being kicked accompanied by grunts of pain from unfit men and groans of disappointment from a very small crowd.

In a quiet empty street of terraced houses leading up a hill, MRS EILEEN OTTERSHAW, *an aproned housewife, with hair in curlers and a headscarf, is beating a doormat against a wall. She looks up towards the sound of the football match, not very happily, finishes banging the mat and turns to go indoors.*

Back at the ground there is stuck on a rather dilapidated wooden door a poster, in handwriting, 'YORKSHIRE PREMIER LEAGUE, BARNSTONEWORTH v BRIGHOUSE. K.O. 3.00 SHARP'.

There is the sound of much straining as well as hoofing of the ball, accompanied by an occasional cough and clearing of the asthmatic throat.

Shouts of 'Kick it, Brighouse' *are echoed by a lone desperately optimistic shout from* GORDON OTTERSHAW.

GORDON: Get it away! Barnstoneworth. Get rid of it!

A wheeling tackle followed by the thud of a ball. Small smattering of applause. Deep groan of disappointment. A final whistle blows.

Back in the steep streets of downtown Barnstoneworth, EILEEN OTTERSHAW *pauses outside her little back-to-back and gives the carpet momentary relief,*

as she hears the final whistle ring out from the football ground. She listens keenly, then hears a familiar cry.

BARNSTONEWORTH SUPPORTERS (*thinly*): Rubbish! Ru — bbish!

With a weary sigh, EILEEN OTTERSHAW *puts down the duster, hurries into the house and starts to clear away all pictures and ornaments in the sitting room. Most of the pictures are group photos of football teams. As she clears things away she calls out.*

MRS OTTERSAW: Barnstoneworth?

A pallid thirteen-year-old emerges from the kitchen his expression lugubrious, his podgy fingers reluctantly marking the place in the Dixie Dean Football Annual.

BARNSTONEWORTH: Yes, Mum?

MRS OTTERSHAW: Pop down Crightons and get us some lard will you for tomorrow . . .

BARNSTONEWORTH (*glumly*): I'm learning the Barnstoneworth United reserve team of 1922, Mum.

MRS OTTERSHAW: Look . . . don't argue . . . do as I say . . .

BARNSTONEWORTH: But Mum . . .

MRS OTTERSHAW: What d'you want your Sunday lunch cooked in? Tea?

She hurries him out, pressing into his hand some money from a pot on the mantelpiece.

BARNSTONEWORTH: But Dad said he were going to ask me . . .

MRS OTTERSHAW (*ushering him out*): Hagerty F., Hagerty R., Tomkins, Noble, Carrick, Dobson, Crapper, Dewhurst, MacIntyre, Treadmore and Davitt . . .

BARNSTONEWORTH (*a little impressed*): . . . Thanks Mum . . .

MRS OTTERSHAW: Davitt scored twice in't last three minutes and Frank Hagerty saved a penalty.

BARNSTONEWORTH *gives his Mum a quick smile and goes out through the front door.* MRS OTTERSHAW *takes a quick, and a little fearful look up the street and hurries back into the house.*

As BARNSTONEWORTH *walks out of the gate he looks up to see a man appearing from round the corner . . . it's* GORDON OTTERSHAW, *his Dad.*

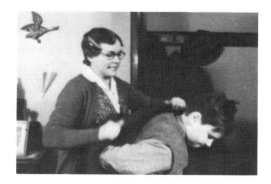

BARNSTONEWORTH (*cheerily*): Hello Dad!

GORDON looks up momentarily, then picks up a brick off a nearby wall and flings it at his son.

Back in the house, EILEEN OTTERSHAW *has quite efficiently stripped the sitting room of most of the ornaments. She stands and smoothes down her apron. The front door flies open with a crash of splintering glass. She suddenly notices she's left the clock on the mantelpiece. She makes to grab it, and is holding it when* GORDON *appears at the door of the sitting room. Their eyes meet for a moment.*

GORDON (*with anger dulled by years of inevitability*): Eight-one! Eight *bloody* one!

Then, quite slowly, he lifts the living room door off its hinges and smashes it to the floor. He picks up a chair and smashes it to pieces on the table, turns to the mantelpiece and finding nothing nice and breakable on top of it pulls it out from the wall bodily and hurls it across the room. He wrenches a cabinet off the wall, emptied of its normal complement of football treasures. He rips down the curtains. Then his anger still unassuaged, he leaps on the pile of rubble again, jumping up and down on it until he has no more strength. Then he turns his piteous gaze on his long suffering wife.

GORDON: Eight-one . . . To Brighouse! *Brighouse!* They're a team of old age pensioners. A tortoise with its legs tied together could dribble round that centre half. The centre-forward wears spectacles! During the game! *Eight* goals . . . four of *them* from back passes to the goalkeeper . . . oh . . . (*He holds his head.*) It was the worst . . . it was the worst . . . Oh!! (*He gives an anguished howl of pent-up anger.*)

MRS OTTERSHAW (*softly*): I'm sorry, love.

She proffers the clock she's holding — a warm and selfless gesture. He accepts it with a weary but grateful nod and hurls it through the plate glass window into the street outside.

A few hours later, GORDON *sits on the edge of a chair staring morosely ahead of him. The room looks very patched together, everything is at strange angles.*

Brown gumstrip holds together the broken window glass. The curtains are torn, the tall cabinet is roped to the wall and the mantelpiece is propped in position with a couple of sticks.

MRS OTTERSHAW   (*from the kitchen*): Gordon! Yer tea's ready.

Wearily GORDON *rises and slowly, and, as if in a trance, walks through to the little kitchen. As soon as he enters* BARNSTONEWORTH *swallows a hunk of bread and dripping and proudly begins to recite.*

BARNSTONEWORTH: Yorkshire Premier League 1922 . . . er . . . Hagerty F., Hagerty R., Tomkins, Noble, Carrick, Dobson, Crapper . . . Dewhurst, MacIntyre, Treadmore, Davitt.

GORDON   (*staring, shell-shocked at the fruit-cake in the middle of the table*): Played nineteen . . . Won None, Drawn One, One abandoned due to illness, Lost seventeen . . .

BARNSTONEWORTH: Barnstoneworth United Reserve Team: Yorkshire Premier League 1922, Holton, Roberts, Carter, Sydney Cave . . . er . . . Ralph Cave, Manningham, Horsewell, Dobkins, O'Grady.

GORDON: Goals for . . . six, Goals against . . . seventy-one . . .

BARNSTONEWORTH   (*brightly*): *Junior* Team: Yorkshire Premier League 1922: Bunn, Wackett, Buzzard, Stubble, Boot, Bowman, Baxter, Broadhurst, B . . .

GORDON: Oh shut up!

He pushes his chair back and stands up.

GORDON: I'm going out.

MRS OTTERSHAW: No dripping?

GORDON: No.

MRS OTTERSHAW   (*getting up from the table and following him to the door*): . . . Gordon . . .

GORDON   (*putting his coat on*): . . . Yes . . .

MRS OTTERSHAW: Gordon . . . I've been meaning to tell you . . .

GORDON   (*abstractedly*): Mm?

MRS OTTERSHAW: I'm going to have a baby!

GORDON   (*puts his woolly supporter's hat on*): Oh right . . . don't wait up for me . . . (*He pulls open the front door.*)

MRS OTTERSHAW: Where are you going?

GORDON: Somewhere to cheer myself up . . .

A door of a nissen hut with light above it and a sign which reads BARNSTONEWORTH UNITED SOCIAL CLUB. GORDON *pushes the door open. Inside is a large empty space. An air of desolation hangs over the place. A bar at one end. A* BARMAN *stands cleaning glasses. Another man sits on a bar stool with a half-drunk pint of light and bitter, staring morosely ahead. At one of the tables sits the only other occupant of this bleak and melancholy room — another supporter staring silently into his beer.*

GORDON *walks up to the bar.*

GORDON (*to the* BARMAN): Hello Cyril.
BARMAN: Hello . . . Gordon.
GORDON (*nods briefly to the* MOROSE MAN AT THE BAR): Ron . . .

RON barely acknowledges the greeting.

GORDON (*to the* BARMAN): Brown, please . . .

The BARMAN *uncaps and pours him a brown ale.* GORDON, *with a bleak smile of acknowledgement, takes it and goes to a table. He takes a sip of ale and sits broodily staring into the glass for a minute. Then quite suddenly with a bellow, like a wounded rogue-elephant, he stands up, and hurls the table onto the ground. He picks up his chair and hurls it down on top of the table. He walks across to the dartboard and wrenches it from the wall, hurling it full tilt into a table in the corner which is full of neatly laid out cups and saucers that smash noisily on the floor.*

BARMAN (*after a respectful pause*): I know how you feel, Gordon.

GORDON turns and looks at a painted 'Honours' board which is screwed against one wall. His eye reads: BARNSTONEWORTH UNITED: YORKSHIRE PREMIER LEAGUE: RESULTS:
1925-26: DIVISION ONE: Played 40, Won 29, Drew 8, Lost 3
1928-29: DIVISION ONE: Played 40, Won 18, Drew 10, Lost 12
1930-31 DIVISION ONE: Played 38, Won 10, Drawn 6, Lost 22
1932-33: DIVISION TWO: Played 40, Won 1, Drawn 2, Lost 37
1933-34: DIVISION THREE: Played 40, Won 0, Drawn 0, Lost 40

He kicks the board savagely. It collapses and falls in two bits off the wall.

GORDON (*with feeling*): The *useless,* useless bastards. (*He turns disconsolately for the door.*)
BARMAN: Coming to training on Tuesday night, Gordon?
GORDON (*wearily, hand on the door*): . . . Yeah . . .

Tuesday night.

A street outside Barnstoneworth's ground. GORDON, *hands in pockets, scarf and supporter's cap on as usual, hurries along the street to the door of the ground. It's a cold day, in the greyness of an approaching evening.*

On the door a hastily scribbled sign reads:
BARNSTONEWORTH UNITED. TRAINING 5.30.

GORDON pushes the rickety door open and goes in. The pitch is in reasonable condition, and there is a stand, built during more prosperous times. It now only serves to emphasize the emptiness and lack of support. A couple of supporters — the BARMAN, CYRIL, and another are there, blowing on their hands and stamping their feet to keep warm. A handful of players, one with no shorts on, are dragging themselves on a 'run' round the pitch. Much coughing, and stopping to spit. In the centre circle, a worried-looking man with sparse hair and the 1930's equivalent of a track suit, stands holding a ball and talking to a determined little middle-aged lady. She is MRS ROCKWORTH, mother of eight, one of whom is Barnstoneworth's star player. He is the Manager.

MRS ROCKWORTH:	I'm sorry, but I'm not having our Barry come out on a night like this . . .
MANAGER:	But, Mrs Rockworth, he's our centre-forward.
MRS ROCKWORTH:	I don't care if he's Tommy Lawton. He's my son and he's not coming out on a night like this with his boils.
MANAGER:	He's a professional footballer, Mrs Rockworth.
MRS ROCKWORTH:	Is that what they call him? Six pounds a match — professional! I tell you, if it weren't for his brother being a Director of the Midland Bank and a financial adviser to the Rothschilds we'd not have two pence to rub together — so don't come 'professional footballer', wi' me!
MANAGER:	Will he be fit for Saturday . . . ? It's the Cup.
MRS ROCKWORTH:	It may be the Cup for you, it could be the coffin for him if his neck goes septic.

She turns with a flourish and marches off, she stops and turns.

MRS ROCKWORTH:	. . . Oh and Mrs Hargreaves said to tell you her Kevin's got a nasty cold sore and she's keeping him at home while Thursday . . .
MANAGER	(*bleakly*): Thank you . . .

MRS ROCKWORTH hurries out, passing the three supporters.

GORDON:	Good evening, Mrs Rockworth.
MRS ROCKWORTH:	Nowt good about it as far as I can see.

She goes off. In the centre circle the MANAGER blows his whistle and summons the half-dozen wheezing wrecks who make up the backbone of his team.

MANAGER:	Righto! Come over here, lads. I want to talk about tactics for Saturday.
FIRST PLAYER	(*plaintively*): 'E's got my shorts on . . .
MANAGER:	What?
FIRST PLAYER:	Roger Hickfield's got my shorts on . . .
SECOND PLAYER:	I have 'eck . . .
MANAGER:	Now then . . .

THIRD PLAYER: Can I go at half past six?

MANAGER: Yes . . . now then . . . Saturday as you all know is Cup-tie day . . . and it's our chance to show . . . What's the matter . . . ?

The FIRST PLAYER is sobbing.

FIRST PLAYER: He's got my shorts on, he won't give 'em back.

SECOND PLAYER: I bloody haven't . . . They were on top of my bag in't changing room.

FIRST PLAYER: They were on *my* peg.

THIRD PLAYER: They were never on his peg! I share't peg wi' 'im and I never saw 'em.

FIRST PLAYER: You're a bloody liar you are, Dobson.

THIRD PLAYER: Don't you call me names, you Pansy . . .

He hits him.

SECOND PLAYER: They were out of my bag . . .

FIRST PLAYER: They bloody weren't . . .

A punch-up starts. They all join in. The MANAGER suddenly snaps. He leaps into action, shrilling on his whistle with piercing vehemence and pulling the would-be combatants apart.

MANAGER: Stop that! D'you hear! Stop it! STOP . . . IT!

The players pull apart. The MANAGER is breathing heavily, and is clearly in a state of barely controlled nervous turmoil.

MANAGER: What the hell do you think's going on! Who the hell do you think you are! (*He glares round at the players.*) I didn't come here on a free exchange from Walsall to stand and watch a bunch of morons arguing about shorts! I came here to create a football team — a hard tough ruthless fighting unit. I don't care if your bloody shorts are on or off so long as you can do a quick one-two with an overlapping half-back . . . You can wear the sodding things over your head if it'll help you drop a long ball right at the centre-forward's feet. You can run the length of this pitch stark bollock naked if you tuck one in the corner of the net at the end of it! Shorts don't matter — d'you hear?

Shorts aren't what it's all about! I don't care if they're blue serge shorts, or white cotton shorts, or green flannel shorts, or sky-blue shorts with elastic-supported hand-stitched Italian-style waistbands. I don't care if they're short shorts or long shorts or three-quarter length shorts or initialled shorts or monogrammed shorts or Billy Meredith signed shorts or shorts made in Ireland or shorts made in Austria or shorts made in Timbuc-bloody-too with pink stars on that light up at night. They're *not* important! D'you hear! They're nothing to do with bloody football! The only things that matter are what's inside them . . . the machine that you've got pounding away in there. Up and down, up and down for ninety minutes.

He starts to grab and tear at the top of his shorts.

You can wear all the shorts you want . . . You can wear fifteen woolly pairs on top of each other. But it won't make a ha'porth of difference if that punching, pounding, pulsating pair inside them can't keep running and fighting and tackling . . .

He pulls his shorts down messianically.

Those are what's important. (*He slaps his marble white legs.*) Not these . . . (*He starts whirling his shorts around his head.*) Chuck 'em away! Fling 'em out . . . Forget 'em!

He races past the spectators.

Throw 'em in the bloody canal! Goodbye shorts . . . hello football!

He disappears out of the ground, buttocks glinting in the late afternoon sun. The spectators shake their heads sadly. The players stand around rather uneasily. The wind blows.

The OTTERSHAWS' *kitchen.* GORDON *tips a custard jug and spreads its contents liberally over sponge pudding.*

GORDON: . . . Indecent exposure in a bakery . . . He'll probably get three years. And that's only the manager . . . Centre forward's off wi' boils. Two half-backs are going to a wedding and the goalie's got a cold sore . . .

MRS OTTERSHAW: Gordon.

GORDON: Chairman's called an emergency meeting.

MRS OTTERSHAW: Gordon?

BARNSTONEWORTH: Dad, when were Barnstoneworth made full members of the Yorkshire Premier League?

GORDON: — 1907, Division two. *He'll* sort the whole bloody thing out . . .

MRS OTTERSHAW: Gordon, I'm going to have a baby.

GORDON: About bloody time, that's all I can say.

He stands up. MRS OTTERSHAW *isn't quite sure how to take this last remark, but at least it's better than no reaction at all.*

MRS OTTERSHAW: You what, love . . . ?

GORDON (*pulling his coat on*): It's about bloody time the Chairman got up off his arse and took an interest in't club. (*He puts his coat on and goes for the door.*) . . . Don't wait up for me . . . (*He leaves.*)

At the social club. The room has been heavily repaired since Gordon wrecked it. There are about ten people in the room. A table is laid up at the front, at which three notable Barnstoneworth citizens are sitting, watching people coming in. GORDON *enters and moves to a seat at the back.*

GORDON (*to the man he's sitting next to: — it's* CYRIL, *the barman*): 'Allo, Cyril.

CYRIL: Hello, Gordon.

GORDON: What's up 'ere then?

CYRIL: I think we're going to buy Arsenal's manager . . .

GORDON (*laughs briefly*): We need Arsenal's team an' all. How's Vera?

CYRIL: Not bad. Farting's stopped.

The CHAIRMAN, *a short, balding, prosperous-looking little man bangs on the table for silence. He stands up and clears his throat self-importantly.*

CHAIRMAN: Gentlemen and fellow supporters. The last few years have not been kind to Barnstoneworth United. One look at the Results Board will tell you that . . .

Quick cut away to the results board. It's split in two halves, which have been roughly nailed back on the wall. One half, however, has been nailed upside down.

. . . Er, this continued lack of success and consequent damage to the financial situation of this club, coupled with the loss of our manager, Mr Dainty, has impressed upon your Board of Directors the need for urgent action.

GORDON   (*and others*): Hear! Hear! 'Bout time! . . .

CHAIRMAN: We have therefore decided, as from Tuesday next week, to sell Barnstoneworth United Football Club, its players, premises and ground to the Arthur Foggen Scrap Corporation for redevelopment . . .

GORDON's *face freezes.*

. . . They have assured us that the name of Barnstoneworth United will not be forgotten and have kindly consented to name one of their steel scrap crushing mills after the club . . .

Some time later. The lonely figure of GORDON *standing beside the pitch at evening. His eyes are watery as he looks out of the empty stand, the* CHAIRMAN's *last words echoing in his head.*

CHAIRMAN'S VOICE: Saturday's cup-tie against Denley Moor Academicals will be the last game at the Sewage Works ground. Believe me, we have not taken such a decision lightly — mindful as we all are of the fine traditions of our Club. But with attendance dropping consistently below the eighteen mark, with only six goals in three years, and bearing in mind the very generous financial terms offered by Mr Foggen, we feel that we have no option but to accept the redevelopment as an inevitable result of economic forces in a modern industrial society.

GORDON *wanders slowly, with utter dejection down the hill towards his house. He turns into the gate (see* GREAT MAGIC TRICKS OF HISTORY *by U. Geller, unbent editions, £5 — slightly bent, £20), and pushes the front door open.*

He enters the kitchen as if in a trance. He picks up a note on the table and reads:

'Your supper is in the oven. P.S. I am going to have a baby.'

GORDON *stands a moment then with a rumble of rage picks up the kitchen table and is about to hurl it at the wall when he stops in his tracks. Ahead of him is a day-by-day calendar. It's called 'Beautiful Barnstoneworth 1935'. It shows a suitably attractive little scene and underneath the words: 'Foggen Scrap Corporation . . . Barnstoneworth's Premier Company'.*

He slowly lowers the table, an idea is dawning. He looks at the clock. It's ten o'clock. He looks back at the calendar . . .

GORDON *appears to make up his mind . . . he turns and hurries out of the kitchen. The front door slams . . .*

In the kitchen, smoke comes from behind the closed oven door. Upstairs EILEEN OTTERSHAW, *her look of hopeful anticipation shattered again by the sound of the slamming door, sadly clicks the bedside light off.*

GORDON *cycles, suddenly hopeful, through the silent, rain-glistening street, out of the town to the gates of a very big smart house, with wide driveway. He goes boldly to the front door. He is about to ring the bell, but his determination suddenly fails him. He stops, indecisively, before the massive front door, then looks to one side, and catches sight of a sign:*

'Tradesmen's Entrance'

He turns and makes for the tradesmen's entrance. He stops again and with renewed determination retraces his steps up to the front door.

He rings the bell.

He pauses and rubs his shoes on the back of his trouser legs. He notices he has his supporter's club scarf and hat on, pulls the hat off and quickly tries to take the scarf off too. This is more difficult. An outside light goes on above his head as he's scrabbling with the scarf. He reacts . . . it makes him rush even more. He pushes his scarf into his pocket. It trails out. He pushes it in, but his hat drops out. The door opens as he's bending to retrieve the hat. A portly, impressive man, with thinning, but distinguished, brilliantined hair, stands looking down on him. He blows cigar smoke out aggressively. The epitome of the self-made Yorkshire millionaire.

FOGGEN: Foggen.
GORDON: Could I have a word with you for a moment?
FOGGEN: Is it about scrap?
GORDON: Well, it's about the Football Club . . .
FOGGEN: Then it's about scrap . . . Come in.

GORDON enters. An opulent but tastefully furnished hall makes GORDON catch his breath in admiration, until he nearly trips over a large pile of scrap. At that moment a very elegant, expensively dressed lady, with pearls and a beautiful gown on, walks into the hall, carrying a couple of heavy railway bogie wheels, which she drops on a pile.

FOGGEN: My wife . . .
GORDON: How d'you do?

FOGGEN's WIFE smiles graciously, a real lady.

FOGGEN   (*indicating the pile of railway wheels as he steps over them*): Just came in today, fourteen bogies from the Scottish Railway Company. That's heavy scrap, that is . . . Worth about fifteen thousand on the open market, and I can get twenty for it . . .

As they talk the sophisticated WIFE continues transferring the bogie wheels from the elegant drawing room on to the pile in the hall, with periodic clunks and bangs. GORDON's eyes keep being diverted by her activity.

FOGGEN: Drink?
GORDON: No thank you.
FOGGEN   (*pouring himself a scotch from a cut glass decanter*): I love scrap, Mr . . . er . . . ?
GORDON: Ottershaw, Gordon Ottershaw.
FOGGEN: I've always loved scrap. Ever since I was big enough to walk I've wanted to be deeply involved with it. Well now, I've got twelve heaps in four major

cities . . . and why? Because there's only one thing I love more than scrap . . .

He sees something behind a Chippendale armchair. It's an old bicycle wheel. He picks it up and throws it across the room onto a pile. It lands accurately with a crash.

. . . and that's success. I wouldn't have anything other than success. I see it, I want it, I get it. That's my motto. In fact that's one of my many mottoes. I love mottoes. I love mottoes almost as much as I love scrap. Now, what d'you want?

GORDON: Well . . . er.

FOGGEN: Come on! *I've* been blunt with you. You be blunt wi' me.

GORDON: I . . . I . . . er . . . I want Barnstoneworth United to stay as a football club.

FOGGEN   (*approvingly*): 'I want'. I like the sound of that. Why do you 'want' Barnstoneworth United to stay as a football club?

GORDON: Well . . . er . . . well, because that's . . . what it is.

FOGGEN: Wrong! Barnstoneworth United hasn't been a football club for years. It's been a rest home for the physically incompetent. I could have had cows on that pitch for the last three years. They'd have paid for themselves *and* scored more goals.

GORDON: Well . . . we've been going through a bad patch.

FOGGEN: Bad patch! You don't know what you're talking about. D'you know when they last won a game at the Sewage Works ground, well I'll . . .

GORDON   (*leaping up, eagerly*): October 7th 1931. Two-nil against Pudsey.

FOGGEN   (*momentarily thrown*): . . . Right, but . . .

GORDON: Hagerty, Noble, Ferris, Codron, Crapper, Davidson, Sullivan, O'Grady, Kemble, Hacker and Davitt. Davitt scored both goals, one in the twenty-first minute one in the twenty-eighth.

FOGGEN: Davitt! Kenny Davitt . . .

GORDON: Neville Davitt.

FOGGEN: *Neville* Davitt, that's right. He were a player. Bald, wasn't he?

GORDON nods enthusiastically.

FOGGEN: Head like stainless steel. Ball came off it like a point two two rifle bullet. (*His eyes go misty.*) Could have got two hundred quid scrap for that head.

GORDON: Once he scored from twenty-eight yards with the back of his head against Barnsley Reserves in 1922.

FOGGEN: That was a night. Cup, wasn't it?

GORDON   (*eagerly*): Yorkshire Cup. Fourth round replay. Hagerty F., Hagerty R., Tomkins, Noble, Carrick . . .

FOGGEN: Carrick! He were a player too.

GORDON: . . . Dobson, Crapper, Dewhurst, MacIntyre, Treadmore and Davitt . . . three all. Five-three after extra time. Davitt scored twice in last three minutes, and Frank Hagerty saved a penalty.

FOGGEN: Oh aye . . . (*He pulls on his cigar.*) That were a night. There must have been ten thousand folk down there . . .

GORDON: Ten thousand, one hundred and eighteen . . . they had coaches from Leeds.

FOGGEN (*reflecting nostalgically*): Coaches from Leeds . . . eh . . . coaches from Leeds . . . (*He suddenly snaps out of it.*) Still, then's then, and now's now. First rule of scrap, never get sentimental. Time is the General Manager on our board, Mr Ottershaw. It marches on relentlessly waiting for no-one, hand in hand with the scrap merchants of this land. (*He pauses a moment.*) I wonder whatever became of Neville Davitt . . . ?

GORDON: He's got a butcher's shop over in Bradley.

FOGGEN: Old Baldy! . . . running a butcher's shop . . . ?

GORDON: Ken Carrick works in a glue factory in Todmorden.

FOGGEN: Carrick? — what a bloody waste. A glue factory for a man who could crack a goalpost in two from the halfway line.

GORDON: He works in the same shed as Harry Treadmore . . .

FOGGEN: Harry Treadmore? (*His eyes light up.*) By God, they were a team in those days.

GORDON: It can be like that again Mr Foggen, if you'll give them a chance.

FOGGEN considers. Then his distant smile of nostalgia is replaced by the calculating frown of the businessman.

FOGGEN: What's it to you?

GORDON: Oh, I'm just a supporter . . .

FOGGEN: I didn't know there were any of *them* left.

GORDON: Oh, there's a few of us . . . We get laughed at . . . but the way I look at it . . . that's when a team needs supporters. During the hard times . . .

FOGGEN: Listen, fifteen hundredweight of cast iron couldn't support a team that's lost its last ninety-six matches . . .

GORDON: Well, I always keep hoping something'll turn up. Another Neville Davitt, another Kenny Carrick . . .

FOGGEN (*throwing his cigar butt decisively into the fireplace, and picking up a piece of scrap*): You're getting soft again, Mr Ottershaw. Those days are gone. And they'll never come back. If they did, people like me'd be out of business. Now if you don't mind . . . (*He walks towards the door, dropping the piece of scrap on a pile as he goes.*) I've got to sort out a gross of steel filings by tomorrow . . . (*He gets to the front door and pulls it open.*) . . . Nice to talk to you . . .

He holds the front door open rather finally. GORDON *emerges and puts his cap on.*

GORDON: Yes . . . er . . . (*He's almost got tears in his eyes.*) Well, Saturday'll be last game then . . .

FOGGEN: There's plenty of good games over at Leeds these days . . . you know. You ought to get a season ticket.

GORDON: Aye well . . . I'll probably give up football for a bit.

FOGGEN: Well, goodnight.

GORDON *walks slowly down the steps, suddenly* FOGGEN *calls after him.*

FOGGEN: Mr Ottershaw!

GORDON (*turns, with a sudden resurgence of hope*): Yes?

FOGGEN: Have you ever thought of a job in scrap?

GORDON's *face falls. He turns bitterly, picks up his bicycle and pedals off into the night.*

Next morning, in the OTTERSHAWS' *kitchen.*

A hand comes in and tears off Wednesday March 7th 1935 from the Foggen Corporation's 'Beautiful Barnstoneworth' calendar revealing Thursday March 8th 1935.

GORDON *stands staring at the calendar, with scrumpled up Wednesday in his hand.*

GORDON (*blearily: he's red-eyed and clearly hasn't slept all night*): They *can* win. I know they can.

MRS OTTERSHAW *looks rather despairingly at her husband in between rushing to get her son ready for school. She's packing him sandwiches . . . whilst he's finishing his last mouthful of breakfast.*

MRS OTTERSHAW: Come on Barnstoneworth, Let's hear them again.

BARNSTONEWORTH: Er . . . Hagerty F., Hagerty R., . . . Tomkins . . .

MRS OTTERSHAW (*angrily*): No! . . . Gladstone, Rosebery, Salisbury, Balfour, Campbell-Bannerman . . .

BARNSTONEWORTH (*tentatively*): Braggit?

MRS OTTERSHAW: No! Asquith!

She shoves the sandwiches into his hand and hurries him out of the room. We hear her shouting down the hall . . .

Asquith! Asquith! ASQUITH!

The front door slams. She comes back into the kitchen. She's very angry.

Gordon! Did you hear that? That boy's got History School Certificate today and he still gets his British Prime Ministers muddled up with the Barnstoneworth reserves for 1914. You've got to stop filling his head with football. It's not healthy! And it's no bloody use!

GORDON: Well he's not going to be a Prime Minister.

MRS OTTERSHAW: And he's not going to be a footballer, is he . . . ?

This hits hard.

GORDON (*quietly*): He may be . . . yet.

MRS OTTERSHAW: You know he can't kick a ball straight. He hates it. And how would you like to be called 'Barnstoneworth'?

GORDON: He's got another name . . .

MRS OTTERSHAW: United! What sort of name's that? I wish you'd let him do what he wants, Gordon. Hagerty, F., Hagerty, R., Tomkins, Noble, Carrick, Davitt . . . It doesn't matter! When will you realize, Gordon, that it doesn't matter who the hell played for Barnstoneworth bloody United in 1922!

She stops, suddenly anxious that she's gone too far. But amazingly, as she looks, a big grin spreads across GORDON's *face.*

GORDON: Yes . . . oh, yes . . . (*Dawning realization.*) Of course! (*He makes for the door.*) Of course!

He turns and grins at her as he pulls his coat on. She follows him to the door.

MRS OTTERSHAW (*following*): Where are you going?

GORDON (*he picks up his bike*): Bradley!

MRS OTTERSHAW: Bradley! What for?

GORDON (*calling back*): Shopping!

MRS OTTERSHAW: Gordon, before you go *any* where, we must talk.

GORDON: Don't wait up for me love.

He cycles off.

MRS OTTERSHAW (*reacts for a moment, then yells after him*): Gordon! *I'm going to have a baby!*

A passer-by, a sallow spotty young man, looks up . . . and reacts to this with some embarrassment.

MRS OTTERSHAW with an angry little cry of frustration, slams the door.

GORDON cycles, with newly-found enthusiasm, along lanes, by dry-stone walls, and across the Yorkshire moors until he coasts down a hill and past a sign 'Bradley'.

He cycles up to a corner shop and looks up at the name with a hopeful smile . . . E. & R.J. DAVITT, HIGH CLASS BUTCHER. He parks his bike . . . pushes open the door to the butcher's shop, a man looks up from behind the counter. He has a very obvious thick head of artificial hair.

GORDON: Mr Davitt? Neville Davitt?

DAVITT looks round in rather quick, furtive alarm.

DAVITT (*cautiously*): Yeah . . .
GORDON: Er . . . my name's Gordon Ottershaw. (*He finds himself staring at DAVITT's luxuriant hairpiece, fascinated.*) . . . er . . . I'm from Barnstoneworth.
DAVITT (*unhelpfully*): Oh yes . . .
GORDON: Oh yes . . . I was a great fan of yours when you used to play for United . . . I remember your . . . er . . .
DAVITT: Yes?
GORDON: Your er . . . Well . . . before you . . . well when you still had er . . .
DAVITT: Fastest legs in West Yorkshire?
GORDON: Er . . . yes . . . and er . . . of course your specialities . . . you know . . . all those goals from the er . . . er . . . (*He can't stop himself looking at the elderly ex-footballer's bonce.*)

DAVITT: Penalty spot?

GORDON (*embarrassed now*): Yes . . . yes . . . and with the er . . . well, with the headers, you know . . .

DAVITT: No. Never scored with my head. Couldn't afford to with a head of hair like this . . . I was always proud of my hair, always will be.

But GORDON *perseveres with* DAVITT. *A few remarks are exchanged and when* GORDON *re-emerges, he looks encouraged and mounts his bike jauntily.*

At the doorway of a factory, marked BRITISH GUM LTD. TODMORDEN WORKS GORDON *is talking to a couple of old men, both in caps. At first much shaking of the head . . . one has no teeth at all. Then one of them gives a bit of a smile, a nod . . .*

An elderly man is being pushed by a nurse along a path at an old folks' home. He coughs a little and looks around. Obviously very frustrated and bored. Suddenly he looks up . . . A figure cycles up the drive. It's GORDON. *He stops, gets off his bicycle, and goes up to the man in the chair . . . He talks for a moment. The man looks puzzled.* GORDON *explains. The man nods eagerly, shakes his hand, and* GORDON *runs back to his bicycle . . .*

GORDON *cycles to a group of railway cottages, and shouts up. A man at an upstairs window in a dressing-gown nods at* GORDON *down below on his bike. They talk a while, then both nod, wave and* GORDON *cycles off again.*

GORDON *cycles off to a church in a small village. He stops his bike, gets off and walks into a graveyard. He walks amongst the mass of gravestones. Suddenly he looks ahead and down and his eyes light up. He calls down to the gravedigger in a hole. The man turns, puzzled.* GORDON *walks up to him, shakes his hand, the man nods . . .* GORDON *talks . . . and sets off again . . .*

Saturday afternoon.
The main, and indeed only, gate of the Sewage Works ground. There is a bold sign on the door: YORKSHIRE CUP. BARNSTONEWORTH UNITED VERSUS DENLEY MOOR. K'O. 3.00.

A couple of people go in. A large smart Riley saloon comes to a halt outside the ground. The door opens. The CHAIRMAN *gets out with his wife, in a fur, looking as though she's loathing every minute of it. He scowls as he sees the sign on the door, and walks briskly past it and into the ground.*

CHAIRMAN: Bloody embarrassing this is going to be . . . Should have called the whole match off — half the team sick or missing. Why the hell we couldn't . . .

He turns and finds himself confronted by FOGGEN.

CHAIRMAN: Oh, Mr Foggen . . . haven't seen you here for a few years. Come for a look at the premises eh? Make a lovely scrapheap this will.
FOGGEN: No, I've come to see Barnstoneworth win a match.
CHAIRMAN: (*laughes dismissively*): Well, I shouldn't hang around getting cold if I were you, Mr Foggen. We haven't even got a full team . . .
FOGGEN: Your Mr Ottershaw thinks they'll win . . .
CHAIRMAN: Ottershaw! Don't go worrying about him, Mr Foggen.
FOGGEN: He's enthusiastic . . . I like enthusiasm.
CHAIRMAN: Obsessed, I call it. It's a form of madness, you know . . . wearing your scarf in bed, calling your kids 'Barnstoneworth'.
FOGGEN: I'd like to see them win again, though.
CHAIRMAN: I'd like to see them turn up . . .

There is a cheer from the massed Denley Moor supporters as their team runs out.

CHAIRMAN: That's Denley Moor . . . good team. They've got young Olthwaite at number eight.
FOGGEN: Oh aye . . . the bank robber?
CHAIRMAN: It were never proved.

A few shouts from Denley Moor supporters, who wave flags and make a lot of noise.

CHAIRMAN: Oh come on Barnstoneworth, where are you?

He looks at his watch, then looks towards the pavilion. On the pitch the Denley Moor team are whistled to the centre by the REFEREE. *They turn towards the pavilion waiting.*

CHAIRMAN (*checking his watch*): Three o'clock!

He looks anxiously round for any trace of his team.

After a moment a figure emerges. It's the MANAGER, ERIC DAINTY, *in a long brown mac from which his white but knobbly legs protrude rudely. He hurries towards the* CHAIRMAN *rather pathetically.*

FOGGEN: Who the hell's that?
CHAIRMAN (*embarrassed*): . . . Our ex-Manager . . .
FOGGEN: What the *hell's* going on?

YORKSHIRE CUP

BARNSTONEWORTH
UNITED
V.
DENLEY MOOR

K.O. 3%

MANAGER: There's only four turned up sir, and only one of them's got shorts.
CHAIRMAN: I don't believe you.
MANAGER: *I could play . . . I could show them a thing or two . . .*
CHAIRMAN: Yes I'm sure you could Mr Dainty . . . but that's not what they've come to see. No, I'll go and cancel . . . What a bloody way to go . . .

He makes to walk to the REFEREE, *when suddenly he is stopped by the sound of a coach drawing up outside. The coach doors slam, then the gate to the ground flies open . . .* GORDON OTTERSHAW *comes running through.*

CHAIRMAN: Ottershaw . . .
GORDON (*holding the gate open*): Sorry we're late!

Into the ground come eleven elderly and middle-aged men in Barnstoneworth colours and long shorts led by NEVILLE DAVITT (*with his wig on*), *bouncing the match ball, followed by the two men from the glue factory, the gravedigger and all the others* GORDON *recruited. All heads turn as they run on to the pitch. The last of all in the team is the* OLD MAN *from the old folks' home.*

He's pushed on in a wheelchair by his same reproving nurse. She pushes him t[o] the touch-line. He throws off the rug and reveals himself in the full splendour of the Barnstoneworth strip. He canters on to the pitch. Some startled applause. The Denley Moor team look on with amazed, somewhat disdainful smiles.

The REFEREE *whistles the captains together.* DAVITT *(60) and the young Denley Moor captain come together. They toss. After the toss the teams line up. Just as the whistle's about to go,* DAVITT *with a dramatic timing throws aside his toupee, to reveal the deadly pate, freshly greased and shining. Now there really is a reaction. Even the Denley Moor players know who it is. A rustle of excitement.*

FOGGEN's *face lights up. Then cheering breaks out . . .* GORDON *looks proud fit to burst . . .*

The whistle goes. The ball goes out from the gravedigger, to the man from old folks' home, who manages to turn past a player and fire a long pass out to the wing with amazing accuracy. The nurse winces as she watches. The ball goes to BALDY DAVITT *who swerves and twists, quite magically to the almost extinct sound of Barnstoneworth cheers.*

The CHAIRMAN *is still stunned as* DAVITT *weaves past a back and cracks in a shot and it's a goal. As the team rush up to congratulate him, the Denley Moor goalie picks himself up from the mud, goes up to a bewildered small fan who stands beside the goal, grabs his autograph book and pencil, thrusts the fan rudely to one side and rushes up to* NEVILLE DAVITT, *proffering the book.*

The REFEREE *points to the centre-spot. Cheers and applause. The Denley Moor supporters are stunned into silence.*

Ninety minutes later outside the little Ottershaw home.

MRS OTTERSHAW *is beating the doormat again when she hears the whistle go. Instinctively she makes to go in to protect her home, when suddenly she freezes.* BARNSTONEWORTH, *her son, appears silently behind her, and he too gazes up the road in disbelief, for what they can hear is cheers, not groans.*

SUPPORTERS: Barnstoneworth! Barnstoneworth!

As the cheers die away, the sound of running feet getting nearer. Round the

corner of the top of the hill comes GORDON. *He races down the road* . . .

MRS OTTERSHAW *ushers her son into the sitting-room. She's a bit worried by this unexpected turn of events.* GORDON *crashes into the house and flings the sitting-room door open. His face is hot, radiant and suffused with joy!*

GORDON: Eight-one! Eight . . . Bloody . . . One!

A slight pause, then all three of them as sheer delight dawns on their faces, turn and start to smash the sitting-room up. With joyous abandon they take the little place apart. Celebrating in an orgy of destruction the almost unbelievable fact that Barnstoneworth United have won a match. At last the OTTERSHAW *family are truly happy.*

*The Ripping Tale of a Young Man
caught in a World of Changing Values
and forced by Circumstances to the
Most Despicable Act known to the British Army*

ROGER
OF THE RAJ

India

ROGER OF THE RAJ

England 1914

Deep in the heart of the English countryside stands the stately edifice of Bartlesham Hall — home of the Bartlesham family for six proud generations (or probably less). This is the story of the son and heir to the Bartlesham estate, Roger Bartlesham, and how he stooped to the most despicable act known to the British army. It is he who now takes up the tale.

The reasons for what I did in India that fateful night in 1917 really began in my childhood . . . I was luckier than most boys of my age in that my father did have enormously large amounts of money, enabling us to be mercifully free of the everyday anxieties of life — such as lack of houses and tennis courts. The endless leisured days at Bartlesham Hall began, as always, with the family breakfast.

A typical family breakfast finds ROGER *marooned in the middle of a lengthy refectory table, with his mother,* LADY BARTLESHAM, *at one end and his father,* LORD BARTLESHAM, *at the other.*

On a sideboard behind him stretches the vast profusion necessary to sustain life at Bartlesham Hall during the long hours before lunch. There are devilled kidneys, eggs and bacon, scrambled eggs, kedgeree, sausages, scotch woodcock, steaks, toast, halibut, kippers and little pastry brioches, all lavishly laid out in silver serving dishes, heated by spirit lamps. Bread and butter, a tea canteen and numerous coffee pots also stand at the ready. On another, even larger, sideboard silver salvers groan with a choice of cold meats — pressed beef, ham, tongue, pheasant, grouse, partridge, ptarmigan. There is also a side table, heaped with fruits — melons, peaches, raspberries, nectarines.

LORD BARTLESHAM *is quite elderly, and is reading a paper as is clearly his wont. He is an amiable man, with a vaguely distant, reflective air.* LADY BARTLESHAM *is a dominating tight-lipped, rather severe lady. She sits bolt upright, eating toast with a sharp staccato crackle. This is the only sound*

in the room, apart from the deep tick of a clock . . . until LADY BARTLESHAM *finally breaks the silence.*

LADY BARTLESHAM:	The toast is frightfully good today, Barty.
LORD BARTLESHAM:	Yes . . . yes . . . it was awfully good.
LADY BARTLESHAM:	Very pleasantly brittle.
LORD BARTLESHAM:	Yes . . . really very good toast.
LADY BARTLESHAM	(*after a short pause*): I think it's some of the best toast we've ever had.
LORD BARTLESHAM:	Yes . . . yes . . . could be . . .
LADY BARTLESHAM:	I wonder who made the toast today?
LORD BARTLESHAM:	Well . . . whoever it was — they're a dab hand.
LADY BARTLESHAM:	Mrs Angel?

The HOUSEMAID *turns from the sideboard.*

Who made the toast today?

MRS ANGEL:	Er . . . Judy, I think, your Ladyship.
LADY BARTLESHAM:	Well, commend her most highly.
MRS ANGEL:	Yes, your ladyship . . .

She curtseys and withdraws.

As she passes LORD BARTLESHAM *he looks up from his paper.*

LORD BARTLESHAM:	Set her free, Mrs Angel . . .
LADY BARTLESHAM	(*exchanging a brief glance with* MRS ANGEL): She *is* free, dear.

MRS ANGEL *leaves.*

LORD BARTLESHAM:	Judy . . . free? Surely not.
LADY BARTLESHAM:	They're all free, dear . . . all the servants. There's been no slavery in this country for donkey's years.
LORD BARTLESHAM:	But Judy — little slip of a girl, washes floors all day long . . .
LADY BARTLESHAM	(*a hint of impatience*): She's still free, dear . . .
LORD BARTLESHAM:	Well, I think it's a great shame . . .

LADY BARTLESHAM: *What* is a shame, dear?

LORD BARTLESHAM: Not being able to free people. (*He lays his paper down and his eyes begin to glisten.*) It must have been a wonderful thing to do . . . just sort of free a chap . . . some poor miserable wretch in chains . . . and along you come and say . . . 'You're free! You're a free man . . . Off you go! Run around wherever you want!' Imagine the new life that's about to open up for him.

LADY BARTLESHAM: Not in front of the boy, Barty.

LORD BARTLESHAM (*as if awaking from a reverie*): What?

LADY BARTLESHAM: You're not to become emotional in front of the boy.

LORD BARTLESHAM: Sorry.

LADY BARTLESHAM: And what are you going to do today, Roger?

The boy is taken off guard.

ROGER: Oh . . . er . . .

I dreaded these moments, when mother would suddenly talk to me. Fortunately, they were mercifully few, but I never seemed to have an answer ready.

ROGER: I . . . shall be doing some Latin translation with Mr Hopper.

LORD BARTLESHAM: Hopper? He's a child-molester, isn't he?

LADY BARTLESHAM: He *was* dear. He is no longer.

LORD BARTLESHAM: Are you sure?

LADY BARTLESHAM: Yes, dear.

She cracks some toast rather conclusively.

Another part of the house. Some time later.
ROGER is sitting with an open exercise book and pencil ready.

A youngish man, gaunt and rather good-looking in a dark, wild-eyed way and in a well-worn suit, turns from a bookshelf and strides across the room, gesticulating, rather dramatically.

Mr Hopper knew no Latin at all. In fact his only qualification as my tutor

was a forged degree from the Department of Botany at Bangkok University. Instead, he used to teach me social revolution.

From ten in the morning until six in the evening, he told me all there was to know about Socialism, Marxism, the State Ownership of Capital and the bloodshed that would inevitably follow the armed uprising of the proletariat.

A shotgun shatters the quiet.

The shotgun is held by LADY BARTLESHAM. *She,* LORD BARTLESHAM, ROGER *and* MR HOPPER *are on the grouse moor, concealed behind a magnificently constructed hide.* LADY BARTLESHAM, *however, is the only one doing any firing. She is wreathed in smoke and firing off volley after volley of shot, whilst a gamekeeper supplies her with freshly-loaded shotguns from a large pile.*

LADY BARTLESHAM:	Come on, Roger. (*Bang.*) Shoot away!

ROGER *looks fed up, but nevertheless fires.*

LADY BARTLESHAM	(*Bang*): And another! (*Bang.*) And another! There we go! (*She turns to* LORD BARTLESHAM.) Come on, Barty, kill something.
LORD BARTLESHAM:	Oh sorry dear. (*He, too, fires, but without tremendous enthusiasm.*)
LADY BARTLESHAM:	Come on, Hopper! (*Bang.*)

My mother had killed more grouse than any other woman in history.

LADY BARTLESHAM:	There's a nice fat one! (*Bang.*)
GAMEKEEPER	(*handing her another gun*): That's Mr Barlow, ma'am.
LADY BARTLESHAM	(*peering rather crossly out of the hide*): So it is. Oh drat! Barty, we must *not* choose beaters that look like grouse. I've just shot Barlow.
ROGER	(*in some alarm*): I'll go and get him!

LADY BARTLESHAM *fires another volley, whilst* MR HOPPER *restrains* ROGER.

HOPPER:	Ssh!
GAMEKEEPER	(*helpfully*): He's been shot before, ma'am. I'm sure he won't mind.
LADY BARTLESHAM:	It's just such a waste of cartridges!

Bang.

LORD BARTLESHAM	(*to* HOPPER): Jolly decent sort of chap you know . . . the average slave.
LADY BARTLESHAM	(*automatically*): Servant, dear.

Bang.

ROGER:	Are you just going to *leave* him there?

LORD BARTLESHAM: Well all right, 'servant' if you like . . . (*Aside to* HOPPER.) I don't know what's wrong with a good old-fashioned word, sometimes.

HOPPER (*smiles*): Well yes, sir, I often find modern jargon offensive. (*He lays a resting hand on* ROGER, *calming his indignation*.) Sssh!

LADY BARTLESHAM (*Bang*): It's inaccurate, that's what's wrong, dear. (*Bang.*) Barlow is a servant. He's a free man. Isn't that right Kenton?

GAMEKEEPER (*touching his forelock*): Yes, ma'am.

LADY BARTLESHAM (*Bang.*)

LORD BARTLESHAM: Well, wonderful chap, anyway.

LADY BARTLESHAM (*Bang bang.*)

LORD BARTLESHAM (*starting to go into a reverie again*): Being free and yet willing to be constantly shot.

ROGER: I don't think he *wants* to be shot, Father. I don't think anyone *wants* to be shot in the back.

LADY BARTLESHAM (*overhearing*): You'd be surprised . . .some of these people quite like it (*Bang.*) . . . gives them a certain security (*Bang.*) . . . not everyone can cope with success and good health all the time. Isn't that right, Mr Hopper? (*Bang.*)

HOPPER: Oh yes, there's a lot in that, your ladyship.

LORD BARTLESHAM: Well it makes me feel humble . . .

LADY BARTLESHAM (*Bang.*)

HOPPER: What, sir?

LORD BARTLESHAM: Chap like Barlow — with all the world to choose from — will repeatedly lie face downwards in the field without a single word of complaint . . . God! I know of chaps who'd moan about the skin on top of their porridge — and they're rich chaps too . . . intelligent, well-educated . . . and yet there's Barlow — a simple slave — lying in the mud without the slightest murmur of animosity.

LADY BARTLESHAM: Do stop talking, Barty, you haven't shot anything for ages . . . (*Bang.*) Fire up, Roger, come on . . .

ROGER *throws his gun down and climbs out of the hide.*

ROGER: Shoot your own beaters!

LADY BARTLESHAM: Roger!

ROGER *walks away.*

LADY BARTLESHAM: What on earth's the matter with the boy . . . ? What's wrong with shooting, for heaven's sake . . . ?

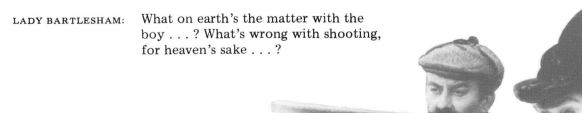

In the twinkling of an eye, however, Lady Bartlesham's shotgun is replaced by the blast of cannon and the boom of heavy artillery, as mud-soaked troops race across the benighted battlefields of Belgium and France.

Besides being immensely rich, my father was also Honorary Colonel of the Dorsetshire Rifles. And in 1914 we found ourselves uprooted from Bartlesham Hall. We were sent four thousand miles away to the Punjab, to do our bit in the Great War for Civilization . . .

India 1914.

The scene changes abruptly to a gentle croquet match on the elegant lawns outside the Colonel-in-Chief's Residence in the Punjab. All the family is there, including MR HOPPER, *who now sports an unmistakably Russian hat.*

Mr Hopper was so pleased to be near Russia, he changed his name to Leon Hopper and bought a new hat.

At this moment, it becomes clear that the young ROGER's *attention is being attracted by the delicately beautiful features of a young girl who is also playing.*

LADY BARTLESHAM: Your turn, Barty.

An INDIAN SERVANT *walks up to* LORD BARTLESHAM *and takes his mallet. The* INDIAN *then proceeds to hit an extremely accurate shot which wins the game. He hands the mallet back to* LORD BARTLESHAM *and everyone applauds.*

ALL: Oh well done, sir!
ROGER: Nice shot, father!

Once again, however, the scene changes — this time to an elaborate dinner amidst the candle-lit splendour of the Colonel-in-Chief's dining-room. The officers are all resplendent in their elegant dress uniform, and the ladies look beautiful.

The evenings were taken up with endless regimental dinners . . . the same people . . . the same talk . . . until one memorable night, as the women were retiring . . .

LADY BARTLESHAM: Well, shall we retire, ladies?

The ladies rise. Pleasant smiles are exchanged all round, as LADY BARTLESHAM *indicates the withdrawing room.*

CAPTAIN MORRISON, *a rather dashing young buck, leans expansively back into his chair, glass of wine in hand.*

CAPTAIN MORRISON: We'll be in to spank you later — you firm-buttocked young Amazons!

The whole room freezes. A ghastly silence falls.

CAPTAIN MORRISON (*rising, ashen faced*): I'm terribly sorry . . . I don't know what came over me . . .

The ladies are ushered quickly out by LADY BARTLESHAM. LORD BARTLESHAM *stares fixedly at the table.*

LORD BARTLESHAM: That's all right, Morrison. I think you know what to do.
CAPTAIN MORRISON: Yes, yes . . . of course, sir.

MORRISON *walks to the door. He turns.*

CAPTAIN MORRISON: I apologize to you all.

He leaves, closing the door behind him. There is a brief pause, followed by a gunshot and the thud of a falling body. At this the silence is broken. Everyone loosens up, the conversation starts to flow again, and the port is passed around.

RUNCIMAN: Pity really, he was a nice enough chap . . .
DAINTRY: Yes . . . talented, too. He could have been number two in the War Office if he'd lived.
MEREDITH: Friend of yours, wasn't he, Clive?
COOPER: Yes . . . he was my best friend in the Regiment.

Meanwhile, at the other end of the table LORD BARTLESHAM *is talking to* RUNCIMAN, *his second-in-command.*

LORD BARTLESHAM: I can't understand what makes a man ruin a career like that.

There is general agreement at this, and then everyone lapses into table talk once more. COOPER, *however, suddenly turns to* MEREDITH, *on his right, and pushes the port towards him.*

MEREDITH: Hey, Clive, what are you doing?

COOPER: Don't you want any port?

MEREDITH (*with a quick, alarmed glance at the others*): Dammit, Clive . . . don't be a fool.

COOPER: I thought you liked port.

MEREDITH (*as if the joke's gone far enough*): Not like *that* . . . come *on! Right* to *left!*

COOPER: Let's pass it the other way for once.

MEREDITH (*in genuine alarm*): Clive, don't be a bloody fool! Think of your wife and children and the Regiment . . .

COOPER: (*recklessly pressing the port on the reluctant* MEREDITH): Come on! Take it!

MEREDITH shies back. LORD BARTLESHAM notices for the first time.

LORD BARTLESHAM: I say, Cooper! What's going on?

MEREDITH (*covering up*): It's nothing, sir . . . he was just asking me . . .

COOPER: I was passing the port from left to right.

There is a stunned silence. All heads turn to COOPER, who looks defiant.

LORD BARTLESHAM: Off you go, Cooper.

Everyone looks down at their plates as if avoiding seeing COOPER. You can cut the atmosphere with a butter-knife, as COOPER rises.

COOPER: All right! I'll go! But I want you to know that I don't care . . . d'you hear me . . . I don't care . . . If that's the way you want to pass the port — you pass it. But you can pass it without me.

He turns and stalks out slamming the door behind him. There is a pause. Then a shot.

LORD BARTLESHAM: Well perhaps we can carry on . . . cigar, Runciman?

MEREDITH pushes his chair back and stands up.

MEREDITH: I want to go too! I think it's about time someone said what Cooper has

257

just said! I think *anyone* should be allowed to pass the port any way they want . . .

LORD BARTLESHAM (*sympathetically, but anxiously*): Meredith!

MEREDITH: Left to right! Right to left! Diagonally!

LORD BARTLESHAM (*more sharply*): Meredith!

MEREDITH: Under the table! Over the table! Behind one man, in front of the next . . . one-handed, two-handed . . . first one way, then the other.

LORD BARTLESHAM: Meredith!

MEREDITH (*in full swing*): Two to the left and three to the right! Missing every third person on one side! Every alternate person on the other!

LORD BARTLESHAM (*as commandingly and definitively as possible*): MEREDITH!

MEREDITH stops. He tosses his head back and looks at them defiantly.

Then he too, rises and leaves. The door shuts. There is a pause. A gunshot.

Everyone relaxes and the conversation starts up again amongst those who are left. But more is to come . . . DAINTRY gets up . . . fiery-eyed.

DAINTRY: May I say it's more than just *passing* the port that's at stake here? I believe . . . that the *women* should be allowed port as well . . .

Gasps of disbelief from all. This really is heresy.

LORD BARTLESHAM (*more in kindness than in anger*): Daintry, sit down . . . (*To RUNCIMAN.*) It must be the heat . . .

DAINTRY: No no! I want to speak! I feel that women should be allowed to drink port *and* brandy *and* madeira!

LORD BARTLESHAM: *Daintry!* You're overtired!

DAINTRY: And they should be allowed to sing! And dance! And throw their heads back in laughter, and toss their beautiful hair! And smile and make the world a finer, happier, saner place!

LORD BARTLESHAM (*with weary resignation*): Off you go . . .

DAINTRY walks out. There is a shot and the sound of breaking china from the hallway, and DAINTRY's voice drifts back.

DAINTRY: Damn.

There is another shot followed by a satisfied grunt, and the thud of a body hitting the floor.

LORD BARTLESHAM and RUNCIMAN (an older, more distinguished and experienced officer) are left alone at the end of the table.

LORD BARTLESHAM takes a sip of port and shakes his head sadly.

LORD BARTLESHAM: Such a damn fine soldier, Daintry . . . don't you agree?

RUNCIMAN	Yes! Damn fine, Barty, damn fine . . . and honest. (*He stands.*) I've wanted women in here for years.
LORD BARTLESHAM:	What?
RUNCIMAN:	Yes, *I've* wanted to pass the port from left to right just as young Daintry did . . . but more than that! (*Pause.*) I've wanted to do away with the Loyal Toast!
LORD BARTLESHAM:	Oh no! Runciman! Not you. (*He shakes his head in disbelief.*)
RUNCIMAN:	I've wanted to abolish the National Anthem! I've wanted to set up a Socialist Republic in this land . . . a state where those who *do* the work shall be given the full reward of that work . . . where privilege and patronage shall be cast away and one man shall be equal with his fellow! *Smash* the Monarchy! . . . *Smash* the Ruling Classes! *Break up* the homes of the Rich and Privileged and let all humanity share equally, as God surely intended them to do!

He marches proudly out. There is another shot and the sound of a body smartly hitting the floor.

LORD BARTLESHAM *hangs his head wearily, sitting in pathetic isolation at the head of the table.*

Suddenly, as if for the first time in his life, he looks up and notices his son, sitting silently, head hung in embarrassment at the end of the table.

Mr Hopper had once told me that a moment like this would come, when the old order would finally collapse, and I was to let him know if it happened while he was out.

Suddenly ROGER *stands up, hurls his glass into the fireplace and stalks out.*

But I had plans of my own.

ROGER *marches down the corridor and out of a side door, and runs towards the servants' quarters.*

Finally he arrives in the main larder. He runs his eye around the fine stock

of pheasant, grouse, duck, chicken, beef and pork, selects the two largest legs of lamb and makes off, out of the house and down the drive. He has almost reached the end of the drive when a guard dog leaps out at him, barking fiercely. ROGER *throws one of the legs of lamb to the dog, who immediately stops barking and gratefully sets to ripping it apart.*

ROGER *runs on, unharmed, through the gates and down the road. Turning in at the drive to the next big house, he is once again faced by a fearsome guard dog. He throws the second leg of lamb for it, and then continues up to the house. Scaling the outside of the house with some agility, he reaches the window of Miranda's bedroom. He lets himself in to find the* HONOURABLE MIRANDA *at her dressing table, combing out her fine, long hair.*

ROGER: Miranda!

MIRANDA: Roger! What are you doing here?

ROGER (*eyes shining eagerly*): Have you thought it over, Miranda?

MIRANDA: Yes, but my parents would never allow it.

ROGER: Why not?

MIRANDA: We just can't Roger . . . we're too different . . .

ROGER: Different? How?

MIRANDA: Oh in a hundred ways . . . I mean, for a start I'm a woman and you're . . . you're a *man* . . .

ROGER: Well, people of the same sex don't get married.

MIRANDA: My fathers did.

ROGER: We'll run away together and start a little shop somewhere and sell things.

MIRANDA: Go into trade?

ROGER (*eyes shining*): Yes! Trade's exciting — it's a challenge . . . I've thought it all over, Miranda . . . that's where the future of our country lies. Buying and selling . . . profit margins . . . cost-effective management . . . sales projections . . . those are *real* . . . those are things that *count!*

MIRANDA (*laying aside her ivory handled hairbrush and standing*): You're mad! You'll own sixteen mansions all over the world when your father dies, and yet you want to throw it all up and go into trade!

ROGER (*following her*): Don't you see it? It's beautiful! Suppose I buy six dozen gross of elastic stocking hose — I'm thinking of a chemists' sundries shop — at two shillings a dozen . . . I sell them for four shillings a dozen — that's a gross profit of twelve shillings per dozen . . . allow a shilling for overheads — transport, wages, heating — that's eleven shillings clear profit . . .

ROGER pauses expectantly . . . breathless with excitement. His eyes shining.

The beautiful and slightly mysterious MIRANDA frowns.

MIRANDA: That's *net* profit is it?
ROGER: Yes.

MIRANDA turns away, preoccupied with her own thoughts.

MIRANDA   (*wilfully*): Supposing one stocked a herbal remedy . . .
ROGER   (*cautioningly*): Not the kind you need a prescription for?
MIRANDA: Obviously not . . . a herbal remedy in gallon cans and dispensed it in two-ounce bottles at the same price. What percentage return would that mean?

ROGER stops close behind her, his eyes glistening.

ROGER: You're talking of a profit margin of . . . two thousand per cent!
MIRANDA   (*her lips part and her heart races a little*): Oh . . . but we couldn't do that . . .
ROGER: Why not? We can do anything!
MIRANDA   (*her voice husky with passion*): We could sell . . . toilet requisites . . .
ROGER: And shaving accessories . . .
MIRANDA: And douches! We could sell douches . . .
ROGER: Oh, Miranda . . . say yes.

MIRANDA hesitates — her eyes aglow. Suddenly she turns away.

MIRANDA: No, no, Roger . . . I can't . . .
ROGER: But Miranda! (*He takes her by the arm.*)
MIRANDA: No no no, Roger — we're too rich! Don't you understand?
ROGER: We could have a surgical goods section as well . . .
MIRANDA   (*anguished*): No, Roger . . . we must have country houses, and croquet parties and grouse shoots . . . you know that . . .
ROGER: Why?
MIRANDA: Someone has to, Roger.
ROGER: Miranda . . .
MIRANDA: No, please, I can hear Father. You *must* go. He's terribly rich!

ROGER, after a moment's brave indecision, rushes to the window, and makes his escape.

A few days later.
Once again it is breakfast time. The only discernible difference from Bartlesham Hall is that the servant dealing with the silver trays of food is Indian. LORD and LADY BARTLESHAM sit at either end of the long table, as usual. ROGER sits despondently in the middle, toying with his food. Four large uneaten platefuls of cornflakes and kidneys surround him.

LORD BARTLESHAM lays aside the Times of India *for a moment and looks up reflectively.*

LORD BARTLESHAM: You know they're extraordinary people . . . the Pathans . . .

LADY BARTLESHAM: Who? Derek and Edna?

LORD BARTLESHAM: No — the Pathans . . . the local tribe we're fighting . . .

LADY BARTLESHAM: (*losing interest*): Oh yes . . .

LORD BARTLESHAM: They respond amazingly well to kindness . . .

LADY BARTLESHAM: (*unimpressed*): Hmm.

LORD BARTLESHAM: They may be very violent, often cruel and senselessly vindictive, but if you're kind to them, they respect you in a strange . . . way . . . Jellicoe was telling me of a chap who was kind to them . . . they wouldn't leave him alone — slept outside his door every night . . .

LADY BARTLESHAM: Really?

LORD BARTLESHAM: Mind you, he was *very* kind to them . . .

LADY BARTLESHAM: Have you tried the Oxshott Cherry Preserve?

LORD BARTLESHAM: You know, I often think that if people had been a little more kind to each other, we could have avoided many of the wars which have plagued society through the ages . . .

LADY BARTLESHAM: Rubbish, dear.

LORD BARTLESHAM: Well . . . maybe . . . but just suppose for a minute that when Wallenstein reached the gates of Magdeburg in 1631, instead of razing the city to the ground and putting its inhabitants to the sword, he'd said . . . 'What a lovely place! How lucky you are to live here . . . I live in Sweden . . . you must come and see me some time' . . . Just think what a difference it would have made . . . he'd have gone down in history as a nice chap, instead of the Butcher of Magdeburg . . .

LADY BARTLESHAM: Eat up dear, and stop talking piffle.

ROGER looks up. His eyes widen, for at the window he can see the HONOURABLE MIRANDA. She signals to him and disappears.

ROGER pushes his chair back noisily and stands up.

LADY BARTLESHAM:	Where are you going, Roger?
ROGER:	To see Mr Hopper.
LADY BARTLESHAM:	There are eight more courses yet . . .
ROGER:	We're doing Horace today.
LORD BARTLESHAM	(*looking up from his paper*): Child molester, wasn't he?
LADY BARTLESHAM	(*impatiently*): No . . . no . . . Horace is a Latin author, Barty.

ROGER makes good his escape.

LORD BARTLESHAM:	Knew a child molester at Eton called Horace.
LADY BARTLESHAM	(*looking round at the door after ROGER*): I don't know what's come over the boy, I really don't. He's been off his kedgeree for weeks.
LORD BARTLESHAM:	Perhaps we should have given him more love and affection . . .
LADY BARTLESHAM:	More brute force, if you ask me — like we did with Nigel.
LORD BARTLESHAM:	Nigel died.
LADY BARTLESHAM:	Yes, but think what he'd have been like if he'd lived!

Out in the garden, ROGER appears looking around for the HONOURABLE MIRANDA.

An Indian servant watches him disapprovingly.

Suddenly he hears a 'Pssst!' and sees MIRANDA behind an urn on the lawn, beckoning him over.

ROGER:	Miranda! What is it?
MIRANDA:	I've decided to come with you.
ROGER	(*slightly nonplussed*): Where?
MIRANDA:	I've bought the option on a two-floor lock-up in the Euston Road . . . complete with stock.
ROGER	(*in some alarm*): But I'm not ready!
MIRANDA:	It's haberdashery mainly, but we could open an accessories section and move into surgical appliances when we've built the business up.
ROGER	(*excited but alarmed*): Look, Miranda . . . I . . .
MIRANDA:	I'll call for you tonight. I'll bring Rover.

MIRANDA gives him a neck-breaking kiss and disappears.

ROGER is left incredulous. Suddenly it's all happening for him.

Nightfall finds ROGER sitting, fully dressed, on the edge of his bed, waiting. His excited face illuminated by the pale rays of the moon.

That night I waited, ready . . . ready for the chance of a lifetime. This time it *had* to work . . .

Suddenly there is the sound of gravel being thrown at the window.

ROGER starts. His hands tighten on his bundle of clothes and he moves towards the window. He opens it.

A ladder has been set against the wall, but coming up the ladder is not the dainty sylph-like form of his beloved, but the hairy-faced, Russian-hatted figure of HOPPER.

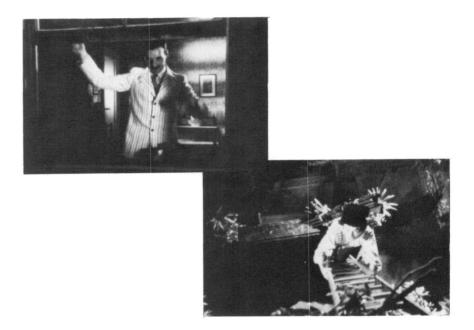

HOPPER is armed to the teeth, and has a carbine slung over his back. He's pulling behind him a formidable bundle of weapons tied together on the end of a rope.

ROGER: Mr Hopper!

HOPPER looks up, his eyes are shining and he is clearly excited.

HOPPER: Roger . . . you heard the news then?
ROGER: What news?
HOPPER: The Tsar of all the Russias is dead — isn't it wonderful?
ROGER: Well . . . yes of course . . .

HOPPER has climbed in by now, he pulls the weapons after him.

HOPPER: Russia's up in arms. The Revolution's begun . . . (*He points to the pile of arms.*) . . . stack that lot in your room, Roger . . .

HOPPER turns and starts to haul up yet another load of small arms and machine guns.

ROGER: Mr Hopper . . . I'm leaving.

HOPPER: No need! We'll start our uprising here! The entire regiment's with us . . . the armed struggle of the proletariat has begun! Today — the Empire! Tomorrow . . . England itself!

ROGER: I can't, Mr Hopper.

HOPPER: What? (*He stops hauling in the next load.*)

ROGER: The Honourable Miranda and I are going back home to start a little shop.

HOPPER: But I need you for the coup . . .

ROGER: I'm sorry, Mr Hopper . . .

ROGER starts to go into the corridor.

HOPPER makes towards him . . . as he does so he lets go of the rope.

There is an almighty crash of arms hitting the drive below.

The sound carries as far as LORD and LADY BARTLESHAM's bedroom. LORD BARTLESHAM sits bolt upright.

LORD BARTLESHAM: The Pathans!

LADY BARTLESHAM: Derek and Edna?

LORD BARTLESHAM: No — the violent but proud race of hill people who threaten our very existence. I must go and be kind to them.

LADY BARTLESHAM: Don't be silly, dear. The servants have orders to come and tell us if there's a Pathan uprising.

Meanwhile, out on the landing, ROGER is backing away from HOPPER, who is now advancing menacingly towards him.

HOPPER: I spent fourteen years teaching you . . . training you for this moment . . . You can't walk out on me now, d'you hear?

ROGER: 'No man owns another,' Mr Hopper.

HOPPER grabs ROGER and flattens him against the wall.

ROGER kicks HOPPER, and slips out of his grasp, and then races down the corridor towards his bedroom door.

Whereupon HOPPER picks up a rifle and takes aim.

HOPPER (*in a hissed whisper*): Stay where you are! You'll do as I say. Now turn around.

ROGER slowly turns round, as he does so he grabs a vase, perched on a conveniently high stand, and flings it at HOPPER, *throwing himself to the floor.*

HOPPER fires wildly.

Back in Lord and Lady Bartlesham's bedroom the shot is still echoing. LORD BARTLESHAM *sits up in bed again.*

LORD BARTLESHAM:	My God! They're armed!
LADY BARTLESHAM:	Nonsense, dear . . . it's probably just Mr Muckbee shooting an intruder . . .
LORD BARTLESHAM:	I'd better go and treat them well.
LADY BARTLESHAM	(*firmly*): Lie down and go to sleep.

They lie down. There is another gunshot and another.

LADY BARTLESHAM: Probably shooting the intruder's family as well . . . I don't know *why* they bring them with them . . .

By now ROGER *has managed to get back into his own room. He slams the door behind him and locks it.*

HOPPER starts rattling the handle.

ROGER looks around for his clothes, grabs a few, and runs for the window. It is stuck.

HOPPER (*loud whisper*): Roger, listen . . . I want you to *lead* the Revolution.

ROGER (*in an equally loud whisper*): Go away!

HOPPER batters away at the door and it starts to splinter.

Back in Lord and Lady Bartlesham's bedroom, the sound of splintering wood is unmistakably audible. LORD BARTLESHAM *sits bolt upright once again.*

LORD BARTLESHAM: They're breaking the place up! They need sympathy . . .

There is another splintering crash.

LADY BARTLESHAM: Don't be silly Barty, go to sleep!
LORD BARTLESHAM   (*rising*): Perhaps I'd better go and check . . . give them all some hot soup and blankets . . . make them full members of the Club . . .

He reaches for his dressing gown.

In the meantime ROGER *has succeeded in opening the window. He climbs out onto the roof of the verandah and drops down, landing spectacularly.*

At this moment, HOPPER *finally bursts into the room.*

He dashes to the window, looks out and takes aim and fires.

ROGER *sprints across the gravel driveway into the bushes. Under this cover he starts to make his way towards the gates, where the* HONOURABLE MIRANDA *has just arrived.*

His escape is cut short, however, when he parts some bushes, and comes face to face with a huddle of officers from his father's Regiment.

FIRST OFFICER: Ah, there you are, sir. Mr Hopper told us to wait here for you.

ROGER: Look . . . I'm not in all this.

FIRST OFFICER: What do you reckon now, sir? Do we wait for Mr Hopper?

ROGER: Look, it's no good asking me . . . I'm off to start a little shop somewhere, with —

The OFFICER slaps a hand over ROGER's mouth and pulls him to one side, looking round anxiously at the bushes behind him.

FIRST OFFICER: Look sir . . . the men are expecting you to lead them. You can't let them down now . . .

ROGER becomes aware of the rest of the Regiment, armed to the teeth, and crouching in the bushes behind.

ROGER: I can't help that. (*He starts to go.*)

There is a click.

The FIRST OFFICER produces a loaded revolver and points it at him.

FIRST OFFICER: I'm sorry sir, but you'd better do just as I say.

There is another shot from the house. They all look up.

Back in ROGER's bedroom.

HOPPER has just fired again, when LORD BARTLESHAM bursts in, holding a tray with some drinks on.

LORD BARTLESHAM: Hello Pathans! How about a drink and some hot sou— Good Lord! Hopper . . .

HOPPER looks distinctly uncomfortable being caught at a window with a smoking rifle and wearing a complete Russian outfit.

LORD BARTLESHAM: You haven't killed any of them, have you?

HOPPER (*confused*): What sir?

LORD BARTLESHAM: The Pathans . . .

HOPPER: It's not the Pathans sir . . . it's . . . it's your own men.

LORD BARTLESHAM: Disguised as Pathans?

HOPPER: No, no, your own men are firing.

LORD BARTLESHAM: You mean . . . like in a mutiny, Hopper?

HOPPER (*takes a big breath — this is the moment of truth*): Yes, sir! I'm afraid this *is* a mutiny.

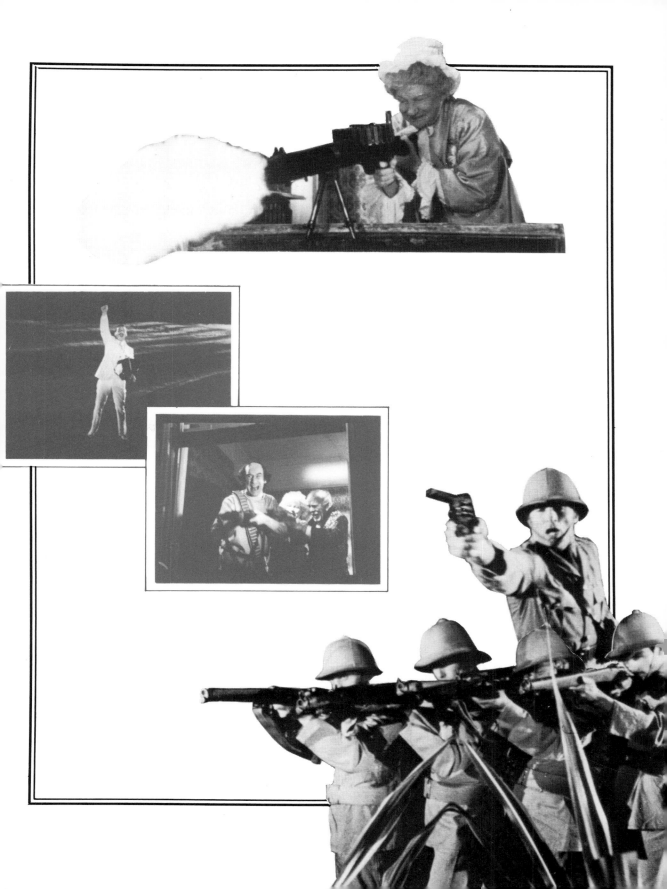

HOPPER points his rifle at LORD BARTLESHAM in a vaguely coercive manner.

LORD BARTLESHAM: Thank God you're still with me, Hopper.
HOPPER: Er no . . . no . . . I'm . . .

LORD BARTLESHAM walks past HOPPER, not noticing the rifle, and giving him a reassuring pat on the shoulder.

LORD BARTLESHAM: The wife and I always had a soft spot for you. (*He peers out of window.*)
HOPPER: Look, I've . . . er . . . I'm . . .

HOPPER tries to bring himself to point the rifle at LORD BARTLESHAM but the old man is awkwardly close.

LORD BARTLESHAM (*scanning the bushes*): What do they want? Money? Double beds? Who the hell's behind this?
HOPPER: Sir . . . (*Swallows.*) I have to tell you . . .

LORD BARTLESHAM turns and peers closely into HOPPER's face . . . obviously intrigued by the tension in HOPPER's voice . . .

LORD BARTLESHAM: What?

HOPPER cannot stand the close eye-contact with his patron of twenty years.

HOPPER: Er . . . I have to tell you . . . it's your son.
LORD BARTLESHAM: They've got him too?

LORD BARTLESHAM grabs the rifle and aims out of the window.

HOPPER: No . . . he's leading them, sir . . .

LORD BARTLESHAM freezes, lowers the rifle and pulls it back into the room.

He slowly turns to HOPPER, very subdued.

LORD BARTLESHAM:	My son? Leading a mutiny?
HOPPER:	I'm afraid so.
LORD BARTLESHAM:	You mean . . . little .. . little what's his name?
HOPPER	(*now sold on shopping* ROGER): Thingy . . . yes . . . He's the ringleader.

LORD BARTLESHAM *is thunderstruck.*

LORD BARTLESHAM:	But *why*? We gave the dear boy everything. A good home . . . several good homes — initialled croquet mallets, hand-tooled books on etiquette . . . What more does he want?
HOPPER	(*can't resist the opportunity*): Perhaps he wants to found a Socialist State with centralized ownership of capital to be used for the benefit of all.
LORD BARTLESHAM:	He wants *what?*

HOPPER *is a little terrified but decides to brave it out.*

HOPPER:	A . . . a . . . Socialist State with centralized ownership of capital to be used for the benefit of all . . . your lordship.
LORD BARTLESHAM:	Oh . . . if that's all he wants he shall have it.
HOPPER	(*taken off guard*): I'm sorry?
LORD BARTLESHAM:	No son of mine shall ever want for anything, Hopper.
HOPPER:	Oh . . . (*with dawning realization.*) . . . *Oh!* Ah . . . Ah well . . .

LADY BARTLESHAM *appears.*

LADY BARTLESHAM:	What's going on, Barty?
LORD BARTLESHAM:	Boy wants the centralized ownership of capital to be used for the benefit of all, dear.
LADY BARTLESHAM:	The ungrateful little bastard!

LADY BARTLESHAM *grabs the rifle and gives it an automatic and professional examination, cocking it as she does so.*

Meanwhile, at the gates, the HONOURABLE MIRANDA *can bear the tension no longer.*

MIRANDA: I'm going to find out what's happening. Wait for me here, Rover.

Her Indian serving-lady nods obediently.

MIRANDA *makes her way through the garden. She sees the lights on in the big house through the trees.*

Suddenly she freezes as she sees the group of mutinous soldiers, with ROGER *at their head.*

FIRST OFFICER (*to* ROGER): Tell them the place is surrounded and that you are taking over personal command.

ROGER: Look, I really . . .

The FIRST OFFICER *cocks his pistol.*

ROGER *realizes he means business, and allows himself to be pushed forward into the driveway. He walks warily towards the house.*

ROGER: Hello . . .

LADY BARTLESHAM takes careful aim.

LADY BARTLESHAM: There he is now. One shot and we can all go back to bed.

ROGER: Can everybody hear me?

LORD BARTLESHAM: Perhaps we should just hear what he has to say, dear.

LADY BARTLESHAM: This is no time to be sentimental, Barty. We do have other children.

ROGER's *voice rises up from below. It sounds more plaintive than threatening.*

ROGER: It is important you listen carefully . . . er . . . to everything I say . . . er . . . and act accordingly . . .

The mutinous soldiers train their guns on his head, their fingers squeezing slightly on the triggers.

Roger's mother follows suit.

Meanwhile, the HONOURABLE MIRANDA *has edged her way up behind the soldiers. She reaches down and picks up a heavy stick.*

ROGER: The house . . . is surrounded . . . and I am taking personal command of the Regiment . . .

For the first time, it is LORD BARTLESHAM's *turn to be outraged.*

LORD BARTLESHAM: Good Lord — *my* Regiment! Give me that!

He makes a grab for the rifle, but LADY BARTLESHAM *hangs on to it.*

LADY BARTLESHAM: Oh Barty, leave it to me.

Meanwhile ROGER *is biting his lip, but carrying on bravely, if a trifle quietly.*

ROGER: This is at the insistence of the officers and men of the Regiment. (*He hears the noise of a scuffle at the window as* LADY BARTLESHAM *and* LORD

BARTLESHAM *argue.*) Though . . . I must point out I'm doing this under duress . . .

In the bushes, fingers tighten on the triggers and gunsights are retrained on his slight figure.

ROGER: Despite my high regard for the ideals of the men.

The FIRST OFFICER *however, raises his hand for them to wait. Meanwhile,* MIRANDA *closes in on the hindmost soldiers.*

Suddenly ROGER *turns towards the soldiers in the bushes.*

ROGER: But I would say to them first of all that obviously Mr Hopper has been talking revolution to you as he has talked revolution to me for the last fifteen years of Latin classes . . .

LORD and LADY BARTLESHAM stop fighting for a moment and turn on HOPPER.

HOPPER smiles hopelessly, as ROGER continues to spill his beans.

ROGER: And no doubt, when I've taken over command of the Regiment, Mr Hopper will expect to take over ultimate power through me . . .

At this, the mutineers look at each other with slightly furrowed brows.

ROGER (*gaining a little confidence*): So I ask the officers and men of the Regiment, what will they have achieved? They will have substituted one figure of authority for another.

The soldiers frown behind their rifles.

What guarantee have they that Mr Hopper — or I for that matter — will treat them any better than my father?

The political tenor of ROGER's train of thought, however, has got HOPPER really agitated, and he cannot stop himself yelling out of the window.

HOPPER: Don't listen to him! That's not Marxism. That's Bakuninite Anarchism..

LORD and LADY BARTLESHAM are looking at HOPPER in a new light, but MR HOPPER is so incensed by ROGER's unorthodoxy that he has forgotten all about his former patrons. He makes to grab the rifle from LORD BARTLESHAM.

Meanwhile ROGER is getting carried away with his own oratory.

ROGER: So I say, let us grasp this opportunity to renounce the violence implicit in

any centralized authority, and aim for a total decentralization of power!

Several of the soldiers have trouble trying to keep up with this change of political direction.

HOPPER *however, has no doubts. He has grabbed the rifle and is now aiming it at* ROGER.

HOPPER: Anarchist!

At this moment MIRANDA *looms up behind one of the hindmost soldiers. She clubs him (rather effectively for such a delicate beauty) and takes his rifle.*

The FIRST OFFICER *runs out from the bushes.*

FIRST OFFICER: Listen! He's got our position slightly wrong. We're not *against* a centralized authority as such . . .
SECOND OFFICER: (*from the bushes*): I am!
FIRST OFFICER: No you're not!
ANOTHER VOICE (*from the bushes*): I agree with the last speaker.
HOPPER: This isn't a bloody debate! It's time for action.

LORD BARTLESHAM *makes a grab for the rifle and they wrestle.*

MIRANDA has climbed into the branches of a tree, she produces a rifle, takes aim and fires at the window from which HOPPER is shouting. She extinguishes the lamp within, with expert marksmanship.

HOPPER and LORD and LADY BARTLESHAM still continue to struggle in the dark. The rifle goes off.

ROGER ducks as the bullet whistles past his head and dodges behind a stone urn.

FIRST OFFICER
VOICE *(panicked by the gunfire):* Fire!
(from bushes, by now extremely confused): Who at?

MIRANDA fires again. Another light goes out in the house.

HOPPER fires back, as bullets hit the window frame around him.

Suddenly LADY BARTLESHAM re-appears at the door of the room carrying a machine gun.

LADY BARTLESHAM *(joyfully):* Look what I've found!

A bullet smashes through the window.

All this time ROGER is cowering behind the urn.

MIRANDA, however, coolly fires at another light.

A soldier wheels round to fire at MIRANDA in the tree.

LADY BARTLESHAM looking as happy as she ever will be, rakes the grounds indiscriminately with machine gun fire.

The mutinous soldiers whirl round in confusion and fling themselves to the ground.

FIRST OFFICER:	Charge!
SECOND OFFICER:	Which way?
ANOTHER:	Where are we?

MIRANDA fires and puts out yet another light.

LADY BARTLESHAM turns the machine gun towards her and fires, raking her tree and knocking the rifle from her hands.

ROGER notices MIRANDA for the first time.

| ROGER | (*shouts*): Miranda! |
| MIRANDA: | I'm coming! . . . Rover! |

The Indian lady pricks up her ears, does a great leap on to the back of the horse leading the trap and whips it furiously. The trap speeds off up the garden drive into the maelstrom of bullets and noise.

As the trap speeds past the urn, the Indian lady leans down from the horse and scoops ROGER up with an Errol-Flynnish flourish.

They career on round the drive and as they come to the other gates, pass under the tree where MIRANDA has been perched, she drops down into the trap and they speed off into the night, leaving chaos behind them, shouting and firing.

The trap hurtles away down the moonlit track.

Exactly what happened that night in India will probably never be known, for no one lived to tell the tale save myself and the Honourable Miranda. After many adventures we found our way back to England, and there we achieved our impossible dream . . .

Outside an old-fashioned chemist's shop hangs a sign which reads:

'Lord Bartlesham and the Honourable Miranda Fyffe-Moncrieff, Duchess of Lincoln: Chemists' sundries, accessories, douches a speciality'

Outside stand the proud owners — ROGER *and* MIRANDA.

. . . To be able to throw off the shackles of wealth and privilege, and live as we'd always wanted to live, as simple shopkeepers . . .

It is noticeable, however, that the shop is actually built on to the imposing front entrance of Bartlesham Hall. And so, as music swells in our ears, we leave ROGER *and his bride happy at last — with Bartlesham Hall and its gardens in all their splendour — undiminished.*

THE END

Tomkinson's Schooldays: First transmitted on BBC-2, January 7th 1976

Directed by Terry Hughes; *Photographed by* Peter Hall; *Designed by* Martin Collins;
Sound Recordist Ron Blight; *Film Editor* Ray Millichope; *Costume Designer* Odette Barrow;
Make-Up Artist Jackie Fitz-Maurice
Cast: *Tomkinson, Headmaster, Mr Craffit* Michael Palin; *Mr Ellis* Terry Jones; *Mummy* Gwen Watford;
School Bully Ian Ogilvie; *with* John Wentworth, Sarah Grazebrook, Lindsay Dunn, Mark Dunn, Chai Lee
Filmed on location in Dorset and at BBC T-V Studios, White City

The Testing of Eric Olthwaite: First transmitted on BBC-2, Sept 27th 1977

Directed by Jim Franklin; *Photographed by* Peter Hall; *Edited by* John Jarvis; *Designed by* John Stout;
Sound Recordist Brian Showell; *Costume Designer* Linda Woodfield; *Make-Up Artist* Jean Speak;
'The Ballad of Eric Olthwaite': *music by* André Jacquemin and Dave Howman
Cast: *Eric Olthwaite* Michael Palin; *Mrs Olthwaite* Barbara New; *Mr Bag* John Barrett;
Irene Olthwaite Anita Carey; *Mr Bag* Reg Lye; *Mrs Bag* Liz Smith; *Enid Bag* Petra Markham;
Bank Manager Michael Palin; *Arthur the Robber* Ken Colley; *Chauffeur* Roger Avon;
Lord Mayor Clifford Kershaw; *Stuntmen* Marc Boyle and Jim Dowdall
with Norman Mitchell, Anthony Smee
Filmed at Beamish and Tow Law, Co. Durham and High Force, N. Yorkshire

Escape From Stalag Luft 112 B: First transmitted on BBC-2, Oct 4th 1977

Directed by Jim Franklin; *Photographed by* Peter Hall; *Edited by* John Jarvis; *Designed by* John Stout;
Sound Recordist Ron Blight; *Costume Designers* Robin Stubbs and Linda Woodfield;
Make-Up Artist Jean Speak
Cast: *Major Phipps* Michael Palin; *Herr Vogel* Roy Kinnear; *Colonel Harcourt Badger-Owen* John Phillips;
Biolek Julian Hough; *Second Guard* David English; 'Buffy' Attenborough* David Griffin;
Nicolson Timothy Carlton *with* Philip Graham, Roland McLeod, Hugh Janes, James Charles,
Glen Cunningham, Nicholas Day, David Machin
Filmed on location on the Salisbury Plain

Murder at Moorstones Manor: First transmitted on BBC-2, 11th Oct 1977

Directed by Terry Hughes; *Photographed by* Peter Hall; *Edited by* Ray Millichope;
Designed by Martin Collins; *Sound Recordist* Brian Showell; *Costume Designer* Barbara Lane;
Make-Up Artist Jean Speak
Cast: *Charles* and *Hugo Chiddingfold* Michael Palin; *Lady Chiddingfold* Isabel Dean;
Dora Chiddingfold Candace Glendenning; *Ruth* Anne Zelda; *Sir Clive Chiddingfold* Frank Middlemass;
Manners Harold Innocent; *Dr Farson* Iain Cuthbertson
Filmed on location at Harefield, Middlesex and Glencoe in Scotland

Across The Andes By Frog: First transmitted on BBC-2, Oct 18th 1977

Directed by Terry Hughes; *Photographed by* Peter Hall; *Designed by* Martin Collins;
Sound Recordist Brian Showell; *Costume Designer* Barbara Lane; *Make-Up Artist* Jean Speak
Cast: *Captain Snetterton* Michael Palin; *Mr Gregory* Denholm Elliott; *R.S.M. Urdoch* Don Henderson;
Peruvian Mountain Guide Eileen Way; *Native with radio* Louis Mansi;
Weedy Whining native Charles McKeown
Filmed at Pinewood Studios and Glencoe, Scotland

The Curse Of The Claw: First transmitted on BBC-2, 25th October 1977

Directed by Jim Franklin; *Photographed by* Peter Hall; *Designed by* John Stout; *Edited by* John Jarvis;
Sound Recordist Brian Showell; *Costume Designer* Robin Stubbs; *Make-Up Artist* Jean Speak
Cast: *Sir Kevin Orr, Uncle Jack* Michael Palin; *Grosvenor* Aubrey Morris; *Captain Merson* Keith Smith;
Kevin's mother Hilary Mason; *Kevin's father* Tenniel Evans; *Young Lady Agatha* Diana Hutchinson;
Grown-Up Lady Agatha Bridget Armstrong; *Chief Petty Officer Russel* Judy Loe
Kevin as a boy Nigel Rhodes; *Stoker* Michael Stainton; *First Engineer* Vanessa Furse
Filmed at Rippingale, Lincolnshire and the Medway Estuary

Roll of honour: The plucky stalwarts, without whom there would have been no Ripping Yarns.
So blame them. Jackie Tyler, Bill '24 Jokes per second' Dudman, Eddie Stuart, Marcus Plantin,
Alfie Williams, Desmond O'Brien, Derry Haws, Sue Bide, Liz Cranston, John Bishop, John Stout,
John Bristow, John Horton, John Adams, John Stevens, Steve Diamond, Tony Caruana, Stuart Fell,
Ian Scoones, Roy Spratley, Jimmy Monks, Les Thomas, Morton Hardacre, Mike Mungarvan,
Robert Smythe, Mervyn Bezar, Maggie Smith, Steve Bowman, Andy Lazell, Brian Bissin,
Tony Newman, Christian Dyall, Derek Sumner, Liz Dixon, Janet Budden, Len Hutton, Brian West,
Dave Phelps, Bob Warrens, Billy Rose, John Phillips, Ken Cooper, Ian Gosling, Bob Johnson,
Des Stewart, John Van Dyken, Don Lee, Janice Booth, Steve Pokol, Brian Willis, Jane Fox,
Dick Norwood, Hamish MacInnes and Jill Foster . . . to name but a few . . . .

Whinfrey's Last Case: First transmitted on BBC-2 October 10th 1979

Directed by Alan J.W. Bell; *Photographed by* Alan Stevens and Mike Radford;
Edited by Glenn Hyde; *Designed by* Gerry Scott; *Sound Recordists* Ron Blight and Ron Pegler;
Dubbing Mixer Ron Edmonds; *Costume Designer* Roger Reece; *Make-Up Artist* Jill Hagger;
Visual Effects John Horton; *Graphics Designer for the series* Ian Hewitt
Production Assistants John Adams and Sue Bennett-Urwin; *Director's Assistant* Carol Abbott;
Assistant Sound Recordist Morton Hardaker; *Grips* Malcolm Sheehan;
Assistant Designer Alan Spalding; *Property Buyer* Enid Willey; *Lighting Gaffer* Ricky Wood;
Make-Up Assistant Caroline Becker; *Assistant Floor Manager* Julie Mann;
Assistant Film Editor Brian Douglas; *Design Assistant* Sarah Leigh
Cast: *Introducer, Whinfrey* Michael Palin; *Meat Lorry Driver* Steve Conway;
General Chapman Jack May; *Lord Raglan* Gerald Sim; *Admiral Jefferson* Antony Carrick;
Man in club Anthony Woodruff; *Barmaid (Lotte)* Ann Way; *Mrs Otway* Maria Aitken;
Mr Carne Richard Hurndall; *Mr Ferris* Charles McKeown; *Mr Girton* Edward Hardwicke;
Mr Vinney Patrick Bailey; *Smooth German* Michael Sharvell-Martin;
Another Eddie Philip Clayton-Gore; *Army Captain* Roy Sampson; *Germans* Members of
the Royal Marines, Exmouth

Filmed on location in London; Torbryan, Devon; Staverton Bridge, Devon (Dart Valley Railway);
Cape Cornwall; and at the BBC Television Film Studios, Ealing

Golden Gordon: First transmitted on BBC-2 October 17th 1979

Directed by Alan J.W. Bell; *Photographed by* Alan Stevens; *Edited by* John Jarvis;
Designed by Gerry Scott; *Sound Recordist* Ron Blight; *Dubbing Mixer* Ron Edmonds;
Costume Designer Roger Reece; *Make-Up Artist* Jill Hagger; *Visual Effects* John Horton;
2nd Unit Cameraman Michael Radford;
Production Assistants John Adams and Sue Bennett-Urwin; *Director's Assistant* Carol Abbott
Assistant Sound Recordist Morton Hardaker; *Assistant Designer* Alan Spalding;
Prop Buyer Enid Willey; *Lighting Gaffer* Ricky Wood; *Grips* Malcolm Sheehan;
Assistant Cameraman Steve Albins; *Assistant Costume Designer* Sarah Leigh;
Assistant Film Editor Christine Pancott; *Make-up Assistant* Caroline Becker
Cast: *Mrs Ottershaw* Gwen Taylor; *Barnstoneworth Ottershaw* John Berlyne;
Gordon Ottershaw Michael Palin; *Barman (Cyril)* Ken Kitson; *Football Manager* David Leland;
1st Footballer David Ellison; *2nd Footballer* Colin Bennett; *3rd Footballer* Matthew Scurfield;
Chairman Teddy Turner; *Arthur Foggen* Bill Fraser; *Mrs Foggen* Pat Taylor;
Baldy Davitt Roger Sloman; *Goalkeeper* Charles McKeown; *Passer-by* John Cleese;
and members of Salts A.F.C. (who didn't mind having their hair cut)
Filmed entirely on location in Keighley (the Ottershaw home), Kildwick (the Foggen home),
Saltaire, Bradley, Bingley and Guiseley in Yorkshire

Roger of the Raj: First transmitted on BBC-2 October 24th 1979

Directed by Jim Franklin; *Photographed by* Reg Pope; *Edited by* Dan Rae;
Designed by Nigel Curzon; *Sound Recordist* Bob Roberts; *Dubbing Mixer* Alan Dykes;
Costume Designer Valerie Bonner; *Make-up Artist* Cecile Hay-Arthur;
Production Assistant Peter R. Lovell; *Producer's Assistant* Elizabeth Cranston;
Visual Effects Designer John Horton; *Assistant Floor Manager* John Bishop;
Design Assistant Richard Brackenbury; *Costume Assistant* Tessa Hayes;
Make-Up Assistant Margaret Magee; *Property Buyer* Eric Baker;
Assistant Cameraman Richard Gauld; *Sound Assistant* John Corps; *Grips* Tex Childs;
Lighting Gaffer Ted Bird; *Assistant Film Editor* Arden Fisher
Cast: *Roger* Michael Palin; *Lord Bartlesham* Richard Vernon; *Lady Bartlesham* Joan Sanderson;
Miranda Jan Francis; *Colonel Runciman* John le Mesurier; *Hopper* Roger Brierley;
Major Daintry Allan Cuthbertson; *Captain Meredith* David Griffin;
Captain Morrison Charles McKeown; *Captain Cooper* David Warwick;
The Gamekeeper Michael Stainton; *1st Mutinous Officer* Ken Shorter;
2nd Mutinous Officer Douglas Hinton; *Housemaid* Dorothy Frere;
Stunts Stuart Fell, Roberta Gibbs
Filmed on location at High Halden and Godington Park in Kent